DATE DUE

UNDERSTANDING
THE NEW BLACK POETRY

By the same author

The Militant Black Writer in Africa
and the United States (with Mercer Cook)

Understanding the New Black Poetry

Black Speech and Black Music as Poetic References

By Stephen Henderson

An Institute of the Black World Book

William Morrow & Company, Inc.
New York   1973

Printed in the United States of America.

Henderson, Stephen Evangelist, comp.
   Understanding the new Black poetry.

   Includes bibliographical references.
   1. American poetry—Negro authors. I. Title.
PS591.N4H37   811'.008   79-170234
ISBN 0-688-00139-4
ISBN 0-688-05139-1 (pbk.)

Grateful acknowledgment is made to:

Samuel Allen for permission to reprint "In My Father's House: A Reverie," "Ivory Tusks," "To Satch" by Samuel Allen from *Ivory Tusks and Other Poems* by Samuel Allen, Kriya Press, 1968.
Lebert Bethune for permission to reprint "A Juju of My Own," "Black Fire," "The Nature of . . ." from *A Juju of My Own* by Lebert Bethune.
Black World for permission to reprint "To a Negro Preacher" by James A. Emanuel, Copyright © September, 1965, by *Negro Digest;* "A Tribute to Duke" by Sarah Webster Fabio, Copyright © January, 1971, by *Black World;* "For All Things Black and Beautiful" by Conrad Kent Rivers, Copyright © September, 1967, by *Negro Digest.*
The Bobbs-Merrill Company for permission to reprint: "Prettyditty," "A Poem for Black Hearts," "SOS," "Black Art," "Three Movements and a Coda," and "I Am Speaking of Future Good-ness and Social Philosophy" by LeRoi Jones (Imamu Amiri Baraka) from *Black Magic Poetry 1961–1967* by LeRoi Jones, Copyright © 1969 by LeRoi Jones.
Sharon Bourke for permission to print "People of Gleaming Cities, and of Lion's and the Leopard's Brood," "I Know She Will Pray for Me," "Sopranosound, Memory of John," and "I Remember That Day."
Paul Bremem Ltd. for permission to reprint: "In Defense of Black Poets," "Watts," "Underground," by Conrad Kent Rivers from *The Still Voice of Harlem*, Volume 5 in the Heritage series, 1968; "A Mourning Letter from Paris," by Conrad Kent Rivers from *The Wright Poems*, Volume 18 in the Heritage series, 1972.
Broadside Press for permission to reprint: "This is an African Worm" and "Passive Resistance" by Margaret Danner from *Poem Counterpoem* by Margaret Danner and Dudley Randall; "For Malcolm, U.S.A.," "Emmett Till," "Freedom Rider: Washout" by James Emanuel from *The Treehouse and Other Poems* by James A. Emanuel, Copyright © 1968 by James Emanuel; "My Blackness Is the Beauty of This Land," "Breath In My Nostrils" by Lance Jeffers from *My Blackness Is the Beauty of This Land* by Lance Jeffers, Copyright © 1970 by Lance Jeffers; "The Idea of Ancestry," "Hard Rock Returns to Prison from the Hospital for the Criminal Insane," "To Dinah Washington," "For Langston Hughes," "On Universalism" by Etheridge Knight from *Poems from Prison* by Etheridge Knight, Copyright © 1968 by Etheridge Knight; "My Name is Afrika," "Origins (for melba)" by W. Keorapetse Kgositsile from *Spirits Unchained* by Keorapetse Kgositsile, Copyright © 1969 by Keorapetse Kgositsile; "The Wall" by Don L. Lee from *Black Pride* by Don L. Lee, Copyright © 1968 by Don L. Yee; "Don't Cry, Scream" by Don L. Lee from *Don't Cry, Scream*, Copyright © 1969 by Don L. Lee; "Move Un-noticed to Be Noticed: A Nationhood Poem" by Don L. Lee from *We Walk The Way of The New World* by Don L. Lee, Copyright © 1970 by Don. L. Lee; "Black Poet, White Critic" by Dudley Randall from *Cities Burning* by Dudley Randall, Copyright © 1968 by Dudley Randall; "Ballad of Birmingham" by Dudley Randall from *Poem Counterpoem* by Margaret Danner and Dudley Randall; "Poem at Thirty,"

[*vi*]

To Jeanne, my wife,
Who knows the reasons why,
And to our children
Steve Jr.
Tim
Philip
Alvin Malcolm

PREFACE

In this anthology certain glaring omissions are evident from the beginning. This, of course, is deliberate, but implies no slighting of those works. What it does imply is a certain embarrassment of riches, especially for the poetry of the sixties. Another peculiarity of my selection which warrants explanation is the inclusion of material which many people would include in a separate category, if at all. I refer now to what can be called "folk poetry" and "street poetry." I also include several poems from important student publications such as *Dasein* and *Burning Spear*, by the "Howard Poets" of the fifties and from *Ex Umbra*, of North Carolina Central University in Durham. In the street poetry I have included some "traditional" pieces as well as modifications of the tradition by such volatile poets as Reginald Butler and H. Rap Brown.

In fact, it is this oral tradition, both rural and urban, which forms an infrastructure for the anthology. In Section I, the work of James Weldon Johnson and Paul Laurence Dunbar is placed in the context of the folk sermon and the spiritual. The intense poetic vision often found in these compositions has been commented on before. It should also be noted that the tradition is far from dead, that it flourishes, in fact, in the gospel song and in the sermons of innumerable Black preachers and orators ranging from Martin Luther King, Jr., Malcolm X, Rev. C. L. Franklin, and Minister Louis Farrakhan, to the preacher who is known only in his immediate community. Paralleling this tradition is the deliberate appropriation of preaching techniques in the communication of artists as diverse as James Brown and the Last Poets. An extension of this is the emergence over the past few years of the "rap" as an authentic Black literary form. In addition, I have included a few "seculars" from Talley's *Negro Folk Rhymes* to suggest in particular some of the cultural roots of the Dunbar selections.

In Section II, the oral tradition is represented chiefly by the blues and the ballad, two forms which were especially appealing to the writers of the Harlem Renaissance and the period immediately following. Langston Hughes and Sterling Brown can thus be better appreciated in the "Soul-Field," so to speak, of these compositions; and it is important to note how the frankness and raciness of their language ring true to their sources of inspiration. There are other folk forms, to be sure, that are not represented, and other influences upon the poets themselves, but it seems to me that these two forms are the crucial ones, and that the critical view of life represented is that of the blues and the universal Black energy of jazz, both problematic from the beginning to the larger American society.

The other poets in this section relate authentically to this tradition as well, though not so obviously or so directly; and in many ways they explore areas of Black sensibility which Hughes and Brown first set down as formal literature.

In Section III, the longest in the book, all of the influences which were suggested in the first two groups are present here also. However, there is a distinct difference in tone and purpose which must be recognized. That difference comes from the streets of the Black Community, and in all probability, dates from the Black northern migrations of pre-World War I days. Sterling Brown and Langston Hughes are certainly conscious of it, but literary conventions forbade their full exploration of it. Still at times they are quite direct. There is the question of drugs, for instance, which Brown makes explicit in "Maumee Ruth," where her son, unaware of her death, is "Hiding in city holes, / Sniffing the 'snow.' . . ." But the chief difference between poetry of the Harlem Renaissance and the Black poetry of the sixties comes in the full exploration and appropriation of the street experience and the formulation of an aesthetic and an ideology based in part upon it. This is no mere literary gesture, as some would have us believe; and for that reason I have included Rap Brown's poem. Its relationship to "Stack O'Lee" and "Shine and the Titanic," should be obvious, at least to Black people. It also should be obvious that for the first time in this nation's history the Black man was putting his oppressors in the *political dozens,* and that, true to form, the oppressor "put stuff in the game." At any rate, to speak about these poems, the crucial difference here is the emergence of the new Black Consciousness and the Black Arts Movements.

Finally, these selections are arranged roughly in the order of their "emergence" or publication, and not always according to the poet's age. Thus, this is a kind of "thesis" anthology, one designed to argue, if you please, a certain point of view. The validity of this argument, I leave to the reader. to judge, not in the isolation of this particular work, but in the context of wider, more conventional selections.

S.E.H.

The author is especially indebted to *The Institute of the Black World,* an independent research center in Atlanta, Georgia, for its aid and comfort while he worked there as a Senior Research Fellow, and to The American Council of Learned Societies for a grant that enabled him to complete the research for this book.

CONTENTS

UNDERSTANDING
THE NEW BLACK POETRY

Introduction:

The Forms of Things Unknown

OVERVIEW

Black poetry in the United States has been widely misunderstood, misinterpreted, and undervalued for a variety of reasons—aesthetic, cultural, and political—especially by white critics; but with the exception of the work of a few established figures, it has also been suspect by many Black academicians whose literary judgments are self-consciously "objective" and whose cultural values, while avowedly "American," are essentially European. This poetry has also been misrepresented in a number of anthologies, not only the so-called integrated ones, but also in some which are exclusively Black. I shall not designate any of these, for my intent is not polemical. Besides, there are many reasons why an anthology may not be "representative." The central problem, however, is one of selection. If we began with Lucy Terry and Phillis Wheatley, then only brief space could be given to the great quantity of poetry produced during the Harlem Renaissance and later during the sixties. Excellent anthologies have been produced which have deliberately focused on either the earlier periods or on the later ones. However, an attempt should be made in which the *continuity* and the *wholeness* of the Black poetic tradition in the United States are suggested. That tradition exists on two main levels, the written and the oral, which sometimes converge. To illuminate the interaction of these two lines of Black poetry, an anthology could profit from a critical framework, an organizing principle, other than chronology; for, indeed, many crucial questions have been leveled at Black poetry, especially that of the sixties, ranging from the spiteful and splenetic to the quick, intellectual probings of Black people themselves as students and teachers, as critics, as poets and performers. While there is a significant number of statements by the poets themselves regarding their intentions, these are often unknown to the critics or ignored or misin-

[*3*]

terpreted by them. In addition, problems arise as a result of philosophical and political preferences. Other problems arise from an impatience to translate ideological positions into aesthetic ones, even when such translation is both possible and useful. This Black poetry deserves much more serious attention than it now receives, especially from Black academicians and others who profess a concern with cultural clarity, historical accuracy, and social justice.

Art, of course, including literature, does not exist in a vacuum, and reflects—and helps to shape—the lives of those who produce it. It is able to do these things, moroever, because of the special heightening and refining of experience that is characteristic of art. Literature, accordingly, is the verbal organization of experience into beautiful forms, but what is meant by "beautiful" and by "forms" is to a significant degree dependent upon a people's way of life, their needs, their aspirations, their history—in short, their culture. Ultimately the "beautiful" is bound up with the truth of a people's history, *as they perceive it themselves,* and if their vision is clear, its recording just, others may perceive that justness too; and, if they bring to it the proper sympathy and humility, they may even share in the general energy, if not in the specific content of that vision. Since poetry is the most concentrated and the most allusive of the verbal arts, if there is such a commodity as "blackness" in literature (and I assume that there is), it should somehow be found in concentrated or in residual form in the poetry.

The formal or written aspect of the poetic tradition that we are dealing with here reaches back to the eighteenth century, and contains a substantial body of compositions which at their best are the equal of much of the other American poetry of the period. Notable Black poets of this era are Lucy Terry, Phillis Wheatley, Jupiter Hammon, and George Moses Horton. This formal aspect of the Black poetic tradition has been carefully and sensitively studied, and this volume makes no pretense at covering that ground.

Still one can profit from the insight afforded by William

H. Robinson's scholarly volume, *Early Black American Poets* (William C. Brown Co., Publishers, 1969). In his introduction Professor Robinson states: ". . . if today a college textbook in 'American Literature' can include such diverse writings as excerpts from travelogues . . . letters, journals and diaries . . . and if the verse of the likes of Philip Pain, John Josselyn, Edward Coote Pinkney can be included in the *Oxford Anthology of American Literature*, which went through ten (10) printings by 1956, then clearly the efforts of early Black American poets deserve student attention also" (pp. xvi, xvii).

However, even if one approaches poetry as formal, written composition, one soon becomes aware of the other side of the tradition—the unwritten songs, the rhymes, and the speech of Black slaves which have also attracted special attention for a very long time. And if confirmation were needed of early enthusiastic judgments on these compositions, one could easily find it in the texts of the songs which were collected in the nineteenth century, but apparently had been in existence long before then. If one still distrusted one's own judgment, one could turn to works like R. T. Kerlin's *Negro Poets and Their Poems* with its sensitive insights into the oral poetry, or to W. E. B. Du Bois's *The Souls of Black Folk*, or to the essays of Sterling Brown or Alain Locke or to *The Negro Caravan*. However, for my purpose the clearest and most intriguing statement is to be found in Richard Wright's essay "The Literature of the Negro in the United States," in which he describes the kind of writing derived from the inner life of the folk as "The Forms of Things Unknown."

This evocative, almost prophetic phrase suggests an interior dynamism which underlies much of the best of contemporary Black poetry. Although others, before and after Wright, were aware of the potential of building upon Black folk roots, no one had named it so explicitly: almost invariably the earlier critics either thought of refining the folk materials, in the manner of the *Lyrical Ballads*, or of absorbing them into forms deriving from European music, the opera, for example, and the symphony. Thus Kerlin observes the similarity of the "folk song of the plantation" to the English folk-song tradition and points to a possible line of development for Black poetry.

> This unstudied poetry of the people, the unlettered common folk, had supreme virtues, the elemental and universal virtues of simplicity, sincerity, veracity. It had the power, in an artificial age, to bring poetry back to reality, to genuine emotion, to effectiveness, to the common interest of mankind. Simple and crude as it was it had a merit unknown to the polished verse of the schools. Potential Negro poets might do well to ponder this fact of literary history. There is nothing more precious in English literature than this crude old poetry of the people. [p. 18.]

Notwithstanding, Kerlin, as others both white and Black, would emphasize the essentially American, i.e., *white* cultural values and norms to be followed by these "potential Negro poets." He warns the reader not to expect or demand "novelty of language, form, imagery, idea—novelty and quaintness, perhaps amusing 'originality,' or grotesqueness . . . ," but, considering the climate of the twenties and the thirties, and, indeed, even the sixties and the seventies, the warning had a certain humane reasonableness. For we remember the patronizing preface which W. D. Howells wrote to Dunbar's *Lyrics of Lowly Life,* and we remember the equally patronizing preface which Allen Tate wrote to Tolson's *Libretto for Liberia,* as well as Karl Shapiro's foreword to *Harlem Gallery,* and the pontifications of an Albert Goldman, on blues singers and Black poets. And for those who see parallels between the Harlem Renaissance and the present, most apparent certainly must be the cult of the Exotic Negro, which so disgusted Langston Hughes. And in the middle ground of the picture, between Langston Hughes and the Last Poets, there is the remarkable achievement of Gwendolyn Brooks, which poet-critic Louis Simpson dismissed in a review in the *New York Herald-Tribune*

(1963) because he was "not sure it is possible for a Negro to write well without making us aware he is a Negro; on the other hand, if being a Negro is the only subject, the writing is not important. . . ." His opinion seems fairly widespread, despite the evaluation by another brilliant poet, Margaret Walker Alexander (*Black Expression,* p. 97).

What we are speaking about now, to be clear, is the question of form, theme, and invention in Black poetry, and the means for assessing them. We thus raise the questions: What is Black poetry? Who is to judge Black poetry? How is it to be judged?

To the first, we may logically say that Black poetry is chiefly:

1. Any poetry by any person or group of persons of known Black African ancestry, whether the poetry is designated Black or not.
2. Poetry which is somehow *structurally* Black, irrespective of authorship.
3. Poetry by any person or group of known Black African ancestry, which is *also identifiably* Black, in terms of structure, theme, or other characteristics.
4. Poetry by any identifiably Black person who can be classed as a "poet" by Black people. Judgment may or may not coincide with judgments of whites.
5. Poetry by any identifiably Black person whose ideological stance vis-à-vis the history and the aspirations of his people since slavery is adjudged by them to be "correct."

Each of these statements poses certain serious and wide-ranging problems of an aesthetic, sociological, historical, political, and critical nature. Each of them suggests a limited means for understanding the scope of Black poetry, and I raise them chiefly to stimulate creative discussion. I have no illusion about answering them completely. Notwithstanding, I do have a position, which is that these questions can not be resolved without considering the ethnic roots of Black poetry, which I insist are ultimately understood only

[7]

by Black people themselves. Be that at is may, let me try, for the sake of clarity, to suggest some of the questions which are implicit in the five formulations.

In No. 1, these questions can be raised. Is there a quality, condition, construction, or composition that can be called "poetry" wherever it is found? Is there, in other words, a poem that everyone would agree to as being a poem, a "universal" poem? Some people obviously think so, and thus we find anthologies of the "best" in American poetry, or the "best" in world poetry, even in world *literature*. And, certainly, there are numerous attempts to define poetry, oftentimes with elaborate theoretical formulations.

Accordingly, there are collections of poetry which contain some "universal" poems that were written by persons who incidentally *happened* to be Black. There is a long and complex history surrounding this kind of argument, involving poets like Countee Cullen on the one hand and some of our most respected critics and scholars on the other. For my part, I confess that the only "universal" commodity that I feel at all certain about is the hydrogen atom.

However, there are working definitions of poetry that are subscribed to by people within the same general cultural framework. Thus, on the basis of criteria developed out of a specific kind of writing, one could say that a certain passage from Phillis Wheatley is better than one from Anne Bradstreet, or that a given passage from Pope is better than both of the others. But whether a passage in the heroic couplet is better or more "poetic" than a passage in blank verse is certainly no easy matter to resolve. Whether everyone should write in a given form because it is accepted by the literary establishment is certainly a relevant and very difficult question.

Statement No. 2 raises the problem of national poetic forms, themes, and temperament. With specific reference to Black poetry, one raises the question of "characteristic" Black forms and expressions. Are there any? What are they? This makes us aware of the need for a serious consideration

[*8*]

of "Negritude" as well as of the historical evolution of poetic forms in the Black World, i.e., Africa and the Diaspora. Statement No. 3 raises the same kinds of questions in more detail. What, for example, distinguishes a Claude McKay sonnet from a sonnet by Longfellow? Is the difference a quality that is common to all, or only to a representative number of Black sonneteers? Is it possible that, given a Black Poetic Structure, a non-Black can create in this form—as whites play jazz, for example? Or as Blacks sing Italian opera?

Statement No. 4 raises the question, Who is a poet? Are the answers the same for all people, in all times? Is the concept of the poet *relevant* to an extended discussion of Black poetry? Is the Baptist preacher who describes the Last Judgment or the Valley of the Dry Bones a poet? Is the blues singer/composer a poet? Is Melvin Tolson a greater poet than James Brown?

Statement No. 5 raises an extremely important question, especially when dealing with contemporary Black poetry. Is the conservative James Weldon Johnson as good a poet as the radical W. E. B. Du Bois? Further, is all of the ideologically "correct" material found in *The Journal of Black Poetry* equally valid as Black poetry? Should one judge? Various poets have said or implied that a relevant criticism is necessary to the development of Black poetry, and some of them have written articles and reviews which express their positions.*

* Stanley Crouch, for example, has made important statements in "Toward a Purer Black Poetry Esthetic," *Journal of Black Poetry*, I, 10, 1968, pp. 28, 29, and in "The Big Feeling," *Negro Digest*, July, 1969, pp. 45–48. Other important statements have been made by Clarence Major in "A Black Criterion," *Journal of Black Poetry*, Spring, 1967, pp. 15, 16; Askia Muhammad Touré, "Black Magic!" *Journal of Black Poetry*, I, 10, 1968, pp. 63, 64; Carolyn Rodgers, "Black Poetry—Where It's At," *Negro Digest*, September, 1969, and more recently in "Uh Nat'chal Thang—The Whole Truth—Us," *Black World*, September, 1971, pp. 4–14; Mari Evans, "Contemporary Black Literature," *Black World*, June, 1970, pp. 4, 93–94. Larry Neal's and Imamu Baraka's statements are well known. To these must be added the observations of Don L. Lee in his new *Dynamite Voices #1*, Broadside Press, 1971.

Besides the poets themselves there are the professional and the academic critics. Some of them sympathize with the views of the poets, some of them do not. At any rate, whether the poets want it or not, readers and listeners will judge. Certainly poets expect it. The question thus should be: Who is best qualified to judge Black poetry? Black people obviously should judge, since the poetry—at least the contemporary poetry—is directed to them. The question then arises: Are all Black people equally endowed with the poetic talent? With the critical talent? Who decides? Black English teachers brought up on English literature? Or the man in the street? Or the ideologue who raises the "correct" questions? Is Maulana Karenga a better critic than Addison Gayle, or Saunders Redding, or Don L. Lee, or George Kent? Or Larry Neal?

There should be, of course, a way of speaking about all kinds of Black poetry, despite the kinds of questions that can be raised. In our attempts to clarify such a method, it might be wise to speak more specifically about the poetry itself, in addition to the critical premises stated above.

Although it is an arbitrary scheme for the purpose of analysis, one may describe or discuss a "Black" poem in terms of the following broad critical categories: (1) Theme, (2) Structure, (3) Saturation.

(1) By *theme* I mean that which is being spoken of, whether the specific subject matter, the emotional response to it, or its intellectual formulation.

(2) By *structure* I mean chiefly some aspect of the poem such as diction, rhythm, figurative language, which goes into the total makeup. (At times, I use the word in an extended sense to include what is usually called genre.)

(3) By *saturation* I mean several things, chiefly the communication of "Blackness" and fidelity to the observed or intuited truth of the Black Experience in the United States. It follows that these categories should also be valid in any critical evaluation of the poem.

THEME

Of the three categories, perhaps the simplest and most apparent is theme. In the following quatrain by George Moses Horton, for example, the "Blackness" is apparent in what he is speaking about, his historical situation as a Black slave in the United States.

> Alas! and am I born for this,
> To wear this slavish chain,
> Deprived of all created bliss,
> Through hardships, toil and pain!

Or another simple example might be Cullen's "To Make a Poet Black," with its bitter concluding couplet:

> Yet do I marvel at this curious thing,
> To make a poet black and bid him sing.*

It could be easily argued that both Horton and Cullen are really dealing with the universal theme of rebellion against oppression, and that Black poets have no monopoly on the theme. To that there can be varied response, but the significant point is that poetry because of its very nature—sensuous and rooted in particular experience—is not the same as philosophy or mathematics. Thus, though "slavish chain" might evoke a sympathetic tear from the eye of a white New York professor meditating upon his people's enslavement in ancient Egypt, that makes the poem no less valid

---

* All thematic materials are certainly not this obvious and direct, but on a very low level of perception we can be alerted to racial content this way. Ambiguities, of course, exist. For example, if a non-Black writer elected to write on a "Black theme" using a Black persona, and if he were as successful in absorbing Black expressive patterns as some musicians are, then, indeed there would be real problems. As far as I know, there are no poems written by non-Blacks which have that degree of success. But there is a considerable body of "dialect" poetry from whites to indicate what I mean. In addition, there are various poetical works like Blake's "Little Black Boy," as well as prose fiction like *Othello, Oroonoko, Uncle Remus.*

as a "Black statement." However, this ambiguity does make it a less precise kind of statement than Cullen's, because in the latter the irony cannot be appreciated without understanding the specific historical debasement of the African psyche in America. Other questions raised under the rubric of "universal theme" can be answered basically in the same way.

It should be understood from the outset that a Black poet may develop a theme which stems directly out of his experience, colored, so to speak, by his Blackness, but not communicate that Blackness, unless one go outside the poem itself. This we may choose not to do. If we do, however, the action, I think, would be perfectly valid. To test the validity of this statement, let us read the following sonnet:

> My mistress' eyes are nothing like the sun;
> Coral is far more red than her lips' red;
> If snow be white, why then her breasts are dun;
> If hairs be wires, black wires grow on her head.
> I have seen roses damask'd, red and white,
> But no such roses see I in her cheeks;
> And in some perfumes is there more delight
> Than in the breath that from my mistress reeks.
> I love to hear her speak, yet well I know
> That music hath a far more pleasing sound;
> I grant, I never saw a goddess go;
> My mistress when she walks treads on the ground:
> And yet, by heaven, I think my love as rare
> As any she belied with false compare.

This, of course, is Shakespeare's sonnet No. 130. But, if we discovered one day that it had been composed by an African at Elizabeth's court, would not the thematic meaning change? Perhaps formalist critics would not publicly admit the point, but a culturally oriented critic would. So, knowledge of the author's race altered our point of view, i.e., going outside of the poem changed our perspective of it.

There are more difficult questions regarding theme, which cannot be discussed abstractly or by simple example. Such questions are: Is there a special theme or cluster of themes which run throughout Black poetry? Are there Black themes which apparently cannot be handled by non-Black writers? This question was raised by W. S. Braithwaite in "The Negro in American Literature," *The New Negro,* p. 35, but in the broader context of all of Black literature, not just poetry. He states, ". . . in spite of all good intentions, the true presentation of the real tragedy of Negro life is a task still left for Negro writers to perform. This is especially true for those phases of culturally representative race life that as yet have scarcely at all found treatment by white American authors." Present-day poets and many critics too— as the response to William Styron's *Nat Turner* shows— would deny the ultimate validity of any white presentation of the Black Experience in art.

Historical surveys such as Brawley's *Early Negro American Writers,* Brown, Davis, and Lee's *The Negro Caravan,* and Robinson's *Early Black Poets* suggest that there are indeed thematic clusters in Black poetry around what could be called the idea of Liberation. And when we move to the present, we must consider certainly the essays by Richard Wright and the critical statements by the poets themselves in which they express their intent that, as a rule, follows the historical consciousness of the people. This is to say, that as Black people in the United States refine and clarify their conceptions of themselves the poetry reflects the process.

The early formal Black poetry reflected the concerns of those who were trained to read and to write. Thus, to follow Sterling Brown's account, there were those poets whose chief object was to demonstrate their ability to write as well as the whites, as in the case of Alberry Whitman and the "Mockingbird School of Poets." Other poets, like James Bell and Frances Ellen Harper, used their talents in the abolitionist cause. Another group wrote in dialect and took for their subject matter the lives of the common folk which they sometimes caricatured in the manner of white writers like Thomas Nelson Page. Others, like Paul Laurence Dunbar and James Edwin Campbell, while still influenced by white stereotypes and the expectations of white audiences, presented wholesome, if not altogether realistic, portraits of Black folk life. The period preceding the Harlem Renaissance not only produced the dialect poets but found many Black poets studiously avoiding overt racial considerations in a manner reminiscent of the late forties and the fifties. "Poetry was a romantic escape for many of them," states Brown, "not a perception of reality. . . ."

Although there were attempts at realistic depiction of Black life before they came on the scene, the writers of the Harlem Renaissance were the first to do this in a systematic manner, as even a cursory look at the period will reveal. One recalls Langston Hughes's famous declaration in "The Negro Artist and the Racial Mountain":

> These common people are not afraid of spirituals, as for a long time their more intellectual brethren were, and jazz is their child. They furnish a wealth of colorful, distinctive material for any artist because they still hold their own individuality in the face of American standardizations. And perhaps these common people will give to the world its truly great Negro artist, the one who is not afraid to be himself. Whereas the better-class Negro would tell the artist what to do, the people at least let him alone when he does appear. And they are not ashamed of him—if they know he exists at all. And they accept what beauty is their own without question.
>
> [*Black Expression*, pp. 259, 260.]

Notwithstanding the bravery of this kind of effort, Hughes and other realistic writers of his generation were sharply censured by middle-class members of their own race, including W. E. B. Du Bois and Benjamin Brawley (*Negro Genius*, p. 248), for portraying the "seamy side" of Black life. Seen in retrospect, the poetry of this group, the poetry of the twenties, helped to balance the pieties of the abolitionist writers on the one hand and the bucolic idylls of the dialect school on the other. Alain Locke's essay entitled "The

New Negro," which appeared in his larger "statement," the epoch-making volume of the same name, brought the issues into focus. Afro-Americans had come of age; they could look at themselves for what they were, without false piety and without shame, rejecting the "social nostrums and the panaceas," and realizing that although religion, freedom, and education were important to their cause, they alone were not sufficient. What was needed was group solidarity and collective effort.

> Each generation . . . will have its creed, and that of the present is the belief in the efficacy of collective effort, in race cooperation. This deep feeling of race is at present the mainspring of Negro life. It seems to be the outcome of the reaction to proscription and prejudice; an attempt, fairly successful on the whole, to convert a defensive into an offensive position, a handicap into an incentive. It is radical in tone, but not in purpose and only the most stupid forms of opposition, misunderstanding or persecution could make it otherwise. Of course, the thinking Negro has shifted a little toward the left with the world-trend, and there is an increasing group who affiliate with radical and liberal movements. But fundamentally for the present the Negro is radical on race matters, conservative on others, in other words, a "forced radical," a social protestant rather than a genuine radical. Yet under further pressure and injustice, iconoclastic thought and motives will inevitably increase. Harlem's quixotic radicalisms call for their ounce of democracy to-day lest to-morrow they be beyond cure.
>
> [*New Negro*, p. 11.]

Locke's analysis was essentially correct. Unfortunately his warning was not heeded, and although the "stupid forms of opposition," the "misunderstanding," and the "persecution" which he warned against seemed to be abating during the Civil Rights Movement of the fifties and sixties, the failure of Dr. King's Northern Campaign which linked the anti-war and the Civil Rights issues, and his assassination in 1968 indicated that the country still intended to keep its Black citizens in subjection.

Disenchantment with the goals and strategies of the Civil Rights Movement led to the Black Power Movement and the subsequent widespread revival of nationalist and internationalist feeling and thought among Blacks. To the extent that Black artists today have influenced their community to view itself in the larger political and spiritual context of Blackness, they have moved beyond the Harlem Renaissance, though obviously influenced by it. The old theme of liberation took on new meaning. Thus the Black Arts Movement, though emerging before the Black Power Movement, is in some respects the cultural dimension of that phenomenon. Numerous eloquent spokesmen have appeared, among them Imamu Amiri Baraka (LeRoi Jones), Larry Neal, Ron Karenga, and Don L. Lee.

In their statements, one can see the process of self-definition made clearer and sharper as the self-reliance and racial consciousness of an earlier period are revived and raised to the level of revolutionary thought.

The present movement is different from the Harlem Renaissance in the extent of its attempt to speak directly *to* Black people *about themselves* in order to move them toward self-knowledge and collective freedom. It is therefore not "protest" art but essentially an art of liberating vision. Larry Neal is probably its most articulate proponent. He states that when Black artists speak of the need to address the psychic and spiritual needs of their people,

> They are not speaking of an art that screams and masturbates before white audiences. That is the path of Negro literature and civil rights literature. No, they are not speaking about that kind of thing, even though that is what some Negro writers of the past have done. Instead, they are speaking of an art that addresses itself directly to Black People; an art that speaks to us in terms of our feelings and ideas about the world; an art that validates the positive aspects of our life style. Dig: An art that opens

us up to the beauty and ugliness within us; that makes us understand our condition and each other in a more profound manner; that unites us, exposing us to our painful weaknesses and strengths; and finally, an art that posits for us the Vision of a Liberated Future.

["Any Day Now: Black Art and Black Liberation,"
Ebony, August, 1969, pp. 55, 56.]

A difference in emphasis, in depth, in scope, and political maturity is thus evident when one considers the Harlem Renaissance, but many of these developments were possible because of the changing world in which Black Americans of the post-World War II generation found themselves, a world in which articulate men and women rediscovered Africa and Pan-Africanism, rediscovered Du Bois and Garvey, rediscovered the Harlem Renaissance itself and built upon its strengths while seeking to avoid its errors. The process is continuing, as a careful examination of Neal's statement would show, for in its polemical dimension it calls attention, in fact, to the problems which still beset Black art. There is still, for example, a sizeable amount of masturbatory art that screams "whitey" and "honkie." But that too is changing under the advice of artists like Mari Evans, in critical essays and in poems like "Speak the Truth to the People." Askia Touré is another who has contributed to a growing general awareness by Black intellectuals that there are more important things to do than to amuse supercilious whites or to respond to their misunderstanding of Black creative efforts.

This awareness is especially meaningful when we hear it expressed by Gwendolyn Brooks. In a lecture at Clark College, in Atlanta, Georgia, April 26, 1971, Miss Brooks stated that she could not imagine herself today writing the kind of poem whose theme was a pleading of her humanity to a larger white society, as she had done years earlier in the words:

Men of careful turns, haters of forks in the road,
The strain at the eye, that puzzlement, that awe—

Grant me that I am human, that I hurt,
That I can cry.*

[*Selected Poems*, p. 65.]

In spite of false starts, meandering, backsliding, and illusory goals, the great overarching movement of consciousness for Black people must be called, in contemporary parlance, the idea of Liberation—from slavery, from segregation and degradation, from wishful "integration" into the "mainstream," to the passionate denial of white middle-class values of the present and an attendant embrace of Africa and the Third World as alternative routes of development. This is not to say, of course, that all contemporary Black poets mean the same thing by Liberation, or even that they speak very precisely for the Black masses when they use that term, but if one substituted the old word "Freedom" for it, there would be no doubt at all that the message is clear. At any rate, it should be clear that not only have the Black professionals organized themselves around varying concepts of Liberation, but so also have innumerable other groups, some representing and having direct contact with the masses. But perhaps the most striking embodiment of this Liberation consciousness has occurred among Black prisoners, as the Attica uprising of September 9, 1971, indicates. Some Blacks see the uprising as a failure of revolutionary resolve because of the divisiveness among the prisoners and their seeming inability to make good on their threats to execute their hostages and fight to the death. Another view appears in a report from

* Because of her importance as a distinguished poet and a catalyst of the present generation of artists and writers, especially of the Chicago-based OBAC group, Miss Brooks's words and attitudes distill the essential heroism of writers like Alain Locke, and makes them meaningful to us in these crucial times. Other writers have served a similar function, among them Langston Hughes, and Sterling Brown, "Black grandfathers of the new poetry." It must be understood, however, that although I have called attention to a few, there are other important and influential writers who have helped to clarify the shift in consciousness from Black endurance and pride to revolutionary awakening, and in any assessment of that function one must certainly name Margaret Walker, Dudley Randall, Sam Allen, Hoyt Fuller, Mari Evans, James Emanuel, and Margaret Danner.

The Institute of the Black World, an independent research organization based in Atlanta, Georgia. The report describes the political significance in these terms:

> Attica is a new event in history. Nothing like it has ever happened before. It is a symbol that black men whom white society has consigned to its deepest dungeons have, instead of succumbing, rediscovered themselves and re-educated themselves to rise up and strike back at the system which intended that they should never survive at all— and certainly not as men. But beyond the symbolism are the immense practical achievements of the brothers.

After listing these achievements, it goes on to state:

> The men of Attica were different from their captors. One brother said, "I am Attica." He meant that he was the new reality, the embodiment of change that Attica and all American institutions must undergo. . . . In order to sustain the revolt at Attica some new moral and political force had to be created, some new set of values. What was it? What was new about the black prisoners which made their revolt unlike any other that had happened before? . . . The prisoners seized Attica and ran it *autonomously* and *humanely*. With compassion for their enemies. This is what is new. This is what the non-official "visitors" who got inside could not believe.
>
> [*IBW Monthly Report*, Sept., 1971.]

Whether the masses of Black people accept this position, the first one, or some other, the cultural dimension of the event lies in the fact that Black writing—not only the works of Malcolm X and Fanon, but the poetry of Etheridge Knight and Don L. Lee and Claude McKay—had helped to shape the prisoners' new values, had increased their self-esteem and sharpened their political awareness, just as it has affected a whole generation of Black college students on all levels. Ironically, for it shows with graphic precision the arrogant ignorance which established institutions have of the Black Arts Movement, and, deeper, of Black history and aspirations

—ironically, a *Time* magazine story which purported to be an in-depth study of the rebellion noted that Black prisoners were inspired by original writings by the prisoners themselves, among which was "a poem written by an unknown prisoner, crude but touching in its would-be heroic style" (*Time*, Sept. 7, 1971, p. 20). And in demonstration of what he meant, the *Time* writer included the opening lines of Claude McKay's famous sonnet, "If We Must Die." This was crude! True, the prisoner who copied the lines had written "unglorious" for McKay's "inglorious." But crude! Winston Churchill, of course, had better taste, and better judgment. In the abysmal early days of World War II when Great Britain was struggling for its very life against Nazi Germany, when all of Western Europe had been overrun, and France itself had been crushed—in those bitter times for the British people—Winston Churchill, the Prime Minister of Great Britain and its greatest leader of modern times, galvanized the British Parliament and the will of the English people with the ringing words of this self-same sonnet, written by a young Jamaican two decades earlier, while he smarted from the same kind of institutionalized racism that Hitler's Germany was inflicting upon its neighbors. The crowning irony, of course, is that few people knew that McKay was Black or bothered to think, if they knew it, that his homeland Jamaica was an exploited British colony with a history of bloody suppression, or, for that matter, that his adopted homeland America though subtle, at times, was hardly less brutal. And now twenty odd years after his death, amidst the intellectual ambivalence which surrounds the Harlem Renaissance, his explosive words, though literally baffled by the sonnet form, still inspire hope and revolutionary courage in the minds of men whom their country had declared to be an economic and spiritual surplus.

But though the great theme of Black poetry, and, indeed, of Black life in the United States is Liberation, there are important complementary patterns, some of which take us outside the dimension of history into the universal realm of the mythical. In the oral tradition, the dogged determination of the work songs, the tough-minded power of the blues, the inventive energy of jazz, and the transcendent vision of God in the spirituals and the sermons, all energize the idea of Liberation, which is itself liberated from the temporal, the societal, and the political—not with the narcotic obsession to remain above the world of struggle and change and death, but with full realization of a return to that world both strengthened and renewed. Thus in the spirituals we have both:

> Go down, Moses, way down in Egypt land.
> Tell ol Pharaoh to let my people go.

and

> Drinkin' of the wine, wine, wine,
> Drinkin' of the wine
> I ought to bin to Heaven ten thousand years
> Drinkin' of the wine.

In the blues we find these haunting lines from Robert Johnson:

> I got to keep movinn', I got to keep movinnn',
> Blues fallin' down like hail, blues fallin' down like hail,
> Mmmmmmmmmmmmm-mmmm-mmm, blues fallin'
>   down like hail, blues fallin' down like hail,
> And the days keep on worryin' me, for a hell-hound
>   on my trail,
> Hell-hound on my trail, hell-hound on my trail.

But we also find this famous anonymous line, which seems a distillation of the blues spirit:

> I got the blues, but I'm too damn mean to cry.

And in Furry Lewis' "White Lightnin' Blues," the blues not only represent spiritual paralysis, but liberation through sexuality.

> Baby, fix my breakfast, so I can go to bed,
> Baby, fix my breakfast, so I can go to bed,

I been drinkin' white lightnin' and it's done gone
to my head.

Got the blues so bad, it hurts my feet to walk,
Got the blue so bad, it hurts my feet to walk;
It wouldn't hurt so bad, but it hurts my tongue to talk.

Not only that, but also this resolution in the affirmative:

The train I ride sixteen coaches long,
The train I ride sixteen coaches long;
She don't haul nothin' but chocolate to the bone.

And even in the contemporary poetry, with all of its pre-
occupation with the immediate problems of political asser-
tion and the raising of consciousness and the celebration of
the Black cities, there is a pronounced concern with the
spiritual, sometimes rooted in the idiom of the Black church,
sometimes exploring religious concepts of Islam and African
religions, sometimes seeking analogues to modern music.
Some of the poets who reflect this concern with the spiritual
are W. Keorapetse Kgositsile, Don Lee, Imamu Baraka
(LeRoi Jones), and Larry Neal. In this volume the pattern
is found in poems like Baraka's "I Am Speaking of Future
Good-ness and Social Philosophy," Sharon Bourke's "So-
pranosound, Memory of John," and Larry Neal's "Morning
Raga for Malcolm," with the lines:

I now calm airily float
lift my spirit—Allah you
am me. space undulates
under me, space, to my sides
and under me nothing
I now calm airily float

There are, of course, other thematic patterns that Black
poetry handles. But even in the purely personal concerns,
say, of some of Paul Laurence Dunbar's "nonracial" poems,
or of Countee Cullen's or Walter Dancy's, there are patterns
that one can call "Black," if one accepts the critical premises
of this essay. So, there are, then, Black poems in which the

theme is apparent, such as the personal concern of Horton as a Black person in the previously quoted quatrain. One might also include in this group Dunbar's bitter lament in "The Poet," Cullen's "Heritage" and some of the poetry of Langston Hughes.

A step toward objectification and distancing of personal involvement occurs when the poet depicts either real or imaginary Black figures. Here the technique, of course, merges with that of other literary traditions, at times rather obviously so, as in the case of the realistic writers of the thirties being under the influence of Carl Sandburg, E. A. Robinson, and other American whites. However, it must be remembered that there is a Black storytelling tradition which is also at work, and sometimes it is consciously being followed. At any rate, this depiction of Black character deals with historical figures like Frederick Douglass, in Robert Hayden's poem; Malcolm X, as in Margaret Walker and James Emanuel; Martin L. King, Jr., as in Mari Evans, Margaret Danner, and Donald Graham; Nat Turner, as in Robert Hayden and Margaret Walker. At times it deals with Black musical figures, whose lives become vehicles for comment by the poet, as in the various poems on Coltrane by Don Lee, Sonia Sanchez, and others; Bessie Smith, by Robert Hayden; Ma Rainey, by Sterling Brown; Duke Ellington, by Sarah Fabio. In addition, there are musical figures who may or may not be historical, such as Dunbar's "Malindy" and "Whistling Sam."

Similarly, Black literary figures also become the subject of various poems. Among the figures thus treated are Countee Cullen, Richard Wright, Paul Dunbar, Langston Hughes, and Gwendolyn Brooks.

A final group of character poems includes larger-than-life figures such as Stack O'Lee, Shine, and John Henry. In all of this, of course, the poet can pursue whatever theme related to the Black Experience he finds meaningful. Of course, few white writers find these subjects meaningful enough to write about.

[23]

Some of these concerns, as I have implied earlier, are common to poets outside of the Black tradition as well, so I need not try to enumerate or to discuss them. Others have been dealt with in summary form, but it might be of value to return to the poetry of the Harlem Renaissance and to compare its concerns with those of the present.

Sterling Brown's succinct statement is an indispensable point of departure. Speaking of the Renaissance poetry, he points out its five chief areas of interest:

> (1) a discovery of Africa as a source for race pride, (2) a use of Negro heroes and heroic episodes from American History, (3) propaganda of protest, (4) a treatment of the Negro masses frequently of the folk, less often of the workers with more understanding and less apology, and (5) franker and deeper self-revelation.
>
> [*Negro Poetry & Drama,*
> Atheneum ed., 1969, p. 61.]

Some of these concerns are also those of contemporary Black poetry, but with an important difference of emphasis. For example, in the rediscovery of Africa as a source for race pride, poets of the sixties were better informed generally about the true nature of African civilizations and, as a rule, were especially concerned about the political relevance of modern Africa to the rest of the Black World. This obviously has been the result of the emergence of free African states during the past two decades as well as the rise of interest among American Blacks in their continental brothers and sisters. The role of the media cannot be overestimated in this phenomenon, especially when Black men in the General Assembly of the United Nations, dressed in their native garb, were shown on television intelligently debating issues of international significance. A further related factor undoubtedly has been the influx of African students into the colleges and universities of the United States, especially into the Black ones. Then, one must consider the Black Power Movement and its extensions in the Black Arts Movement,

[*24*]

the national concern with Black Studies and the subsequent reprinting of quality materials on Africa, and finally the resurgence of interest in Pan-Africanism. In all of this, Alain Locke's essay "The New Negro" presently reads almost like prophecy. In sum, if the concern in the twenties was largely romantic, in the sixties, though at times not unromantic, it has been chiefly political.

With regard to the second point, "a use of Negro heroes and heroic episodes," we have already referred to the contemporary popularity of Black historical figures as subjects of poetry. However, it must be noted that the single most popular hero of contemporary Black poetry is Malcolm X, not Martin Luther King, Jr. And the heroes, whoever they are, do not apologize to America, nor plead, but seek to affirm their right to self-definition and manhood, with all that that implies. And the episodes in American history are viewed as episodes in "Black history," so it is not Peter Salem who interests the present generation but Nat Turner. And Black history also means African history and African heroes, Chaka, Kenyatta, Lumumba, Nyeryere, Nkrumah.

There has been, despite denials, some protest poetry in the sixties, as I have implied, but for the most part the message of that period, unlike that of earlier times, has been directed toward Black audiences, even though the poet knew that the white world was looking over his shoulder.

What Brown stated in his fourth point is still true of Black poetry. Although the "masses" appear frequently in the poetry of the sixties, there is to my knowledge little or no treatment of the Black worker as subject. Perhaps this is due to a comparative lack of sympathy with Marxist thought, perhaps to ideological unclarity, perhaps to a tendency to concentrate on heroic figures, martyrs, hustlers, and other romanticized types who go counter to the "mainstream" of American life.

Point number five, "franker and deeper self-revelation," indicates an important difference between the poetry of the Renaissance and that of the present; the tendency since the sixties has been mainly toward public statement, toward didacticism, and toward collective ritual. Thus it is not surprising that some of the poets are also dramatists and musicians and artists. I think one can safely generalize that much of the poetry of self-revelation written and published during this period is either by poets whose chronological age puts them in the fifties, at least, or by very young poets who are caught up in the introspection of adolescence. Notwithstanding, it is curious that much of contemporary poetry avoids the character drawing which was so prominent a part of the earlier production, from Paul Laurence Dunbar to Gwendolyn Brooks. Again, however, the exceptions are the older poets who have managed to keep attuned to the times. The question of form and personal habit may have something to do with this. At any rate, the younger poet will usually rap or declaim or sing, but if he wants to create a Black character for one purpose or another, he usually turns to drama or to the short story, as in the case of Sonia Sanchez, Carolyn Rodgers, and S. E. Anderson. Perhaps, finally, their method is dictated by their objectives. They want to speak as directly to the community as they can. At times they succeed, even when it entails not only speaking to a college audience but to a cynical gathering of people at a poolroom or bar, as the OBAC writers have done. More recently, the poets have been experimenting with more effective ways of reaching a mass audience, and the result has been the recording of LP albums which are played on the air, the use of the church as a forum, as in the case of Nikki Giovanni, and TV appearances, like those by the Last Poets. As I pointed out earlier, these poets are being heard and they are being understood by the people whom they address.

Sometimes a poet in his effort at self-revelation moves outside of the immediate concerns of the Black Community. Some of the poems of Mari Evans, Gwendolyn Brooks, and Robert Hayden appear to do this. Nevertheless, our mere awareness of them as Black persons helps to shape our response to the poem, and this is so whether or not the poet wants us to consider him as other than a poet pure and simple, or for that matter, pure and complex. The fact of the matter is that the Black Community does not intend to give up any of its beautiful singers, whether Countee Cullen or Melvin Tolson or Robert Hayden. We may quarrel with them sometimes, but ain't never gonna say good-bye.

STRUCTURE

Structure in Black poetry in some respects is the most difficult of the three elements which I have chosen for discussion. In the two examples used earlier, Horton uses a quatrain modeled on the English hymn, while Cullen uses the Shakespearean sonnet. And to complicate the matter, Claude McKay, the most militantly Black poet of his generation, uses the sonnet also, in a manner in which his thematic intention is unmistakable. We and the poets of our day have the problem of form to contend with as well, for often there is little (sometimes nothing) on the page to tell a reader at first sight that a "Black" poem was not indeed composed by e. e. cummings, Jack Spicer, or Paul Blackburn.

Professor W. E. Farrison, one of the outstanding scholars in the field of Afro-American literature, is noticeably peeved, for example, in a review of *Today's Negro Voices: An Anthology by Young Negro Poets,* edited by Beatrice M. Murphy (Julian Messner, 1970). He questions the inclusion of certain poems for their deficiency "in the harmony of sound and clear sense which is essential to good poetry." Then he singles out the kind of typographical stylistics which were popularized by e. e. cummings. He tries to hold his peace, but finds it difficult.

> Now as is evidenced by the long history of the art of writing, if a writer can express himself well without the aid of capitals and punctuation, he can most probably express himself better with it; and if he cannot express himself well with their aid, it is doubtful that he can express himself better without it.
> [*CLA Journal,* XIV, no. 1, 1970, p. 96.]

Although one could quarrel with the excessively stringent concept of poetry found in this review, it isn't difficult to sympathize with Farrison's impatience, because a good deal of modern poetry—white and Black—not only makes excessive demands on the reader's eyesight but tends too often to degenerate into artifice that however clever bears little real relationship to the oral aspect of the poem. Indeed, this emphasis on the visual has extensive and tenacious roots in Western poetry, not only in the cryptograms which Dryden satirized in *Macflecknoe,* but in the poetry of George Herbert, and long before him the Greek poems in the shape of altars, wings, and the like, which date from Simmias' poem in the shape of an egg in 300 B.C. (See *Art News Annual,* XXVIII, 1958, pp. 64–68, 178.) This tradition has also influenced modern Black poets, like Joe Goncalves in his "Now the Time Is Ripe to Be" and "Sister Brother," both appearing in *Black Fire,* LeRoi Jones and Larry Neal, eds. (William Morrow & Co., 1968), and N. H. Pritchard's various "concrete" poems in *Dices or Black Bones,* Adam David Miller, ed. (Houghton Mifflin Co., 1970).

Still if one is seriously interested in contemporary Black poetry, then one must examine some of the bases of this confusion. One must admit that typographically, at least, contemporary Black poets have been greatly influenced by white poets and frequently admit it, at least the older ones do. Imamu Amiri Baraka (LeRoi Jones) has said on several occasions that he owes a great technical debt to William Carlos Williams, and his early poetry embodies many of the attitudes and utilizes many of the techniques of the Beats who were also indebted to Williams. Much the same can be said of Bob Kaufman, who is considered by some to be the greatest innovator among the poets of that generation. But more fundamental than all of this is the fact that along with their immersion in Zen, the Beats themselves were enamored of jazz in particular and the Black life-style in general, and at times sought to communicate what has to be called a "Black feeling" in their work. Often their formal model was alleged to be jazz, so that accurately or not, Allen Ginsberg described Jack Kerouac's writing as a kind of "bop prosody." The words give us an important clue. They let us know that the Beats in their writing were striving to capture the rhythms and phrasings of Black music, to notate somehow those sounds on the printed page. Of course, it was not all printed, and some of the poetry was read to the accompaniment of jazz combos. But the point needs to be made that this was a generation after Langston Hughes had done the same thing—and with greater success. So, in effect, the Beats were approaching through empathy with the Black Experience some of the very same considerations—technical and thematic—that the Harlem Renaissance, the Negritude Movement, and the present generation of Black poets have approached from the *inside,* so to speak.

In their insistence upon jazz as a model and inspiration for their poetry, these writers were and are confronted with enormous technical problems, some of which may be insoluble if they continue to write that poetry down. For their model is dynamic, not static, and although one can suggest various vocal and musical effects with typography, an extensive use of these rather mechanical devices may be ultimately self-defeating. Thus Black poets are rediscovering the resources of their oral traditions and have occasionally been very successful with them. Some *idea* of that success may be obtained by *listening* to Imamu Amiri Baraka (LeRoi Jones), Larry Neal, Don L. Lee, Nikki Giovanni, and Ghylan Kain and the Original Last Poets. In the meantime, however, the question of typography is still quite formidable and still unresolved.

The central problem again is the printed page. Perhaps it will remain with us as a reminder of our compromise with a cold technology. Perhaps not. Though some of the poetry even on the page is highly effective, we still are confronted with Larry Neal's challenge of "the destruction of the text," in which the text of a poem is merely a "score," a single possible form of a poem. Much more theorizing and experimenting remain to be done.

Structurally speaking, however, whenever Black poetry is most distinctly and effectively *Black,* it derives its form from two basic sources, Black speech and Black music. It follows, then, if this is correct, that any serious appreciation or understanding of it must rest upon a deep and sympathetic knowledge of Black music and Black speech and—let us be plain —the Black people who make the music and who make the speech.

By Black speech I mean the speech of the majority of Black people in this country, and I do not exclude the speech of so-called educated people. By Black speech, I also imply a sensitivity to and an understanding of the entire range of Black spoken language in America. This includes the techniques and timbres of the sermon and other forms of oratory, the dozens, the rap, the signifying, and the oral folktale.

By Black music I mean essentially the vast fluid body of Black song—spirituals, shouts, jubilees, gospel songs, field cries, blues, pop songs by Blacks, and, in addition, jazz (by whatever name one calls it) and non-jazz music by Black composers who *consciously or unconsciously* draw upon the Black musical tradition.

These two "referents," as I shall call them, of Black poetry are themselves so closely related that it is quite naive, even foolish, to speak of the spirituals or the blues without considering their verbal components. And even in jazz the verbal component lurks somewhere in the rhythms, in the coloring, and in the phrasing, so that one hears talk, for example, of "speech inflected jazz"; one reads descriptions of the "scream" of Coltrane's horn.

Black Speech as Poetic Reference

There are two simple ways of documenting Black speech and its appearances: (a) in references to the speech and songs of the Black slave in journals, kept by whites, and (b) in the texts of the songs themselves collected since the middle of the nineteenth century. Other sources, of course, are folktales, either recorded by scholars or surviving in the present rural Black communities and the so-called slave narratives.

But the most important source is the living speech of the Black Community, both urban and rural, which forms, as it were, a kind of continuum of Blackness—at one end instantly identifiable in all of its rich tonal and rhythmic variety, at the other indistinguishable from that of the whites. Even those at that far end of "Standard English"— and it is a good, ironically expressive term—respond, however, to the dynamics of the middle range.

The ear, of course, is the best guide to any consideration of Black speech, for there is no adequate way of indicating its rhythmic variety, especially in stylized ceremonial talk or in oratory. Nor is there any adequate way of representing its tonal range or its consonantal ambiguity or its incredible energy. But our poets do attempt this impossible task, and they should. Some bravely, I think, in the face of intolerant, fearful, and sometimes ignorant criticism.

Perhaps the fear of Black speech in poetry comes from a too vivid recollection of the Dunbar School and the "minstrel" tradition which preceded it; perhaps it stems from a genuine desire not to be boxed in by the speech of any particular class. It is a groundless fear, I think, which in both poet and critic is rooted in the narcissism which Richard Wright speaks of and, frankly, ignores the technical breakthroughs of James Johnson, Langston Hughes, Sterling Brown, and others. This is not to say that all poets who try to use "the language of the people" are equally effective, or, indeed, that the language of the "streets" is capable of expressing everything that the poet knows and feels. Nevertheless, no one to my knowledge has demonstrated that the language of the streets *is not* capable of expressing all that a poet needs to say, especially if he is speaking *to* the people. Nor have I seen any contemporary Black poet restrict himself exclusively to the language of the streets. That is, to what critics usually call the language of the streets, because street language is not limited to hip phrases and monosyllabic obscenities—at least not the language that I hear in the streets, because often when I hear a group of brothers or sisters talking I hear poetry—sometimes a very complete poetry.

Poets use Black speech forms consciously because they know that Black people—the mass of us—do not talk like white people. They know that despite the lies and distortions of the minstrels—both ancient and modern, unlearned and academic—and despite all of the critical jargon about "ghettoese" and "plantation English," there is a complex and rich and powerful and subtle linguistic heritage whose resources have scarcely been touched that they draw upon.

Don Lee, for example, can use the word "neoteric" without batting an eye and send us scurrying to our dictionaries. The word is not "Black" but the casual, virtuoso way that he drops it on us—like "Deal with that"—is an *elegant Black linguistic gesture,* a typical gesture, like lightning arpeggios on difficult changes, or on no changes at all. If one has heard the contrasting voices of Malcolm X and Martin Luther King, then further comment is superfluous.

For there is this tradition of beautiful talk with us—this tradition of saying things beautifully even if they are ugly things. We say them in a way which takes language down to the deepest common level of our experience while hinting still at things to come. White people and many academicians call this usage slang and dialect; Black people call it Soul Talk. Some of the song texts which I have included are striking examples of this "talk," especially "Black Woman" (p. 108), recorded in the fifties by Rich Amerson of Alabama, and "Dry Spell Blues" (p. 113), recorded in the twenties by Edward "Son" House, the great Mississippi blues singer. The lovely complex imagery of the one and the highly charged, almost allegorical imagery of the other are worthy of the most serious reflection.

Black linguistic elegance takes innumerable forms, many quite subtle, but some of the more obvious ones may be considered here.

a. *Virtuoso naming and enumerating.* This technique

overwhelms the listener, who assumes that the speaker really must know what he is talking about. Quite often, of course, he does, as in the examples below. The roots of this technique might conceivably lie in the folk practice of riddling and similar kinds of wordplay. It may also be related to the kind of witty gesture involved in nicknaming. It is definitely related to the kind of product brand-name story that Roger Abrahams records in *Deep Down in the Jungle*, and which still flourishes in the Black Community.

> Cavalier took a ride across the desert on a Camel, just 'cause he was in love with somebody called Fatima. Philip was blasting off to Morris. Now Raleigh decided since he had made a Lucky Strike he was going down to Chesterfield's. He had a whole pocket full of Old Gold. And so, last but not least, he decided to go on a Holiday.
>
> [Kid, #100, p. 244.]

In this poem by Reginald Butler the continuity of technique is evident.

> You go round the mulberry bush and I'll go round
>   the CEDAR
> You pull up your petticoat and I'll pull out my
>   PETER MURFEE
> Had a dog, Lorenjo was his name
> Loan him to a lady friend to keep her company.
> Around the house Lorenjo ran; he stumbled
>   on a ROCK.
> His head went up the lady's dress; he tried to smell her—
> Get away, you dirty dog. You make my nature RISE
> There ain't but one man in this town that can
>   lay between my—
> Thank you mam for a glass of beer, pity if you SUCK
>   same, for a man
> who get a wife and don't take time out to roll and
>   tumble
> on a thimble leaning on a ROCK—
> The smallest woman in this town got the biggest
>   COCKtail

gingerale leaning on a STICK
The smallest man in this town got the biggest
DICK Tracy Count Basie

Ted Joans elaborates this technique in two interesting compositions—"Jazz Must Be a Woman" (p. 221) and "The Nice Colored Man" (p. 223). The first is somewhat mechanical because of the alphabetical arrangement of the names, but one soon discounts this and in fact considers it as a structural device that displays the poet's intimate knowledge of his subject. Although it is rather inert on the page, the poem as a spoken composition could be very effective, deriving its force from the fundamental assumption that these names are known, or should be known, because they identify the musicians as creative shapers of reality.

"The Nice Colored Man" is much more effective because the poet succeeds in suggesting the rhythmic variety of the spoken voice on the page. In addition, the witty variations that he plays on the word "nigger" are completely unpredictable, yet, like good jazz, perfectly logical once they are articulated.

b. *Jazzy rhythmic effects.* To an extent "The Nice Colored Man" also illustrates this practice, but certainly there are others. The poem must be read in its entirety for both devices. Even so, as in so much of the Black poetic tradition, many of these effects are lost on the printed page; thus the ear is still the best judge. With that realization, some poets at Broadside Press have begun to record their work, both on tape and record. Especially interesting to the listener is the fact that some of the rhythmic patterns of contemporary Black poetry go back to folk and street sources and are commonly known in the Black Community. Some of these occur in children's games and in the folk rhymes that were recorded by Talley in his *Negro Folk Rhymes.* Others are traceable to the rhythms of the dozens, and even to popular quasi-folk songs like the "Dirty Dozens" and to urban narratives and toasts like "Shine" and "The Signifying Monkey."

Compare these lines from LeRoi Jones's "T. T. Jackson Sings" with the traditional dozens lines which are printed just below them.

> I fucked your mother
> On top of a house
> When I got through
> She thought she was
> Mickey Mouse
>
>   *   *   *   *
>
> I fucked your mother from house to house
> Out came a baby named Minnie Mouse.

[Recorded by R. Abrahams, "Playing the Dozens," *American Folk Music Occasional*, No. 1, p. 79.]

In Mari Evans' poem "Vive Noir!" the rhythms reflect the hipness of the folk tradition as it becomes urbanized.

> I'm tired
>   of hand me downs
>   shut me ups
>   pin me ins
>   keep me outs
>   messing me over have
>   just had it
>   baby
>   from
> you . . .

Etheridge Knight's "Dark Prophesy" (p. 330) is more than a paraphrase of the traditional "Shine and the Titanic." It is to that piece what the blues poems of Hughes and Brown are to blues songs. The essence is retained while the form is altered to make the meaning less dependent upon a musical acompaniment, or upon the spoken voice.

> Yeah, I sing of Shine
> and how the millionaire banker stood on the deck
> and pulled from his pocket a million dollar check
> saying Shine Shine save poor me
> and I'll give you all the money a black boy needs—

Two further examples in this anthology are Carolyn Rodgers' brilliant "The Last M. F." (p. 346) and Ladele X's "O-o-oo-ld Miss Liza" (p. 356), which the reader may examine for himself.

It should also be pointed out that these rhymes are deeply rooted in Black speech and Black oratory as well as in certain kinds of Black song. When we return to prose, to Ellison's *Invisible Man*, we find a demonstration of these jazzy rhythms in a popular Black narrative style. In the following passage the speaker describes the exploits of Ras the Exhorter in a battle with the mounted police during a Harlem riot.

> Before the cops knowed what hit 'em Ras is right
> in the middle of 'em and one cop grabbed for that
> spear, and ole Ras swung 'round and bust him across
> the head and the cop goes down and his hoss rears up,
> and ole Ras rears his and tries to spear him another
> cop, and the other hosses is plunging around and ole
> Ras tries to spear him still another cop, only he's
> too close and the hoss is pooting and snorting and
> pissing and shitting, and they swings around and the
> cop is swinging his pistol and every time he swings
> old Ras throws up his shield with one arm and chops
> at him with the spear with the other, and man, you
> could hear that gun striking that ole shield like
> somebody dropping tire irons out of a twelve-story
> window.
>
> [Signet ed., pp. 487, 488.]

c. *Virtuoso free-rhyming.* This occurs both in speech and in poetry, and seems to be related to the impulse to lard speech and conversation with proverbs and aphoristic sayings, both sacred and secular, but there is a pronounced emphasis upon wordplay either as an indication of hipness or seemingly an end in itself. There may be present also certain residual linguistic habits that might have been carried over from the tonal elements of African languages. These verbal habits are found in both the older and the younger members of the community. For example, a Black man in his fifties recently said the following in an interview which I conducted on the meaning of "Soul":

> I don't want nothin' old but some gold;
> I don't want nothin' black but a Cadillac!

A few years ago it was commonplace for a preacher to announce the following sermon text:

> I can't eat a bite, I can't sleep at night,
> 'Cause the woman I love don't treat me right.

This, of course, was a ploy to get people interested; what they were treated to was the idea of depending on God, not on human beings, for solace. Let us recall too that this kind of rhyming is found in the speeches of Malcolm X and in those of Martin Luther King, Jr., as in the "I Have a Dream" speech with its dryly comical "every hill and mole hill" reference. In this collection, interesting examples from the street tradition can be seen in Rap Brown's poem, in lines like the following:

> They call me Rap the dicker the ass kicker
> The cherry picker and city slicker the titty licker . . .

d. *Hyperbolic imagery.* The breathless virtuoso quality of free-rhyming comes from the utilization of single rhyme sound, the object being to get in as many rhymes as one can. Oratorically, this is balanced by a passage in which there is no rhyme at all, and the wit and the energy expend themselves in a series of hyperbolic wisecracks, rooted in the tradition of masculine boasting.

These wisecracks also illustrate *hyperbolic imagery* as the passage is balanced with material, like that below (also Rap's poem), with resonances in the folk tradition. Note, however, that the last two lines present a kind of hyperbolic coolness—supercoolness.

> I'm the man who walked the water and tied the
> whale's tail in a knot
> Taught the little fishes how to swim

Crossed the burning sands and shook the devil's hand
Rode round the world on the back of a snail
carrying a sack saying AIR MAIL.

Some idea of Rap's relationship to the folk tradition may be
seen in the resemblance between the passage just quoted and
the following secular rhyme quoted by Sterling Brown in
Negro Poetry and Drama, p. 21:

I seen Solomon and Moses
Playing ring around the roses . . .
I seen King Pharaoh's daughter
Seeking Moses in de water . . .
Seen Ole Jonah swallowin' de whale
And I pulled de lion's tail;
I've sailed all over Canaan on a log.

Hyperbolic imagery, in short, is common in Black speech
and often reveals striking poetic talent. In the account of Ras
the Destroyer's battle with the Harlem police, Ellison's genius
illuminates this cultural feature. Ras, for example, is de-
scribed thus:

And man that crazy sonofabitch up there on that
hoss looking like death eating a sandwich . . .

We recall that some of the most imaginative images of this
type are found in the sermons, both folk and learned. See
the *Book of Negro Folklore,* pp. 232–42, for folk examples.
Listen to contemporary urban preaching for others. Rev.
C. L. Franklin of Detroit, famous in his own right and the
father of the gifted Aretha Franklin, continues a sophisti-
cated version of the folk sermon in imagery like this:

I want God's Word to be shaped like a vessel,
And I want my soul to step on board.

e. *Metaphysical imagery.* When hyperbolic imagery merges
into the kind of figure in which precise intellectual statement
is coupled with witty far-reaching comparison in a unified
and passionate image, it is called metaphysical imagery

[*39*]

after the practice of Samuel Johnson. This kind of imagery abounds in the work of English religious poets of the first half of the seventeenth century and in poetry from the Eliot school. It appears also in Black poetry, sermon, and song. A good example is this passage from Big Bill Broonzy's "Hollerin' the Blues" (p. 110):

> You'll never get to do me like you did my buddy Shine
> You'll never get to do me like you did my buddy Shine—
> You worked him so hard on the levee—
> Till he went stone blind.
> I can hear my hamstrings a-poppin', and my collar cryin'
> I can hear my hamstrings a-poppin', and my collar cryin'.

The last two lines are anatomically precise, though hyperbolic, and the pun on "cryin'" (the slipstream from his running and the emotion that he feels) picks up the effort which goes into his frenzied attempt to escape his buddy's fate. And we hear the steady stream of wind and tears punctuated by the rhythm of his Achilles tendon as it "pops" like a whip as he runs. Frankly, the image is worthy of John Donne, one of the master poets of the English Metaphysical School.

f. *Understatement.* A supreme example would be these tragic blues lines:

> I'm gonna lay my head on some lonesome railroad line;
> I'm gonna wait on No. Nine, just to pacify my mind.

g. *Compressed and cryptic imagery.* This can be seen by the arcane references to what I have called "mascon" imagery as well as lines like Ted Hunt's poem in this volume and Muddy Waters' "Just to Be with You" (Chess 1620, LP 1501). For comparison here is the street cleaner's rap to Ellison's hero.

> All it takes to get along in this here man's town
> is a little shit, grit and mother-wit. And man,
> I was bawn with all three. In fact, I'maseventh-

sonofaseventhsonbawnwithacauloverbotheyesandraised-
onblackcatboneshighjohntheconquerorandgreasygreens—
[*Invisible Man*, Signet ed., p. 155.]

h. *Worrying the line*. This is the folk expression for the device of altering the pitch of a note in a given passage or for other kinds of ornamentation often associated with melismatic singing in the Black tradition. A verbal parallel exists in which a word or phrase is broken up to allow for affective or didactic comment. Here is an example from Rich Amerson's "Black Woman":

> Say, I feel superstitious, Mamma
> 'Bout my hoggin' bread, Lord help my hungry time,
> I feel superstitious, Baby, 'bout my hoggin' bread!
> Ah-hmmm, Baby, I feel superstitious,
> I say 'stitious, Black Woman!
> Ah-hmmm, ah you hear me cryin'
> About I done got hungry, oh Lordy!
> Oh, Mamma, I feel superstitious
> About my hog Lord God it's my bread.

Aside from elegance of gesture, there is the opposite aspect of the tradition—frankness, bluntness of language, obscenity—a kind of verbalized social dissonance. Despite the fact that the poets, like the blues singers and the dozens players, use it with great virtuosity and even (in the case of Carolyn Rodgers) a certain charm, it remains perhaps the least understood aspect of the tradition. In the classroom, ironically, it causes a great deal of confusion because instructors are unaware of, underestimate, or refuse to acknowledge the "Soul-Field," the complex galaxy of personal, social, institutional, historical, religious, and mythical meanings that affect everything we say or do as Black people sharing a common heritage. The same students who read and understand Don Lee's "The Wall," for example, are tongue-tied in the classroom because they have to pretend that they do not know the meaning of that powerful Oedipal word in the last line, and

[*41*]

our own special employment of it. But the word is important to an understanding of the Black Experience within the context of the poem. It is charged with more experiential energy than perhaps any other, with the possible exception of the word "nigger."

This blunt style is certainly familiar to the general reader by now. However, it still has not been appreciated as *literature,* at least as a valid aspect of *Black* literature. Too, it is difficult to isolate specific structural aspects of this style since it may in fact employ the forms of the elegant style with the difference lying chiefly in the usage of obscenity. Here, however, one has to be honest. The use of obscenity is frequently brilliant, at times inspired, whether it occurs in literature or in real life. However, convention forbids us to treat it seriously until the inventor has either achieved "universal fame" (in which case no one challenges his prerogative to dirty words) or has been dead for two hundred years (in which case he is unable to defend himself either way *any*way). Notwithstanding there are certain "ground rules," as it were, by which one can judge the skill or the art employed in the rough style. For example, one can devastate an opponent by sheer dint of dirty detail. On the crudest, least imaginative level the dozens can degenerate to that. Unfortunately some contemporary Black poetry suffers from the same defect, prompting warnings by craftsmen like Stanley Crouch and Larry Neal. A more skillful use of the style would lie in concluding an "elegant" passage (satirical or otherwise) with a rush of prurient detail as in Rap's poem, for instance.

Perhaps the hallmark of successful use is wit, which listeners and readers instantly recognize and respond to in a manner similar to their response to metaphysical imagery, but in addition to the pleasure of intellectual surprise there is the added dimension of defying social taboo. Frankly, at times one arrives at a kind of rock-bottom truth which is memorably expressed. Compare, for example, the following

[*42*]

passages, one from English literature, the other from the Black street tradition:

(a) A rag, a bone, a hank of hair . . .
(b) Pussy ain' nothin' but meat on the bone . . .

Here the words "meat on the bone," with echoes perhaps of biblical imagery distilled in the folk mind, challenge literary prejudice with their essential rightness.

In this anthology, several of the poems embody the blunt style. For example, Imamu Baraka's (LeRoi Jones) "Pretty-ditty" (p. 211) hinges on the last line and especially on the hyperbolic but subtle in-group meanings of "motherfucker." Although Don Lee's "The Wall" (p. 334) hinges on the same word, also in a hyperbolic sense, the meaning suggests appreciative awe and scales off into personally and communally recognized meanings which are more felt than named, in other words, into a condition of *saturation*.

Close to the directness of street talk are poems like Ahmed Alhamisi's "The Black Narrator" and Ebon's "Presidential Press Parley" (p. 351); and in Carolyn Rodgers' "The Last M. F." (p. 346), the rough tradition is gradually and delightfully subsumed in the intellectually elegant.

Finally, it is perhaps in the appropriation of the dozens techniques that contemporary Black poetry has been most effective in the use of the rough aspect of the tradition. For example, one could profitably study Imamu Baraka's (LeRoi Jones) "Word from the Right Wing." It is especially significant since it involves the political element with the dozens on the one hand, and it illustrates the dozens as a political weapon on the other. Baraka, of course, was not alone in this, for while he was employing this much imitated device in poetry, Stokely Carmichael and H. Rap Brown, who were engaged in direct political action, employed the dozens as a mode of attack, and of entertainment, which their opponents, accustomed to the golden sonorities of the sermon, were unable to deal with. The technique was too flexible for the establishment, too allusive, too cryptic, too dangerous.

This brings us to a curious and very important aspect of Black speech in this country. Certain words and constructions seem to carry an inordinate charge of emotional and psychological weight, so that whenever they are used they set all kinds of bells ringing, all kinds of synapses snapping, on all kinds of levels. I am not speaking merely of words like "nigger" and "the big M. F.," as Ron Welburn calls it, since they are rather obvious. I am not speaking of "code words." Nor am I speaking merely of what literary critics mean by the word "resonance." I am speaking rather of words which are innocent enough—words like "rock," "roll," "jelly," "bubber," "jook," and the like, which have levels of meaning that seem to go back to our earliest grappling with the English language in a strange and hostile land. These words, of course, are used in complex associations, and thus form meaningful wholes in ways which defy understanding by outsiders. I call such words "mascon" words, borrowing from (of all places!) the National Aeronautics and Space Administration. NASA invented the acronym to mean a "massive concentration" of matter below the lunar surface after it was observed that the gravitational pull on a satellite was stronger in some places than in others. I use it to mean *a massive concentration of Black experiential energy* which powerfully affects the meaning of Black speech, Black song, and Black poetry—if one, indeed, has to make such distinctions.

Let us take the word "roll," for example. Here are some instances of its use: "Rock and Roll," "Rollin' with My Baby," "I'm Rollin' Through an Unfriendly World," "Let the Good Times Roll," "He was sure rollin' today," "Roll 'em, Pete," "If you can roll your jelly like you roll your dough . . . ," "Let the church roll on," and so on. The meanings connote work, struggle, sexual congress, dancing, having a good time, and shooting dice. They cut across areas of experience usually thought of as separate, but they are not mutually exclusive. In fact, the meanings overlap and wash into each other on some undifferentiated level of common experience. The poetic potential of all this should be obvious, so I shall not belabor the point.

However, here is a more complex example. Take the line from the hymn "Hold to His hand, God's unchanging hand." Compare it with the blues line, "If you don't want me, baby, give me your right hand." Compare Faye Adams' song from the fifties, "Shake a Hand, Shake a Hand." White critics of Black folk song call these expressions clichés. I *know* that they are mistaken. What has happened is that the experiential energy of the expression is lost to the outsider, so consequently all that he can sense *is* the "outside," the morphology of the term, and any criticism is, as a result, merely superficial or distorted. Black people have used these expressions over and over because they are deeply rooted in an apparently inexhaustible reality, in this case, a highly compressed secular/sacred experience. I think that I need only mention "the right hand of fellowship" and the crossed hands of the Civil Rights Movement, both dating back to the earliest days of our life in this country, and I suspect even to Africa itself.

The same kind of mascon term occurs in music. Although I am neither musician nor musicologist, I can cite, in addition to my own observations, the following statements from trained musical observers, which are all the more important because these observers are "outsiders," i.e., non-Blacks. The first is from Martin Williams' article in *Down Beat* (January 21, 1971, p. 12), in which he discusses the recurrence of certain blues and boogie-woogie figures in the history of jazz. With regard to one figure he acknowledges:

> But my brief account of the recorded history of the phrase probably doesn't scratch the surface of its use as a basis for written themes, nor its use as an interpolation, in hundreds of variants and permutations, by soloists as they improvise.
>
> It is one of those phrases that just seem to have been indigenous parts of Afro-American musical lore from the beginning, as it were, and whose meaning for each successive generation of players has been tenacious.

With empathic insight, Charles Keil points out the Black oratorical technique of repetition, which characterizes both the preacher and the blues singer, in this case, Martin Luther King and B. B. King. The repetition is not tiring because it deals with mascon structures. He is speaking here of the "I Have a Dream" speech:

> This relentless repetition of phrases, the listing of American landmarks and the long enumeration of Negro goals, gradually moved the audience to an emotional peak, a fitting climax to a stirring demonstration. Employing a standard twelve-bar blues form, repeated over and over again in song after song, turning out well-known phrases in every chorus yet always introducing novel combinations and subtle new twists in each performance—in short, using the same patterns—B. B. King rarely fails to give his listeners much the same kind of emotional life.
>
> [*Urban Blues*, pp. 96–7.]

The net effect of this, Keil correctly concludes, equals "soul."

However, most outsiders are neither so sensitive nor so knowledgeable as Keil, and the viewpoint which he describes below not only represents that of the contemporary American public, but of an earlier one as well, including professional music commentators.

> To the uninitiated—and a surprising number of music critics are included in this category—Jimmy Smith's funky runs, Coltrane's sheets of sound, or B. B. King's cliches seem monotonous, tiresome, or just plain boring; but to the people who have been exposed to the music for the longest time and who have listened to it with care and attention, these artists never lose their freshness and vitality.
>
> [*Urban Blues*, p. 97.]

Black Music as Poetic Reference

Now let us formally, though briefly, consider this second referent—music—in further detail. Aside from mascon structures, there are other important ways in which music, Black

music, lies at the basis of much of Black poetry, either con-
sciously or covertly. I have been able to distinguish at least
ten types of usage, but I am certain that there are others. I
shall list them first, then attempt to illustrate them.

1. The casual, generalized reference
2. The careful allusion to song titles
3. The quotations from a song
4. The adaptation of song forms
5. The use of tonal memory as poetic structure
6. The use of precise musical notation in the text
7. The use of an assumed emotional response incorporated
into the poem: the "subjective correlative"
8. The musician as subject/poem/history/myth
9. The use of language from the jazz life
10. The poem as "score" or "chart"

In No. 1, *the casual, generalized reference,* there are mere
suggestions of Black song types. Here are some examples. In
Jean Toomer's "Song of the Son" (p. 118):

> . . . one seed becomes
> An everlasting song, a singing tree,
> Caroling softly souls of slavery,
> What they were, and what they are to me,
> Caroling softly souls of slavery.

Compare Sterling Brown's "Slim Greer" (p. 136), where the
whites left Slim alone in the parlor:

> An' he started a-tinklin'
> Some mo'nful blues,
> An' a-pattin' the time
> With No. Fourteen shoes.

And see Gwendolyn Brooks's "We Real Cool" (p. 176):

> . . . We
> Jazz June. We
> Die soon.

Finally, note the range of the reference in Margaret Walker's "For My People" (p. 163):

> For my people everywhere singing their slave songs repeatedly: their dirges and their ditties and their blues and jubilees . . .

In No. 2, there is a *careful allusion to song titles,* as in James Weldon Johnson's "O Black and Unknown Bards." The entire poem must be read in order to appreciate the effect.

A more subtle use is found in Gwendolyn Brooks's "The Sundays of Satin-Legs Smith" (p. 169), where the poet names and describes the songs coming out of the "vendors," i.e., the jukeboxes: "The Lonesome Blues," the "Long-Lost Blues," and "I Want A Big Fat Mama." For a reader familiar with these songs, the titles evoke a more particularized response, and the effect thus borders on the "subjective correlative" alluded to in type seven. In brief, then, these categories are suggestive and not ironclad and mutually exclusive. In fact, if one knew the various blues songs whose lyrics anticipate "Big Fat Mama," another dimension would obviously be added to his understanding of the scene. Actually, Miss Brooks sums up the meaning in these powerful lines from the poem:

> The pasts of his ancestors lean against him.
> Crowd him.
> Fog out his identity.

Note also how she assumes knowledge of the popular Black songs, but in order to create the proper contrast, she delineates the essential quality of the European composers whom she mentions. Saint-Saëns' name is beautiful enough in itself to evoke his "Meditation" from *Thaïs,* but she goes on to suggest the "piquant elusive Grieg," Tschaikovsky's "wayward eloquence" and "the shapely tender drift of Brahms."

In her "I Love Those Little Booths at Benvenuti's" (p. 174), she uses the technique in a flatter, less evocative but still precise manner as she indicates the music which the Bronze-ville people play: "They All Say I'm the Biggest Fool," "Voo Me on the Vot Nay," and "New Lester Leaps In."

In "Dear John, Dear Coltrane" (p. 238), Michael Harper not only uses the title of the composition as an epigraph, but quotes from the companion poem that Coltrane wrote for the album, building upon the phrase "a love supreme" in a manner suggesting a musician improvising on a motif. It is highly effective. Compare Kgositsile's "Origins" (p. 308) with the line concluding "what is this thing called/Love," where the reference is probably to a specific version of that song, perhaps Charlie Parker's. This usage extends even to conver-sation or, perhaps, arose *from* conversation as, for example, in James Baldwin's reference to Lorraine Hansberry as "Sweet Lorraine," which immediately resolves into a specific version of the song in the incomparably sweet voice of Nat King Cole. These, of course, are not random, "free" associa-tions, but connections which naturally emerge from the "Soul-Field" of the Black Experience.

Both Don L. Lee and Nikki Giovanni, two of the most popular poets of the sixties, make considerable use of this device. See, for example, the references in "Don't Cry, Scream" (p. 336) to "Ascension" and "My Favorite Things" of Coltrane, as well as James Brown's "Cold Sweat." In Nikki Giovanni's "Reflections on April 4, 1968" (p. 279) the con-cluding line is adapted from the title of the Thomas A. Dor-sey hymn "Precious Lord, Take My Hand." The poet makes this "Precious Lord—Take Our Hands—Lead/Us On." Shortly before his assassination, Dr. King had requested the director of the Operation Breadbasket Band to play this song for him. It is important to note that the composer of the song was once a famous blues singer and pianist who accompanied Ma Rainey, under the name of Georgia Tom. The story of his conversion is legendary. Hundreds of Black sacred and secular songs employ this image. It is so powerful that it must be considered a mascon.

Also worth careful attention is Giovanni's "Revolutionary

Music" (p. 280) with its brilliant use of title and quotation from popular Black songs, ending with Sam Cooke's poignantly prophetic "A Change Is Gonna Come," which anchors not only the reality of the Civil Rights Movement but his own untimely death.

Quotations from a song are incorporated into the poem in the third device. For examples, see again J. W. Johnson's "O Black and Unknown Bards" and the poems of Nikki Giovanni mentioned above. Observe, too, that the weaving of song titles and/or quotations from a song into the texture of a poem has a parallel in the use of titles and quotations from literary works, as in Sarah Webster Fabio's "montage" on the death of Langston Hughes, entitled "A Mover," *Negro Digest,* September, 1967, p. 42. Obviously, non-Black writers use similar references, especially literary ones. The important thing here is that the references are *chiefly* to *Black music.*

Adaptations of song forms, the fourth device, include blues, ballads, hymns, children's songs, work songs, spirituals, and popular songs. These are fairly numerous and easily recognizable for the most part, especially the ballad, the hymn, and the blues. The first two have numerous parallels in other literary traditions. But the blues as a literary form was developed and refined by Langston Hughes and later by Sterling Brown, although Hughes clearly overstated his case for the fixity of the blues form in his preface to *Fine Clothes to the Jew.* Notwithstanding, in the poetry of both men it is important to see how they expand and amplify the form without losing its distinctive blues flavor. Poems like Hughes's "The Weary Blues" and "Montage of a Dream Deferred" and Brown's "Memphis Blues" suggest something of their range, even in their respective first volumes of poetry. Their work merits close study for the subtle use which they make of this form. Since all folk blues do not have the "classic" twelve-bar, three-line form, as examples by "Son" House and Charlie

Patton and others clearly show, the poets' blues extensions therefore are not only logical but historically accurate.

In addition, note how Brown combines the blues form and feeling with the ballad and, in effect, "invents" the blues-ballad which, as a literary phenomenon, is as distinctive as Wordsworth's "lyrical ballad." * Moreover, Brown and others like Gwendolyn Brooks, Margaret Walker, Robert Hayden, and Dudley Randall have also mastered the traditional literary ballad in the Anglo-American tradition, even to the Pre-Raphaelite echoic refrain of Dante Rossetti and William Morris.

Another example of blues in this volume is A. B. Spellman's "the joel blues" (p. 263). The reader should also examine the many fine examples in *Poetry for My People* by the late Henry Dumas, edited by Hale Chatfield and Eugene Redmond (Southern Illinois University Press, 1970). Other poets who have built upon this form include Robert Hayden, Owen Dodson, and the West Indian Edward Brathwaite.

An example of the work song can be found in Sterling Brown's poem "Southern Road." By contrast, there is Langston Hughes's delightful "Children's Rhymes." The reader who might question the sophistication of the rhymes should be reminded of the poet's habit of writing down snatches of songs, conversation, and the like from real life. He might, in addition, listen to Harold Courlander's recording of children's rhymes on the Folkways album *Negro Folk Music of Alabama*. Black city and country folks alike may remember their own local variations of these songs.

For religious songs it is difficult to approach the original grandeur of the spirituals, so wisely, I feel, the poets usually allude to them. In this volume Robert Hayden's "Runagate Runagate" (p. 157) is a prime example.

> Runs falls rises stumbles on from darkness into
> darkness

---

* See "Memphis Blues" in Brown's *Southern Road*, and, in this volume, "Ma Rainey."

and the darkness thicketed with shapes of terror
and the hunters pursuing and the hounds pursuing
and the night cold and the night long and the river
to cross and the jack-muh-lanterns beckoning
   beckoning
and blackness ahead and when shall I reach that
   somewhere
morning and keep on going and never turn back and
   keep on going

In this first stanza there are allusions to the songs: "One More River to Cross," "In That Great Getting Up Morning," "Keep on a Inching Like a Po Inch Worm."

However, the traditional English hymn has influenced poets like George Moses Horton. Horton and other early formal poets in whom this kind of influence is documented can be studied in William Robinson's excellent anthology, *Early Black Poets,* and Benjamin Brawley's *Early Negro American Writers.* Still it is somewhat surprising that the whole body of gospel song which influenced Black and white music so deeply in recent years has been virtually ignored by contemporary poets, with the outstanding exceptions of Henry Dumas and Nikki Giovanni, the latter having recorded some of her work with The New York Community Gospel Choir. Perhaps the general lack of interest by the poets stems from the comparative blandness of imagery in the gospels when compared to the spirituals and the blues. Nevertheless, the soul singers like James Brown and Aretha Franklin draw heavily upon both the imagery and the singing and instrumental styles of this tradition. It remains to be seen, then, whether the growing importance of the soul singer as cultural hero will affect the course of the poetry. Perhaps we will have to look to the dramatic and semi-dramatic creations of performing groups like The Last Poets, The Blue Guerilla, and The National Black Theater. Perhaps we will have to build on the roots of Langston Hughes again, after all.

Device No. 5 is the practice, with considerable variety, of *forcing the reader to incorporate into the structure of the*

*poem his memory of a specific song or passage of a song, or
even of a specific delivery technique.* Without this specific
memory the poem cannot properly be realized. Some out-
standing examples may be found in Don Lee's "Don't Cry,
Scream" (p. 336), with its stylized allusion to the Coltrane
sound; Nikki Giovanni's poem referring to Sam Cooke's "A
Change Is Gonna Come" (p. 280); and Sarah Fabio's poem on
Duke Ellington (p. 243). There are, of course, early examples
in Sterling Brown's "Ma Rainey" and "When the Saints Go
Ma'chin' In."

Further examples of this practice can also be seen in Percy
Johnston's "Number Five Cooper Square" (p. 191), with the
lines:

> I remember Clifford tossing
> Bubbles, Scit! Whoom!, from an
> Ante-bellum moon. Scit! And
> Killer Joe's golden chain, Scit!
> While Ornette gives a lecture on
> A Sanskrit theme with Bachian
> Footnotes, scit. . . .

LeRoy Stone's "Flamenco Sketches" (p. 194) is an example
of the kind of precision which is possible with this technique.
Here the poem seeks to realize the musical experience. But
even in its precision it does not lapse into the purely technical
detail for its own sake. Note the "whisper/ intoned in fifths/
slivered through Davis durations," or the last section, "Com-
ment/ on a cloud of Oriental ninths/ comment!"

In Lance Jeffers' "How High the Moon" (p. 200) the precise
descriptions of musical structure gradually give way to the
realization of the social context. Even here, however, the
sense of musical style is still present in the lines:

> . . . the beat of the street talk flares strong,
> the scornful laughter and the gestures cut the air.

Parentheses suggest that this is a distillate of the poet/
listener's mind. It is not mere free-association, however, for
"the beat of the street talk" takes up the question of "speech-

inflected jazz" alluded to earlier. There is a good deal of documentation, especially of the be-bop period, of musicians actually making their horns "talk" either to one another or to the audience. All that was said was not flattery either! The topic needs researching. Observe, for example, the blues singers like Furry Lewis and Mississippi John Hurt telling the audience, "I'm gonna let this guitar talk to you." Compare Rev. Gary Davis, the blind preacher guitarist, who even in his religious songs stops and asks "Miss Gibson" to sing a little while. And the most popular recent example of this is B. B. King and *his* Gibson guitar "Lucille."

So, in fact, the poets are translating what the instruments say, but in order to understand them fully, one must know the original text, as it were. See A. B. Spellman's poem on Coltrane (p. 261), where he says, "Trane's horn had words in it."

In the examples cited above, tonal memory at times provided usually all of the subject matter of the poem, particularly in the examples of Johnston and Stone. In Don Lee's famous poem "Don't Cry, Scream," he draws upon the Coltrane "sound" in a highly effective manner, both in the written poem and in his performance of it. He begins with general descriptions of the music:

> blowing
> a-melodics
> screeching,
> screaming,
> blasting—

It was "music that ached./ murdered our minds (we reborn)." And in the rebirth the poet celebrates the blackness that we were taught to despise. Then follows the stylized *visual* representation of the Coltrane sound. It is merely suggestive, but still precise in its own way. There are stage directions that become part of both written and spoken comment: "sing/ loud &/ high/ with/ feeling" and "sing/ loud &/ long/ with feeling"; then rooted in a sure knowledge of the instrumental style anchored in the vocal style of both sacred and secular music, the directions state: "sing loud/ & high with/ feeling/ letting/ your/ voice/ break." It is that precise technique of "letting/ your/ voice/ break" which is so *Black* and so right. In performance, the poet gives three different pitches to each verbal group of "we-eeeeeeee," "scream-eeeee-eeeeee-ing." The effect is, literally, thrilling. Some academic critics call this poetry "unreadable." One has to smile at their arrogance. There is a story current in the Black Community about a white critic who, after listening to some records by Coltrane and Pharoah Sanders, said with great condescension, "It's interesting, but you can't dance to it," whereupon a young brother said with withering scorn, "*You* can't dance to it!" So we can say to those critics that maybe Don Lee is "unreadable" to you, but then so really is Martin Luther King, Jr., to say nothing of Malcolm X. In this poem, then, the stylized rendition of the Coltrane sound becomes the touchstone of the meaning. The sound, in effect, becomes the *persona*. The Trane sound is the sound of the real, of the natural, of the spiritual. But the separations are arbitrary and Western, for they are part of the same truth.

> i can see my me, it was truth you gave,
> like a daily shit
> it had to come.
> > can you scream————brother?   very
> > can you scream————brother?   soft
>
> i hear you.
> i hear you.
>
> and the Gods will too.

Almost a perfect parallel exists in Lee's use of the spoken Black voice in the poem "Move Un-Noticed to Be Noticed: A Nationhood Poem" (p. 340), where the Black exclamation of surprise, excitement, and astonishment is used to sum up the tremendous natural potential energy of the Black masses. Many writers have called attention to this "exotic" speech habit of Black people. It has been parodied and poked fun of in a thousand ways. White Southerners even seem to have unconsciously adopted it. And Flip Wilson has become rich off it. Don Lee, in the peculiar style of the Black Arts revolution, smashes head-on into it, and through it, and detonates its essence: the energy of Black self-awareness as revolutionary potential.

    woooooooooowe boom boom   woooooooooowe bah
    woooooooooowe boom boom   woooooooooowe bah

The first part, "woooooooooowe," is the essential exclamation. The "boom boom" detonates it, so to speak, releasing its energy in the cosmic dance of a hurricane. It is a dance for righteousness and nationhood that transforms Beaulah from a maligned stereotype of the Black woman to the Mother of the Black nation reborn.

    be the baddddest hurricane that ever came, a black
        hurricane.
    woooooooooowe boom boom   woooooooooowe bah
    woooooooooowe boom boom   woooooooooowe bah

    the baddest black hurricane that ever came, a black
        hurricane named Beaulah,

    Go head Beaulah, do the hurricane.

    woooooooooowe boom boom   woooooooooowe bah
    woooooooooowe boom boom   woooooooooowe bah

    move
    move to be moved from the un-moveable,
    into our own, your/self is own, yrself is own,
        own yourself.

In Sarah Webster Fabio's poem "Tribute to Duke" (p. 243), there is room for at least two spoken voices, both of which evoke specific recollections of the Ellington repertoire. The technique includes the use of song titles as well as descriptions of the sound and empathetic comment from the second voice. In addition there are places where medleys or individual songs are either to be played in the background or imagined—recalled—by the audience/reader. While the poem is sufficient in itself, it assumes a great familiarity with Ellington's music. At times, the second voice becomes a set of directions, or a score.

Earlier examples in this text may be found in Langston Hughes and Sterling Brown. Note Hughes's fascination with the humorous and ironic sounds of bop, and Brown's anticipation of those sounds, in a literary sense, in his "Cabaret" (p. 130), written in 1927, almost twenty years before the birth of bop. In "Jazz Band" (p. 144) by Frank Marshall Davis, that poet's love of the "new" Black music is evident in his description of the orchestral sounds. Besides onomatopoeia, he employs half-humorous figures to suggest the delivery technique: "Chopin gone screwy, Wagner with the blues . . ."

Sonia Sanchez's poem "a/coltrane/poem" (p. 274) provides another interesting example of this technique. It is not too important, perhaps, to know which of the two poems, hers or Don Lee's, was written first. What is important is performance. Lee has his own devastating sound, so anyone reading or writing a Coltrane poem after "Don't Cry, Scream" has the achievement of Lee to contend with. Despite some surface similarities, Miss Sanchez's poem is all her own. Especially startling is her delivery technique, which is suggestive and witty rather than dramatic, like Lee's. She understands her own vocal resources, so she does not attempt the nearly exact duplication of the Coltrane sound which Lee captures. Instead, near the middle of the poem she creates an onomatopoetic pun on the Coltrane sound, and it becomes the violent death cry of the white oppressors.

The most interesting technical feature of the poem, however, is the singing and scatting of two songs connected with Coltrane—one, the English version of the French children's song, "Frère Jacques," translated as "Brother John," and the other, a half-humming, half-scatting of the basic melody of

"My Favorite Things." This amounts, really, to another specific kind of musical referent that we can simply call *singing or humming a specific tune or melody.* Coupled with this, the poet comments on the melody in the traditional manner of the blues singer and the Baptist preacher, modifying this, however, into a coherent Liberation Rap. Although the form on the page is fairly fixed, even with stage directions for stomping the foot for rhythm, the poem is fluid, a kind of score that lends itself to a wide range of dramatic interpretations.

In the sixth kind of musical referent, *precise musical notation is incorporated into the text of the poem,* as in the manner of Paul Laurence Dunbar's "Whistling Sam." The technique suggests a possible solution to some of the problems of contemporary Black poetry. In this connection, one should recall Dr. DuBois' use of musical quotations as epigraphs to the various chapters of *Souls of Black Folk.* It is reasonable to assume that the total meaning of the book cannot be approached without *hearing* these phrases as well as reading the poetic fragments which accompany them.

A variation on this usage can be seen in Langston Hughes's neglected poem "Ask Your Mama," where the poet uses as *leitmotif* the traditional "Hesitation Blues," the music of which is printed before the Contents of *Ask Your Mama* along with the "Shave and a Haircut" "figurine." In the text of the poem, the appearance of the music and its performance are specifically indicated by the poet. One could compare this practice with that of Don Lee and Sarah Fabio. This poem, in fact, is almost the kind of "score" that Larry Neal speaks of. It is certainly more than just a "libretto," or a "lyric." Hughes carries out the musical analogy by calling his glosses to the poem "Liner Notes." In fact, Hughes "performed" this poem with Randy Weston at The Market Place Gallery in Harlem.

In device number seven, the reader's *emotional response to a well-known song is incorporated into the poem* in a manner resembling the use of a "rest" in music or an assumed "obbligato." And sometimes this is done by using a single word, as in Robert Terrell's "Asian Stew," with its play on the word "jelly."

> Wit rice-n-mud-n-bamboo shoots
> Wit sizzled hairs-n-human eclairs
> Wit shrapnel-n-goodwill-n-jelly
> jelly jelly

[*The New Catalyst*, Morehouse College, 1969]

Since the reference is to a state of mind or feeling instead of to an object or structure, the technique could be called the use of the "subjective correlative," in contrast to the "objective correlative" of the New Criticism. The clearest examples in this collection are Carolyn Rodgers' "5 Winos" (p. 344), with the reference to "the most carefully/constructed a-melodic Coltrane psalm . . ." and, especially, "Me, In Kulu Se & Karma" (p. 345), where the basis for the ecstasy of the experience is the assumption that the reader has felt the same way about the music. I distinguish this from "tonal memory" because that category refers more specifically to the actual structure and performance of the music. There is, to be sure, some of that in "Me, In Kulu Se & Karma," but the emphasis is upon *the emotional reaction to the music.* The poet calls this a *bein* poem: "Every poet has written a *bein* poem. In fact, most poets start off writing them. Just writing about the way they be, they friends be, they lovers be, the world be. . . ." And she quotes from this poem. It is significant, I think, that the poet's sense of *bein* is clarified and heightened by the music. See her sensitive essay, "Black Poetry—Where It's At," *Negro Digest*, September, 1969.

The musician himself functions as subject, poem, history, or myth in the eighth device or category. Particular musicians may be so treated, as in Brown's "Ma Rainey" (p. 134), Don Graham's "Soul" (p. 322), or A. B. Spellman's "did john's music kill him?" (p. 261). There is also a more general treatment, as in Hughes's "Jazzonia" (p. 128). In addi-

[*59*]

tion, the music rather than the musician may be the actual subject of the poem. This is probably the largest category of musical referents in Black poetry. The range is wide, even in this anthology, and the reader should compare and study the poems mentioned above and also Ted Joans's virtuoso piece, "Jazz Must Be a Woman" (p. 221), Neal's "Don't Say Goodbye to the Pork-Pie Hat" (p. 290), Henderson's "Elvin Jones Gretsch Freak" (p. 264), Jeffers' "How High the Moon" (p. 200), De Legall's "Psalm for Sonny Rollins" (p. 202), and Graham's Poem for Eric Dolphy" (p. 321).

Language from the jazz life or associated with it, commonly called "hip" speech, constitutes the ninth type of referent. This speech blends into so-called street talk, but one can find instances of precise and specific musical references, as in Larry Neal's "Don't Say Goodbye to the Pork-Pie Hat," or David Henderson's "Elvin Jones Gretsch Freak," or Percy Johnston's "Number Five Cooper Square." Sometimes the language may even be drawn from jazz criticism, as in Neal's use of the expression "rolling sheets of sound," which is a term often applied to the playing of Coltrane. In addition, there is the idiom of "bop" talking and "scat" singing, introduced into poetry, it seems, by Langston Hughes. This language from the jazz life, finally, is evident in many contemporary Black poems, though by no means in all. Nor, obviously, is it necessary to employ it in the writing of a Black poem. Notwithstanding, the world of jazz has had a tremendous impact upon the vocabulary of spoken English in this country, and it is thus quite easy to employ that language without being aware of its origin. Thus, in addition to the overworked words, "soul" and "funky," even relatively precise musical expressions like "going through rough changes," are part of the vocabulary of Blacks and the hip young whites who imitate them.

In the tenth category, *the poem as "score" or "chart,"* we move to the most challenging aspect of Black poetic structure

—the question of limit, or performance, of the text, or better, to use Larry Neal's expression, "the destruction of the text." When I say "limit," I raise the question of the distinction between singing Black songs and reading Black poems. When I say "performance," I refer essentially to the same question. For my own part, the question is merely academic; the distinction between song and poem, never that precise in the oral tradition, is in the context of the New Black Poetry, and some of the old which builds upon the same sources and styles, not at all very useful. By "destruction of the text," Neal, if I understand him correctly, refers both to the relegation of the printed poem to the status of a "musical score," and to a lack of concern with "permanence" in the Western, Platonic sense of IDEAL FORM. A poem may thus differ from performance to performance just as jazz performances of "My Favorite Things" would. Moreover, it implies that there is a Black poetic mechanism, much like the musical ones, which can transform even a Shakespearean sonnet into a jazz poem, the basic conceptual model of contemporary Black poetry. The technique, the fundamental device, would be improvisation, lying as it does at the very heart of jazz music. To this one may add the possibility of the poet's working with a group of mascon images drawn from the Black experience, especially from the spirituals and the blues, upon which he would build his free but disciplined associations. The text in such a case would become a chart, not a score, bringing it even closer to the musical ideal. There are other possibilities, some of which the poets are already trying. If they are successful, the whole thrust of modern poetry could conceivably be changed. That, however, is not their concern, and consequently not mine.

This concludes our discussion, then, of the first two of three broad critical categories which I proposed near the beginning of this essay: Theme, Structure, and Saturation. There remains now the third, which while difficult to formulate, does provide I hope at least a theoretical concept with some validity and usefulness.

SATURATION

By "saturation" in Black poetry, I mean several things, but chiefly (a) the communication of Blackness in a given situation, and (b) a sense of fidelity to the observed and intuited truth of the Black Experience. I postulate this concept as a third category for describing and evaluating Black poetry. As in the other two, theme and structure, this category exists only in relationship to the entire work and is employed merely to deal with an aspect of the poetry that warrants discussion and appreciation. In other words, just as it is misleading to speak of theme to the exclusion of structure and vice versa, it is difficult, if not impossible, to speak honestly about saturation without considering these other two. In addition, one must not consider the poem in isolation but in relationship to the reader/audience, and the reader to the wider context of the phenomenon which we call, for the sake of convenience, the Black Experience.

We may first consider saturation as a *perception* by the reader that a given poem deals with the Black Experience even though there are no verbal or other clues to alert him. He simply *knows* that this is so. He may perceive this on varying levels, either sharply and precisely by gestalt, or obscurely upon reflection. Sometimes the awareness comes through as a kind of "tone," sometimes as "perspective," either that of the poet, or of the reader. Note these two examples from Mari Evans' collection, *I Am A Black Woman* (William Morrow & Co., 1970).

> I am not
> lazy . . . just
> . . . battered

Also (from "Where Have You Gone," p. 35):

> where have you gone
> with your confident

        walk your
        crooked smile the
        rent money
        in one pocket and
        my heart
        in another . . .

With Mari Evans the special despair that seeps through the
jeweled diction, and sometimes the bitter wit itself, is some-
how akin to the blues. In cases like these, the awareness is
largely unverbalized and comes across as a "typical" situa-
tion, which we identify as true-to-life or part of the Black
Experience. Perhaps there are minute linguistic or gestural
clues, but these are highly ambiguous, as in the statement
"I am not lazy." Anybody of any race could say that, of
course, but what makes it special is the reaction to the im-
plied historical stereotype of the lazy darky. Black people
have a kind of hypersensitivity to those stereotypes even
when their use is unintended or unperceived. Therefore, for
one who is totally immersed, as it were, or saturated in the
Black Experience the slightest formulation of the typical or
true-to-life experience, whether positive or negative, is
enough to bring on at least subliminal recognition.

Again, saturation may be viewed in terms of analogy, and
one may use literature itself as a basis for comparison. There
are, for example, passages in a poem that we may designate
as very "English" or "American" without ever being able to
explain ourselves more precisely than that. Or, even more
basically, we may prefer an obviously flawed sonnet to one
which is metrically perfect, and even consider it somehow to
be a better poem or more poetic or meaningful. The same is
true, more dramatically so, in more expansive forms like the
epic or the novel, where some other consideration than mere
structure causes us to prefer, for example, a Dreiser novel to
one by Scott Fitzgerald, or Faulkner to Hemingway. The
same kind of consideration enables Blacks to recognize *Na-
tive Son* as somehow truer to the Black Experience in Amer-
ica, somehow more typical than *Invisible Man,* even though,

paradoxically, the latter deals with a wider range of that experience.

What we are talking about then is the *depth* and *quality* of experience which a given work may evoke. We are also speaking about saturation as a kind of *condition*. The kind of difference, for example, that exists between a Tin Pan Alley "blues" and a blues by Lightnin' Hopkins. Or if one protested because of the identifiable form of the blues, we could turn to the important phenomenon of Blacks taking over certain "white," i.e., general American cultural traits or features, and putting a decidely Black stamp on them. One may think for example of Bessie Smith's rendition of a Tin Pan Alley song like "Muddy Water," which is much better by far than the song deserves. Was it pure commercial concern that motivated her? Didn't she understand the words? At any rate, anyone who has heard Mississippi bluesmen sing of catastrophic flooding in the Delta would perceive some commonality in the singing of Bessie Smith. More to the point is this: What is it, except some fundamental mechanism or set of values, that causes an Aretha Franklin to *select* for her special Black interpretation certain songs that were written and sometimes performed by whites. To speak of universal appeal, I think, is a cop-out, for the obvious rejoinder would be why is one particularly good song chosen and another rejected? Especially when the singer takes the trouble to give it a Black interpretation which is literally a reinvention. To speak purely in musical terms is, of course, a contradiction because of the virtual saturation of all Black music in the conditions which produced it. I would attribute the choice to an inner personal need or to cultural drive. Perhaps to a cultural imperative, to use Harold Cruse's phrase. At any rate, stylistic differences aside, the recognition on the part of the audience that the artist has made a selection based on a set of mutually shared experiences and/or values is another way of talking about saturation.

We may speak more directly of saturation with specific

relationship to both theme and structure. In such cases, where style and subject matter are obviously Black, one may feel, for example, that a word, a phrase, a rhythm, is so *right*, so *Black,* that its employment illuminates the entire composition. An example would be Gwendolyn Brooks's observation of the Bronzeville man with the belted coat, or Sterling Brown's "Sister Lou," where the poem ends with the felicitous words, "Take your time, honey, take your *bressed* time" (my italics).

It is, in fact, in character drawing where questions of saturation become especially dramatic. Here one may feel that a given *objectively* described character, or self-revealed character, may be *perfectly* Black, i.e., that any additional touch would result in caricature or other distortion. The character is thus felt to be saturated in the Black Experience, and the poem itself a saturated one. This perception comes as a kind of gestalt in which the whole is more than the sum of the parts, the character more than his actions, his speech, or his thoughts, although they are in this case identifiably Black. Such characters abound in the poetry of the period from the twenties through the fifties. They may be inventions based on real life observations or they may be historical or legendary figures. There are fine examples in this text by Brown and Hughes, by Dodson, Brooks, Hayden, and others. In brief, the Nat Turner of Robert Hayden (p. 154) and Margaret Walker (p. 166) are Black in ways that William Styron's Turner could not possibly be—or certainly is not. That is, I think, because the Black portrayal of Turner becomes almost a mascon image, as it were, a highly concentrated experienced reality that embodies somehow in a single man a major movement of the racial mind.

That, briefly, is what I mean by saturation as a descriptive category. How now does it function as a critical category, as a means of evaluation? In the first place, it lets us know that the recognition of Blackness in poetry is a value judgment which on certain levels and in certain instances, notably in matters of meaning that go beyond questions of structure and theme, must rest upon one's immersion in the totality of the Black Experience. It means that the ultimate criteria for critical evaluation must be found in the sources of the creation, that is, in the Black Community itself.

In the second place, it lets us know that judgments regarding fidelity to the Black Experience are both objective and subjective, and that although a Joel Chandler Harris may record Black folk tales, the inner truth of those tales must be decided by the people who told them and who listened. Here, of course, we are not speaking merely of *realism* as a literary phenomenon. Notwithstanding, in the history of Black literature generally, and Black poetry specifically, let us remember the circumstances in which the realists worked, and let us remember what they accomplished. Let us, then, assume the same attitude in evaluating the realistic poetry of the sixties.

The concept of saturation as a critical category provides a clue to the philosophical meaning of phrases like "Black Is Beautiful," "Black People Are Poems," and so on. For Blacks the celebration of Blackness is an undertaking which makes value judgments, some of which certainly many American whites would reject. Nonetheless, if a Black celebratory poem is to be *understood* on the most elementary level it must be on these terms. There are none others that are valid.

SUMMARY

I have suggested a critical framework which, hopefully, is flexible enough to facilitate discussion of the entire range of Black poetry produced in the United States, whether it is folk poetry, or escapist poetry, or Black revolutionary poetry. First, I have considered the two main aspects of that tradition, which can be called the "formal" and the "folk." However, I called attention to the usefulness of Richard Wright's corresponding terminology, which is "the Narcissistic level" and "The Forms of Things Unknown." Both of these levels existed simultaneously when the first extant Black poem was composed. Both levels have existed throughout the recorded history of Black literature in the United States, and both exist today.

It is fallacious to think of these two levels as discrete entities, although for the most part the influence has been from the folk to the formal during the periods of greatest power and originality. Notwithstanding, one must consider as well the influence of the formal upon various aspects of the folk source. This, of course, can be seen in the development of the spiritual and other song forms, in the influence of biblical imagery and thought on the sermons, and even the sermon itself as a Western form, albeit fundamentally transformed by African sensibility and the peculiar demands of Black society. These matters are much too involved for discussion here, but it is clear from numerous sources that these two sides of the tradition were, and still are, conscious on various levels of each other.

The relationship is perhaps too subtle to be called dialectic. At any rate, it implies that Black poetry has contour and movement and direction. These latter two qualities I have touched upon in the first of the three categories—theme— which I set up as a basis for describing and evaluating the poetry. The main movement has been in the direction of

Freedom, of Liberation, and has generally followed and illuminated the historical movement of the people, despite apparently contradictory minor patterns. As a critical category, theme is very useful and has been, in fact, the basis of much of the discussion of Black poetry which presently exists.

The next category—structure—has not been spelled out in great detail on its own terms, especially for that poetry which is most distinctly Black, although there have been notable efforts in folk poetry by Brown and others, and ground-breaking monographs on individual poets, such as James Emanuel's distinguished work on Langston Hughes and George Kent's incisive work on Gwendolyn Brooks. But the problem of relating the structure of a Phillis Wheatley couplet to a McKay sonnet to a Ted Joans rap has, to my knowledge, been eschewed. Wherein does the Blackness lie? I have suggested an answer, at least, a hypothesis—in the roots, in Black speech, and in the movement toward the forms of Black music. I have arrived independently at this position, but it is one which is shared by some of the poets themselves, several of whom have expressed it quite precisely on various occasions.

Finally, I have tried to postulate a concept that would be useful in talking about what Black people feel is their distinctiveness, without being presumptuous enough to attempt a description or definition of it. This quality or condition of Black awareness I call *saturation*. I intend it as a sign, like the mathematical symbol for infinity, or the term "Soul." It allows us to talk about the thing, even to some extent to use it, though we can't, thank God! ultimately abstract and analyze it: it must be experienced.

That really is the purpose of this essay—to send us back to the poems themselves and to the people who make them. This is the great challenge of our poets as they incessantly proclaim their miraculous discovery that Black people are poems. What this means for the teacher and the student and the critic is that, like the poets, they must not separate themselves or their work, whatever it is, from the concerns of the people. Nor must they assume that they know all there is to be known about the people, including themselves. Nor all that there is in the Black Experience simply because they are Black. Nor that that knowledge is sufficient unto itself. For the knowledge of Blackness is the knowledge of pain and oppression as well as joy. It is a knowledge rooted in history and the real world, in all of its incompleteness and fragmentation. It is also a knowledge rooted in the spirit, which thus demands real action—social, political, and moral—in the real world, to make it fit for living, not exploitation. For non-Blacks the vision is a challenge to see the world through the eyes of others. It might even mean an enlargement of sensibility and a change of values. They must decide for themselves. But whatever they decide, Black people are moving toward the Forms of Things Unknown, which is to say, toward Liberation, which, however I have stammered in the telling, is what it is all about.

S.E.H.

Section I:

Pre-Harlem Renaissance and Soul-Field

I
Drinkin' of the wine—wine—wine
Drinkin' of the wine
O—yes—my Lord.
I oughta bin to Heaven ten thousand years
Drinkin' of the wine.

Georgia Sea Islands, Traditional

A respectable tradition of formal Black poetry has existed since the eighteenth century, but the poetic picture must be completed by considering those productions that were created by the people themselves. Although this is an area which is large and important enough to warrant exclusive attention, such division is not only unnecessary but misleading, for it assumes that there was no interaction between the two strata of expression, that they were unaware of each other. That would hardly be the case, of course, considering the backgrounds of some of the writers and the general knowledge of Black song, in a rudimentary sense, even among native American whites. In addition, the dialect tradition among Black poets—in imitation of whites—also shows an awareness of the folk tradition. James Weldon Johnson's Preface to the first edition of his *The Book of American Negro Poetry* points out, however, the limitations of traditional dialect—the stereotypes associated with it and the changing circumstances of Black life resulting from urbanization. What was needed, he felt, was "a form that will express the racial spirit by symbols from within rather than by symbols from without, such as the mere mutilation of English spelling and pronunciation." Such a form would be "freer and larger than dialect, but which will still hold the racial flavor; a form expressing the imagery, the idioms, the peculiar turns of thought, and the distinctive humor and pathos, too, of the Negro, but which will also be capable of voicing the deepest and highest emotions and aspirations, and

[73]

allow of the widest range of subjects and the widest scope of treatment" (pp. 41, 42).

Johnson's concerns are still the concerns of Black poets, and it is useful to note the terms "racial spirit" and "racial flavor" which he employs, as well as the more explicit reference to "imagery," "idioms," and "peculiar turns of thought." In the late 1950's the word "Soul" surfaced in the musical community and quickly spread to the wider Black Community, where it came to mean not only a special kind of popular music based on gospel songs and hymns but also the "racial spirit" and "racial flavor" which Johnson had spoken of some forty years earlier. The word is losing some of its popularity now, due perhaps to overuse and to co-optation by young whites, and in its place "funk," an old obscene, maligned word, is now appearing, but even that is now being defined by whites for their own purposes. I have spoken of that pattern elsewhere, so need not repeat myself, but the important thing is that Black Americans during the crucial period of the sixties and the uncertainties of the present have sought a term which epitomizes their unique identity. A generation ago, the Negritude writers sought to do much the same thing. In fact, Dr. Leopold Senghor, in his recent address to the delegates at the Dakar Festival (April, 1971) declared that "Soul," especially as defined by Lerone Bennet, was an even better term than Negritude to express the Blackness which his generation felt, "since the very choice of the term and of the idea—of Soul—recalls a certain manner which is both African and popular" (cf. *Black World*, August, 1971, p. 14). It is in this broad sense of special and explicit racial identity that I use the term. And when I say Soul-Field, I have in mind an analogy to a magnetic field or to a gravitational field, at the center of which would be that unique cluster of forces, events, personalities, and sensibility that have created that complexity which we casually call the Black Experience. Some parts of it are denser than others, as I imply in my notion of mascon imagery, but each affects every other, so that the totality is a kind of cosmos. Within such a cosmos it would be impossible to be both sentient and unaware of one's Blackness, however one responded to that awareness. Thus in terms of this volume, especially of this section, Johnson's poetry must be viewed as part of a system which contains the sermons of John Jasper, and his success must ultimately be measured against that standard. I need not elaborate, except to say that this has not often been the case. I think that I need not point out the obvious importance of W. E. B. DuBois' *The Souls of Black Folk,* which, published in 1903, antedated both Johnson's mature poetry and the efforts of Paul Laurence Dunbar.

Still it might be useful to suggest how a writer like James Corrothers, who is perhaps better known as a "straight" English protest poet than a dialect poet, would show the effect, so to speak, of the Soul-Field. There is a movement from verbal "blackface" in a piece like "Sweeten 'Tatahs" with its stereotyped situation announced in the first lines—"I has always laked good eatin's,/ F'om de minute I wah bo'n"—to a sly incipient realism in "An Indignation Dinner," which deals with the same subject, but with the kind of verve found in the oral literature. And when we come to the famous "At the Closed Gate of Justice," we find lines like these: "To be a Negro in a day like this/ Demands strange loyalty. We serve a flag/ Which is to us white freedom's emphasis." Here we get some idea of the man's real roots. And behind lines like the following from "In the Matter of Two Men" the folk voice is clear and unmistakable, though the sentiment of the poem is the middle-class ethic of work.

> The white man rides in a palace car,
> And the Negro rides "Jim Crow."
> To damn the other with bolt and bar,
>   One creepeth so low; so low!

Compare the folk rhyme, especially the conclusion;

> The white gal's ridin' an aeroplane,
> The yellow gal's ridin' a train . . .
> The black gal's ridin' on a mule's ass,
> But she's ridin' just the same.

This directness is characteristic of folk expression, and has been pointed out many times before. However, directness and simplicity should not be equated with simple-mindedness, as some seem to do. A serious study of the imagery of blues and spirituals would show a highly sophisticated and virtuoso use of language and spectacular leaps of imagination. At its best, in songs like "Go Down, Moses," for example, this style—to speak in comparative terms—is akin to Matthew Arnold's concept of the Grand Style Simple. If the songs are thematically grouped, as Harold Courlander has done in *Negro Folk Music, U.S.A.*, then their spaciousness suggests the epic. But it is the compression, and the evocativeness of these songs that give them enduring meaning and an appeal beyond the picturesque and the quaint, so that eventually all Black poetry in English must be measured against them. There are a few examples here. Others may be found in *The Book of Negro Folklore*, edited by Langston Hughes and Arna Bontemps, Dodd Mead & Co., 1958; *Slave Songs of the Georgia Sea Islands*, edited by Lydia Parrish, reissued by Folklore Associates, Inc., 1965; *The Negro and His Songs*, Howard W. Odum and Guy B. Johnson, reissued by Folklore Associates, Inc., 1964; the two-volume edition of *The Books of American Negro Spirituals*, edited by James W. Johnson and J. Rosamond Johnson, The Viking Press, 1940; and

American Negro Songs, edited by John W. Work, Bonanza Books, 1940. In addition, one should listen to the various collections on record made by Harold Courlander, Alan and John Lomax, and Frederick Ramsey, Jr.

Although a variety of Black song and folk poetry existed in the period preceding the Harlem Renaissance, it was the religious song and the secular rhymes and the folk sermon which seemed to inspire the concious poets like Dunbar and Johnson. There was the influence of the minstrel show also and of ragtime, which subjects Johnson deals with in his highly informative preface. For that reason, then, I make the selections from the Georgia Sea Islands and from the secular folk rhymes. It remained for another generation to explore the ballad and the bitter bawdiness of the blues.

GEORGIA SEA ISLANDS

I Heard the Angels Singin'

Chorus: One mornin' soon
             One mornin' soon
             One mornin' soon
Ah heard the angels singin'.

     All in my room
     All in my room
     All in my room
Ah heard the angels singin'.

Lawd, Ah wuz down on my knees
     Down on my knees
     Down on my knees
Ah heard the angels singin'.

     No dyin' there
     No dyin' there
     No dyin' there
Ah heard the angels singin'.

Ah heard the angels singin' Lawd
Ah heard the angels singin'
Ah heard the angels singin' Lawd
Ah heard the angels singin'.

Well, there's no weepin' there
     No weepin' there
     No weepin' there
Ah heard the angels singin'.

Lawd, it wuz all 'roun' me shine
     All 'roun' me shine

All 'roun' me shine
Ah heard the angels singin'.

Lawd, it wuz all over my head
All over my head
All over my head
Ah heard the angels singin'.

Lawd, it wuz all aroun' my fet
All aroun' my feet
All aroun' my feet
Ah heard the angels singin'.

My God Is a Rock in a Weary Land

"This song belongs to the exhorting-sermon type which has an African counterpart. The old-time preacher rhythmically chanted his sermon; at effective intervals he broke into song, in which he was joined by the congregation."— Lydia Parrish, *Slave Songs of the Georgia Sea Islands.*

Chorus: My God is a rock in a weary land
weary land
in a weary land
My God is a rock in a weary land
Shelter in a time of storm.

Ah know He is a rock in a weary land
weary land
in a weary land
Ah know He is a rock in a weary land
Shelter in a time of storm.

Stop let me tell you 'bout the Chapter One
When the Lord God's work has jus' begun

Stop and let me tell you 'bout the Chapter Two
   When the Lord God's written his Bible through
Stop and let me tell you 'bout the Chapter Three
   When the Lord God died on Calvary.

Chorus: An' Ah know He is a rock in a weary land
                     weary land
               in a weary land
    Ah know He is a rock in a weary land
    Shelter in a time of storm.

Stop and let me tell you 'bout the Chapter Four
   Lord God visit 'mong the po'
Stop and let me tell you 'bout the Chapter Five
   Lord God brought the dead alive
Stop and let me tell you 'bout the Chapter Six
   He went in Jerusalem and healed the sick.

Stop and let me tell you 'bout Chapter Seven
   Died and risen and went to Heaven
Stop and let me tell you 'bout the Chapter Eight
   John seen Him standin' at the Golden Gate
Stop and let me tell you 'bout the Chapter Nine
   Lord God turned the water to wine
Stop and let me tell you 'bout the Chapter Ten
   John says He's comin' in the world again.

JAMES WELDON JOHNSON

The Judgment Day

In that great day,
People, in that great day,
God's a-going to rain down fire.
God's a-going to sit in the middle of the air
To judge the quick and the dead.

Early one of these mornings,
God's a-going to call for Gabriel,
That tall, bright angel, Gabriel;
And God's a-going to say to him: Gabriel,
Blow your silver trumpet,
And wake the living nations.

And Gabriel's going to ask him: Lord,
How loud must I blow it?
And God's a-going to tell him: Gabriel,
Blow it calm and easy.
Then putting one foot on the mountain top,
And the other in the middle of the sea,
Gabriel's going to stand and blow his horn,
To wake the living nations.

Then God's a-going to say to him: Gabriel,
Once more blow your silver tumpet,
And wake the nations underground.

And Gabriel's going to ask him: Lord
How loud must I blow it?
And God's a-going to tell him: Gabriel,
Like seven peals of thunder.

Then the tall, bright angel, Gabriel,
Will put one foot on the battlements of heaven
And the other on the steps of hell,
And blow that silver trumpet
Till he shakes old hell's foundations.

And I feel Old Earth a-shuddering—
And I see the graves a-bursting—
And I hear a sound,
A blood-chilling sound.
What sound is that I hear?
It's the clicking together of the dry bones,
Bone to bone—the dry bones.
And I see coming out of the bursting graves,
And marching up from the valley of death,
The army of the dead.
And the living and the dead in the twinkling of an eye
Are caught up in the middle of the air,
Before God's judgment bar.

Oh-o-oh, sinner,
Where will you stand,
In that great day when God's a-going to rain down fire?
Oh, you gambling man—where will you stand?
You whore-mongering man—where will you stand?
Liars and backsliders—where will you stand,
In that great day when God's a-going to rain down fire?

And God will divide the sheep from the goats,
The one on the right, the other on the left.
And to them on the right God's a-going to say:
Enter into my kingdom.
And those who've come through great tribulations,
And washed their robes in the blood of the Lamb,
They will enter in—
Clothed in spotless white,

With starry crowns upon their heads,
And silver slippers on their feet,
And harps within their hands;

And two by two they'll walk
Up and down the golden street,
Feasting on the milk and honey
Singing new songs of Zion,
Chattering with the angels
All around the Great White Throne.

And to them on the left God's a-going to say:
Depart from me into everlasting darkness,
Down into the bottomless pit.
And the wicked like lumps of lead will start to fall,
Headlong for seven days and nights they'll fall,
Plumb into the big, black, red-hot mouth of hell,
Belching out fire and brimstone.
And their cries like howling, yelping dogs,
Will go up with the fire and smoke from hell,
But God will stop his ears.

Too late, sinner! Too late!
Good-bye, sinner! Good-bye!
In hell, sinner! In hell!
Beyond the reach of the love of God.

And I hear a voice, crying, crying:
Time shall be no more!
Time shall be no more!
Time shall be no more!
And the sun will go out like a candle in the wind,
The moon will turn to dripping blood,
The stars will fall like cinders,
And the sea will burn like tar;
And the earth shall melt away and be dissolved,
And the sky will roll up like a scroll.

With a wave of his hand God will blot out time,
And start the wheel of eternity.

Sinner, oh, sinner,
Where will you stand
In that great day when God's a-going to rain down fire?

GEORGIA SEA ISLANDS

Sangaree

"This ring-play varies in action wherever I see it done. For that reason I will attempt no description. The tune, however, always remains the same. . . ."—Lydia Parrish, *Slave Songs of the Georgia Sea Islands.*

If I live
>Sangaree.
Don' get kill'
>Sangaree.
I'm goin' back
>Sangaree.
Jacksonville
>Sangaree.

Chorus: Oh Babe
>Sangaree.
Oh Babe
>Sangaree.
Oh Babe
>Sangaree.
Oh Babe
>Sangaree.
If I live
>Sangaree.
See nex' fall
>Sangaree.
Ain' goin' t' plant
>Sangaree.
No cotton at all
>Sangaree.

Chicken in the fiel'
>Sangaree.

Scratchin' up peas
Sangaree.
Dog on the outside
Sangaree.
Scratchin' off fleas
Sangaree.

FOLK RHYMES

Did You Feed My Cow?

"Did yer feed my cow?" "Yes, Mam!"
"Will yer tell me how?" "Yes, Mam!"
"Oh, w'at did yer give 'er?" "Cawn an' hay."
"Oh, w'at did yer give 'er?" "Cawn an' hay."

"Did yer milk 'er good?" "Yes, Mam!"
"Did yer do lak yer should?" "Yes, Mam!"
"Oh, how did yer milk 'er?" "Swish! Swish! Swish!"
"Oh, how did yer milk 'er?" "Swish! Swish! Swish!"

"Did dat cow git sick?" "Yes, Mam!"
"Wus she kivered wid tick?" "Yes, Mam!"
"Oh, how wus she sick?" "All bloated up."
"Oh, how wus she sick?" "All bloated up."

"Did dat cow die?" "Yes, Mam!"
"Wid a pain in 'er eye?" "Yes, Mam!"
"Oh, how did she die?" "Uh-! Uh-! Uh-!"
"Oh, how did she die?" "Uh-! Uh-! Uh-!"

"Did de Buzzards come?" "Yes, Mam!"
"Fer to pick 'er bone?" "Yes, Mam!"
"Oh, how did they come?" "Flop! Flop! Flop!"
"Oh, how did they come?" "Flop! Flop! Flop!"

Peep Squirrel

Peep squir'l, ying-ding-did-lum;
Peep squir'l, it's almos' day,
Look squir'l, ying-ding-did-lum,
Look squir'l, an' run away.

Walk squir'l, ying-ding-did-lum;
Walk squir'l, fer dat's de way.
Skip squir'l, ying-ding-did-lum;
Skip squir'l, all dress in gray.

Run squir'l!   Ying-ding-did-lum!
Run squir'l!   Oh, run away!
I cotch you squir'l!   Ying-ding-did-lum!
I cotch you squir'l!   Now stay, I say.

Bedbug

De June-bug's got de golden wing,
De Lightning-bug de flame;
De Bedbug's got no wing at all,
But he gits dar jes de same.

De Punkin-bug's got a punkin smell,
De Squash-bug smells de wust;
But de puffume of dat ole Bedbug,
It's enough to make you bust.

W'en dat Bedbug come down to my house,
I wants my walkin cane.

Go git a pot an'scald 'im hot!
Good-by, Miss Lize Jane!

Walk, Talk, Chicken with Your Head Pecked

Walk, talk, chicken wid yo' head pecked!
You can crow w'en youse been dead.
Walk, talk, chicken wid yo' head pecked!
You can hol' high yo' bloody head.

You's whooped dat Blue Hen's Chicken,
You's beat 'im at his game.
If dere's some fedders on him,
Fer dat you's not to blame.

Walk, talk, chicken wid yo' head pecked!
You beat ole Johnny Blue!
Walk, talk, chicken wid yo' head pecked!
Say: "Cock-a-doo-dle-doo—!"

Wild Negro Bill

I'se wild Nigger Bill
Frum Redpepper Hill.
I never did wo'k, an' I never will.

I'se done killed de Boss.
I'se knocked down de hoss.
I eats up raw goose widout apple sauce!

I'se Run-a-way Bill,
I knows dey mought kill;
But ole Mosser hain't cotch me, an' he never will!

Fattening Frogs for Snakes

You needn' sen' my gal hoss apples
You needn' sen' her 'lasses candy;
She would keer fer de lak o' you,
Ef you'd sen' her apple brandy.

W'y don't you git some common sense?
Jes git a liddle!   Oh fer land sakes!
Quit yo foolin', she hain't studyin' you!
Youse jes fattenin' frogs fer snakes!

PAUL LAURENCE DUNBAR

Scamp

Ain't it nice to have a mammy
  W'en you kin' o' tiahed out
Wid a-playin' in de meddah,
  An' a-runnin' roun' about
Till hit's made you mighty hongry,
  An' yo' nose hit gits to know
What de smell means dat's a-comin'
  F'om de open cabin do'?
    She wash yo' face,
    An' mek yo' place,
  You's hongry as a tramp;
Den hit's eat you suppah right away,
  You sta'vin' little scamp.

W'en you's full o' braid an' bacon,
  An' dey ain't no mo' to eat,
An' de lasses dat's a-stickin'
  On yo' face ta'se kin' o' sweet,
Don' you t'ink hit's kin' o' pleasin'
  Fu' to have som'body neah
Dat'll wipe yo' han's an' kiss you
  Fo' dey lif' you f'om you' cheah?
    To smile so sweet,
    An' wash yo' feet,
  An' leave 'em co'l an' damp;
Den hit's come let me undress you, now
  You lazy little scamp.

Don' yo' eyes git awful heavy,
  An' yo' lip git awful slack,
Ain't dey som'p'n kin' o' weaknin'

In de backbone of yo' back?
Don' yo' knees feel kin' o' trimbly,
  An' yo' head go bobbin' roun',
W'en you says yo' "Now I lay me,"
  An' is sno'in on de "down"?
    She kiss yo' nose,
    She kiss yo' toes,
  An' den tu'n out de lamp,
Den hit's creep into yo' trunnel baid,
  You sleepy little scamp.

In the Morning

'Lias! 'Lias! Bless de Lawd!
Don' you know de day's erbroad?
Ef you don' git up, you scamp,
Dey'll be trouble in dis camp.
T'ink I gwine to let you sleep
W'ile I meks yo' boa'd an' keep?
Dat's a putty howdy-do—
Don' you hyeah me, 'Lias—you?

Bet ef I come crost dis flo'
You won' fin' no time to sno'.
Daylight all a-shinin' in
W'ile you sleep—w'y hit 's a sin!
Ain't de can'le-light enough
To bu'n out widout a snuff,
But you go de mo'nin' thoo
Bu'nin' up de daylight too?

'Lias, don' you hyeah me call?
No use tu'nin' to'ds de wall;
I kin hyeah dat mattuss squeak;

Don' you hyeah me w'en I speak?
Dis hyeah clock done struck off six—
Ca'line, bring me dem ah sticks!
Oh, you down, suh; huh, you down—
Look hyeah, don't you daih to frown.

Ma'ch yo'se'f an' wash yo' face,
Don' you splattah all de place;
I got somep'n else to do,
'Sides jes' cleanin' aftah you.
Tek dat comb an' fix yo' haid—
Looks jes' lak a feddah baid.
Look hyeah, boy, I let you see
You sha' n't roll yo' eyes at me.

Come hyeah; bring me dat ah strap!
Boy, I'll whup you 'twell you drap;
You done felt yo'se'f too strong,
An' you sholy got me wrong.
Set down at dat table thaih;
Jes' you whimpah ef you daih!
Evah mo'nin' on dis place,
Seem lak I mus' lose my grace.

Fol' yo' han's an' bow yo' haid—
Wait ontwell de blessin' 's said;
"Lawd, have mussy on ouah souls—"
(Don' you daih to tech dem rolls—)
"Bless de food we gwine to eat—"
(You set still—I *see* yo' feet;
You jes' try dat trick agin!)
"Gin us peace an' joy.   Amen!"

When Malindy Sings

G'way an' quit dat noise, Miss Lucy—
  Put dat music book away;
What 's de use to keep on tryin'?
  Ef you practise twell you're gray,
You cain't sta't no notes a-flyin'
  Lak de ones dat rants and rings
F'om de kitchen to de big woods
  When Malindy sings.

You ain't got de nachel o'gans
  Fu' to make de soun' come right,
You ain't got de tu'ns an' twistin's
  Fu' to make it sweet an' light.
Tell you one thing now, Miss Lucy,
  An' I'm tellin' you fu' true,
When hit comes to raal right singin',
  'T ain't no easy thing to do.

Easy 'nough fu' folks to hollah,
  Lookin' at de lines an' dots,
When dey ain't no one kin sence it,
  An' de chune comes in, in spots;
But fu' real melojous music,
  Dat jes' strikes yo' hea't and clings,
Jes' you stan' an' listen wif me
  When Malindy sings.

Ain't you nevah hyeahd Malindy?
  Blessed soul, tek up de cross!
Look hyeah, ain't you jokin', honey?
  Well, you don't know whut you los'.

[*94*]

Y' ought to hyeah dat gal a-wa'blin',
   Robins, la'ks, an' all dem things,
Heish dey moufs an' hides dey face
   When Malindy sings.

Fiddlin' man jes' stop his fiddlin',
   Lay his fiddle on de she'f;
Mockin'-bird quit tryin' to whistle,
   'Cause he jes' so shamed hisse'f.
Folks a-playin' on de banjo
   Draps dey fingahs on de strings—
Bless yo' soul—fu'gits to move em,
   When Malindy sings.

She jes' spreads huh mouf and hollahs,
   "Come to Jesus," twell you hyeah
Sinnahs' tremblin' steps and voices
   Timid-lak a-drawin' neah;
Den she tu'ns to "Rock of Ages,"
   Simply to de cross she clings,
An' you fin' yo' teahs a-drappin'
   When Malindy sings.

Who dat says dat humble praises
   Wif de Master nevah counts
Heish yo' mouf, I hyeah dat music,
   Ez hit rises up an' mounts—
Floatin' by de hills an' valleys,
   Way above dis buryin' sod,
Ez hit makes its way in glory
   To de very gates of God!

Oh, hit's sweetah dan de music
   Of an edicated band;
An' hit's dearah dan de battle's
   Song o' triumph in de lan'.
It seems holier dan evenin'

When de solemn chu'ch bell rings,
Ez I sit an' ca'mly listen
While Malindy sings.

Towsah, stop dat ba'kin', hyeah me!
Mandy, mek dat chile keep still;
Don't you hyeah de echoes callin'
F'om de valley to de hill?
Let me listen, I can hyeah it,
Th'oo de bresh of angels' wings,
Sof' an' sweet, "Swing Low, Sweet Chariot,"
Ez Malindy sings.

The Poet

He sang of life, serenely sweet,
With, now and then, a deeper note.
From some high peak, nigh yet remote,
He voiced the world's absorbing beat.

He sang of love when earth was young,
And Love, itself, was in his lays.
But ah, the world, it turned to praise
A jingle in a broken tongue.

Section II:

The Harlem Renaissance and Afterward,
Soul-Field

II
HEY! HEY!

Sun's a risin',
This is gonna be ma song.
Sun's a risin',
This is gonna be ma song.
I could be blue but
I been blue all night long.

Langston Hughes, *Fine Clothes to the Jew*

The Harlem Renaissance is usually dated from the publication of Claude McKay's *Harlem Shadows,* 1922, and Jean Toomer's *Cane,* 1923. However, the Renaissance was anticipated and crystallized by a set of circumstances so complex that the age is also the Jazz Age, the Blues Age, the Age of Garvey, the Age of the New Negro, and the age of the first great migration of Blacks to the North from the farms and plantations of the South.

If the dominant musical impact on the earlier period was the spiritual and the secular lyrics, the major influence on Harlem Renaissance literature came from the folk ballads and epics, the blues, and later—in the thirties—the infectious rhythms of jazz.

Among the most famous of these ballads is the story of Stack O'Lee and Billy Lyons, which appears in various versions, one, a popular song of the fifties. In this volume we have a traditional version and a blues distillation by Mississippi John Hurt. Ballads, it must be noted, contributed significantly to the development of standard blues forms, and many blues singers regularly included them in their repertoires. This practice was especially true of "songsters" like John Hurt, Leadbelly, Mance Lipscomb, and nameless others who provided entertainment as well as solace to their listeners.

Ranking in popularity with Stack O'Lee is the story of "Shine and the Titanic," which one still hears in poolrooms and bars. Note how Leadbelly's Jack Johnson story blends into that ballad. Another version is the "Sinking of the Titanic" by Richard "Rabbit" Brown (Roots R1-304), which emphasizes the tragedy without reference to the bitter viewpoint of the legendary Shine. Note the skillful reworking of the story by Etheridge Knight in "Dark Prophesy: I Sing of Shine," and Larry Neal's powerful evocation in his afterword to *Black Fire*.

Several writers handle the ballad with strength. Among those represented here are Jean Toomer, Langston Hughes, Sterling Brown, Robert Hayden, Margaret Walker, Gwendolyn Brooks, Owen Dodson, and—later—Dudley Randall and James Emanuel. Special note should be made of the different handlings, especially the idiomatic precision of Brown, the historical richness of Hayden, the dramatic power of Brooks, and the authentic juju of Margaret Walker's "Ballad of the Hoppy-Toad."

In this complex age the glamour of Blackness, captured in poems like Cullen's "Heritage" and Hughes's "Jazzonia" and "The Negro Speaks of Rivers," is sharply tempered by the realism of "When Sue Wears Red," "Cabaret," "Jazz Band," and "Roosevelt Smith." The ground tone of this attitude may be found in blues like those presented here. This mingling of glamour and tough-mindedness is everywhere apparent inside the Black Community. "Son" House's "Dry Spell Blues" is almost apocalyptic. How different is this mood from the spirituals and even the bitterest of the early seculars. It foreshadows the urban mood of the sixties; does it presage things to come?

HUDDIE LEDBETTER (LEADBELLY)

Titanic

(Look where and what has been done—1912, twelfth day of May, when the Titanic sink in the sea. When they was getting on board (there) was not no colored folks on. There was not no Negroes died on that ship. But Jack Johnson went to get on board. "We are not hauling no coal," (they said). So Jack Johnson didn't like what the Big Boss said. He went and tried to do something about it, but it was so much Jim Crow he could not have no go. And a few hours later Jack Johnson read the papers where the Titanic went down. Then the peoples began to holler about that mighty shock. You might have been Jack Johnson doing the Eagle Rock so glad that he was not on that ship). [Leadbelly, from a letter to Moses Asch, Folkways]

> It was midnight on the sea
> Band playing "nearer my God to thee—"
> Cryin', fare thee, Titanic, fare thee well.
>
> Titanic, when it got its load,
> Captain hollered, "All Aboard"
> Cryin', fare thee, Titanic, fare thee well.
>
> Jack Johnson want to get on board,
> Captain said, "I ain't haulin no coal"
> Cryin', fare thee, Titanic, fare thee well.
>
> Titanic was comin' 'round the curve
> When it ran into that great big iceberg
> Cryin', fare thee, Titanic, fare thee well.
>
> Titanic was sinking down,

Had them lifeboats all around.
Cryin', fare thee, Titanic, fare thee well.

Had them lifeboats around,
Savin' the women and children, lettin'
    the men go down.
Cryin', fare thee, Titanic, fare thee well.

Jack Johnson heard the mighty shock,
Might 'a' seen him doin' the Eagle
    Rock.
Cryin', fare thee, Titanic, fare thee well.

When the women and children got on the
    land,
Cryin', "Lord have mercy on my man."
Fare thee, Titanic, fare thee well.

TRADITIONAL BALLAD

Stagolee

It was early, early one mornin',
When I heard my bulldog bark,
Stagolee and Billy Lyons
Was squabblin' in the dark.

Stagolee told Billy Lyons,
"What do you think of that?
You win all my money, Billy,
Now you spit in my Stetson hat."

Stagolee, he went a-walkin'
In the red-hot, broilin' sun—
Says, "Bring me my six-shooter,
Lawd, I wants my forty-one."

Stagolee, he went a-walkin'
Through the mud and through the sand.
Says, "I feel mistreated this mornin',
I could kill most any man."

Billy Lyons told Stagolee,
"Please don't take my life,
I've got three little helpless chillun
And one poor, pitiful wife."

"Don't care nothin' about your chillun,
And nothin' about your wife,
You done mistreated me, Billy,
And I'm bound to take your life."

He shot him three times in the shoulder,
Lawd, and three times in the side,

Well, the last time he shot him
Cause Billy Lyons to die.

Stagolee told Mrs. Billy,
"You don't believe yo' man is dead;
Come into the bar-room,
See the hole I shot in his head."

The high sheriff told the deputies,
"Get your pistols and come with me.
We got to go 'rest that
Bad man Stagolee."

The deputies took their pistols
And they laid them on the shelf—
"If you want that bad man Stagolee,
Go 'rest him by yourself."

High sheriff ask the bartender,
"Who can that bad man be?"
"Speak softly," said the bartender,
"It's that bad man Stagolee."

He touch Stack on the shoulder,
Say, "Stack, why don't you run?"
"I don't run, white folks,
When I got my forty-one."

The hangman put the mask on,
Tied his hands behind his back,
Sprung the trap on Stagolee
But his neck refuse to crack.

Hangman, he got frightened,
Said, "Chief, you see how it be—
I can't hang this man,
Better set him free."

Three hundred dollar funeral,
Thousand dollar hearse,
Satisfaction undertaker
Put Stack six feet in the earth.

Stagolee, he told the Devil,
Says, "Come on and have some fun—
You stick me with your pitchfork,
I'll shoot you with my forty-one."

Stagolee took the pitchfork,
And he laid it on the shelf.
Says, "Stand back, Tom Devil,
I'm gonna rule Hell by myself."

MISSISSIPPI JOHN HURT

Stack O'Lee Blues

Police and officers, how can it be
You can arrest everybody but cruel Stack O'Lee
That bad man, O cruel Stack O'Lee!

He said, "Stack O'Lee! Stack O'Lee!
Please don't take my life."
Says, "I got two little babes and a darling loving wife."
He's a bad man, that cruel Stack O'Lee!

"What I care about your two little babes, your darling loving
    wife.
Say You done stole my Stetson hat,
I'm bound to take your life."
That bad man, O cruel Stack O'Lee!

Ummmmmm Ummmmmmmmmm Ummmmmmmmmm
Ummmmmm Ummmmmmmmmm Ummmmmm Ummmm
    Ummm

Boom! Boom!   Boom! Boom! went a .44
Well, when they spy Billy Lyons
He was lying down on the floor
That bad man, O cruel Stack O'Lee!

Gentlemen of the jury,
What do you think of that?
Say Stack O'Lee killed Billy Lyons
About a five dollar Stetson hat
He's a bad man, O cruel Stack O'Lee!

Standin' on the gallows

Stack O'Lee did curse.
The judge say, "Let's kill him
Before he kill some of us."
He's a bad man, O cruel Stack O'Lee!

Standin' on the gallows
His head was way up high.
At twelve o'clock they killed him
They's all glad to see him die.
That bad man, O cruel Stack O'Lee!

Police and officers, how can it be
You can arrest everybody but cruel Stack O'Lee
That bad man, O cruel Stack O'Lee!

RICH AMERSON

Black Woman

Well, I said come here, Black Woman,
Ah-hmm, don't you hear me cryin', Oh Lordy!
Ah-hmm, I say run here, Black Woman,
I want you to sit on Black Daddy's knee, Lord!
M-hmmmm, I know your house feel lonesome,
Ah don't you hear me whoopin', O Lordy!
Don't your house feel lonesome,
When your biscuit-roller gone,
M-hmmm, I know your house feel lonesome,
Mamma, when your biscuit-roller gone!

I say my house feel lonesome,
I know you hear me cryin' oh Baby!
Ah-hmm, ah, when I looked in my kitchen, Mamma,
And I went all through my dinin' room!
Ah-hmmm, when I woke up this mornin',
I found my biscuit-roller done gone!

I'm goin' to Texas, Mamma,
Just to hear the wild ox moan,
Lord help my cryin' time I'm goin' to Texas,
Mamma, to hear the wild ox moan!
And if they moan to suit me,
I'm going to bring a wild ox home!
Ah-hmm, I say I'm got to go to Texas, Black Mamma,
Ah-hmmm, I know I hear me cryin,' O Lordy!
Ah-hmmm, I'm got to go to Texas, Black Mamma,
Ah, just to hear the white cow, I say, moan!
Ah-hmmm, ah, if they moan to suit me, Lordy,
I b'lieve I'll bring a white cow back home!

Say, I feel superstitious, Mamma
'Bout my hoggin' bread, Lord help my hungry time,
I feel superstitious, Baby, 'bout my hoggin' bread!
Ah-hmmm, Baby, I feel superstitious,
I say 'stitious, Black Woman!
Ah-hmm, ah you hear me cryin'
About I done got hungry, oh Lordy!
Oh, Mamma, I feel superstitious
About my hog Lord God it's my bread.

I want you to tell me, Mamma,
Ah-hmmm, I hear me cryin', oh Mamma!
Ah-hmmm, I want you to tell me, Black Woman,
Oh where did you stay last night?
I love you, Black Woman,
I tell the whole wide world I do,
Lord help your happy black time, I love you, Baby,
And I tell the world I do!
Ah-hmmm, I love you, Black Woman,
I know you hear me whoopin', Black Baby!
Ah-hmmm, I love you, Black Woman,
And I'll tell your Daddy, I do, Lord!

"BIG BILL" BROONZY

Hollerin' the Blues

Yes, I'm settin on this old stump, baby, got a worried mind.
Yes, I'm settin on this stump, baby, I've got a worried mind.
Yeah, I'm gonna find my baby, Lord, or lose my life tryin.

Yeah, I shot five dollars, caught a point like nine,
Yes, I shot five dollars, baby, and I caught a point like nine.
Yeah, I stopped that six spot, baby, and that trey come flyin.

Yeah, I hear my hamstring a-poppin, my collar cryin,
Lord, I hear my hamstring a-poppin, baby, and I hear my
    collar cryin.
Now how can I stay happy, Lord, when my baby's
    down the line.

Yeah, you'll never get to do me like you did my buddy Shine,
No, you'll never git to do me like you done my buddy Shine.
You know you worked him down on the levee until he
    went real stone blind.

"MA" RAINEY

Sweet Rough Man

I woke up this morning
My head was sore as a board
I woke up this morning
My head was sore as a board
My man beat me last night
With five feet of chopped up cord

He keeps my lips split
Got eyes as black as day
He keeps my lips split
Got eyes as black as day
But the way he love me
Make me soon forget

Every night for five years
I've got a beaten from my man
Every night for five years
I've got a beaten from my man
People says I'm crazy
How to straighten you understand

My man, my man, Lawd
Everybody knows he's mean
My man, my man, Lawd
Everybody knows he's mean
Cause when he starts to loving
I wring, and twist and sing

Lawd, it ain't no big thing
About my man being rough
Lawd, it ain't no big thing
About my man being rough
But when it comes to loving
He sho can strut his stuff.

LEWIS BLACK

Spanish Blues

Hmmmm, Hmmmm, Hmmmm
Hmmmm, Hmmmm, Hmmmm
Hmmmm, Hmmmm, Hmmmm

Hmmmm, Mama, Mama, Mama, Mama
Hmmmm, Mama, Mama, Mama, Mama
Hmmmm, Mama, Mama, Mama, Mama

Hmmmm, don't mean me no good at all
Hmmmm, don't mean me no good at all
Hmmmm, don't mean me no good at all.

EDDIE "SON" HOUSE

Dry Spell Blues

The dry spell blues have fallen, drove me from door to door.
Dry spell blues have fallen, drove me from door to door.
The dry spell blues have put everybody on the killing floor.

Now the people down south sure won't have no home.
Now the people down south sure won't have no home
'Cause the dry spell have parched all this cotton and corn.

Hard luck's on everybody, and many people are through.
Hard luck's on everybody, and many people are through.
Now besides the shower, ain't got a help but you.

Lord, I fold my arms, and I walked away.
Lord, I fold my arms, Lord, I walked away.
Just like I tell you, somebody's got to pay.

Pork chops forty-five cents a pound, cotton is only ten.
Pork chops forty-five cents a pound, cotton is only ten.
I can't keep no women, no, no, nowhere I been.

So dry, old boll weevil turned up his toes and died.
So dry, old boll weevil turned up his toes and died.
Now ain't nothing to do, bootleg moonshine and rye.

It have been so dry, you can make a powderhouse out of the
    world.
Yes, it has been so dry, you can make a powderhouse out of
    the world.
Then all the money men like a rattlesnake in his coil.

I done throwed up my hands, Lord, and solemnly swore.
I done throwed up my hands, Lord, and solemnly swore.

There ain't no need of me changing towns, it's a drought
    everywhere I go.

It's a dry old spell everywhere I been.
Oh, it's a dry old spell everywhere I been.
I believe to my soul this old world is bound to end.

Well, I stood in my back yard, wrung my hands and screamed.
I stood in my back yard, I wrung my hands and screamed.
And I couldn't see nothing, couldn't see nothing green.

Oh Lord, have mercy if you please.
Oh Lord, have mercy if you please.
Let your rain come down, and give our poor hearts ease.

These blues, these blues is worthwhile to be heard.
Oh, these blues, worthwhile to be heard.
God's very likely bound to rain somewhere.

CLAUDE MC KAY

Harlem Shadows

I hear the halting footsteps of a lass
  In Negro Harlem when the night lets fall
Its veil. I see the shapes of girls who pass
  To bend and barter at desire's call.
Ah, little dark girls who in slippered feet
Go prowling through the night from street to street!

Through the long night until the silver break
  Of day the little gray feet know no rest;
Through the lone night until the last snow-flake
  Has dropped from heaven upon the earth's white breast,
The dusky, half-clad girls of tired feet
Are trudging, thinly shod, from street to street.

Ah, stern harsh world, that in the wretched way
  Of poverty, dishonor and disgrace,
Has pushed the timid little feet of clay,
  The sacred brown feet of my fallen race!
Ah, heart of me, the weary, weary feet
In Harlem wandering from street to street.

North and South

O sweet are tropic lands for waking dreams!
  There time and life move lazily along.
There by the banks of blue-and-silver streams
  Grass-sheltered crickets chirp incessant song,
Gay-colored lizards loll all through the day,
  Their tongues outstretched for careless little flies,

And swarthy children in the fields at play,
  Look upward laughing at the smiling skies.
A breath of idleness is in the air
  That casts a subtle spell upon all things,
And love and mating-time are everywhere,
  And wonder to life's commonplaces clings.
The fluttering humming-bird darts through the trees
  And dips his long beak in the big bell-flowers,
The leisured buzzard floats upon the breeze,
  Riding a crescent cloud for endless hours,
The sea beats softly on the emerald strands—
O sweet for quiet dreams are tropic lands!

Baptism

Into the furnace let me go alone;
Stay you without in terror of the heat.
I will go naked in—for thus 'tis sweet—
Into the weird depths of the hottest zone.
I will not quiver in the frailest bone,
You will not note a flicker of defeat;
My heart shall tremble not its fate to meet,
My mouth give utterance to any moan.
The yawning oven spits forth fiery spears;
Red aspish tongues shout wordlessly my name.
Desire destroys, consumes my mortal fears,
Transforming me into a shape of flame.
I will come out, back to your world of tears,
A stronger soul within a finer frame.

If We Must Die

If we must die, let it not be like hogs
Hunted and penned in an inglorious spot,
While round us bark the mad and hungry dogs,
Making their mock at our accursèd lot.
If we must die, O let us nobly die,
So that our precious blood may not be shed
In vain; then even the monsters we defy
Shall be constrained to honor us though dead!
O kinsmen! we must meet the common foe!
Though far outnumbered let us show us brave,
And for their thousand blows deal one death-
    blow!
What though before us lies the open grave?
Like men we'll face the murderous, cowardly
    pack,
Pressed to the wall, dying, but fighting back!

JEAN TOOMER

Song of the Son

Pour O pour that parting soul in song,
O pour it in the sawdust glow of night,
Into the velvet pine-smoke air to-night,
And let the valley carry it along.
And let the valley carry it along.

O land and soil, red soil and sweet-gum tree,
So scant of grass, so profligate of pines,
Now just before an epoch's sun declines
Thy son, in time, I have returned to thee,
Thy son, I have in time returned to thee.

In time, for though the sun is setting on
A song-lit race of slaves, it has not set;
Though late, O soil, it is not too late yet
To catch thy plaintive soul, leaving, soon gone,
Leaving, to catch thy plaintive soul soon gone.

O Negro slaves, dark purple ripened plums,
Squeezed, and bursting in the pine-wood air,
Passing, before they stripped the old tree bare
One plum was saved for me, one seed becomes

An everlasting song, a singing tree,
Caroling softly souls of slavery,
What they were, and what they are to me,
Caroling softly souls of slavery.

Georgia Dusk

The sky, lazily disdaining to pursue
  The setting sun, too indolent to hold
  A lengthened tournament for flashing gold,
Passively darkens for night's barbecue,

A feast of moon and men and barking hounds,
  An orgy for some genius of the South
  With blood-hot eyes and cane-lipped scented mouth,
Surprised in making folk-songs from soul sounds.

The sawmill blows its whistle, buzz-saws stop,
  And silence breaks the bud of knoll and hill,
  Soft settling pollen where plowed lands fulfill
Their early promise of a bumper crop.

Smoke from the pyramidal sawdust pile
  Curls up, blue ghosts of trees, tarrying low
  Where only chips and stumps are left to show
The solid proof of former domicile.

Meanwhile, the men, with vestiges of pomp,
  Race memories of king and caravan,
  High-priests, an ostrich, and a juju-man,
Go singing through the footpaths of the swamp.

Their voices rise . . the pine trees are guitars,
  Strumming, pine-needles fall like sheets of rain . .
  Their voices rise . . the chorus of the cane
Is caroling a vesper to the stars. .

O singers, resinous and soft your songs
  Above the sacred whisper of the pines,
  Give virgin lips to cornfield concubines,
Bring dreams of Christ to dusky cane-lipped throngs.

COUNTEE CULLEN

Yet Do I Marvel

I doubt not God is good, well-meaning, kind,
And did He stoop to quibble could tell why
The little buried mole continues blind,
Why flesh that mirrors Him must some day die,
Make plain the reason tortured Tantalus
Is baited by the fickle fruit, declare
If merely brute caprice dooms Sisyphus
To struggle up a never-ending stair.
Inscrutable His ways are, and immune
To catechism by a mind too strewn
With petty cares to slightly understand
What awful brain compels His awful hand.
Yet do I marvel at this curious thing:
To make a poet black, and bid him sing!

Heritage
(For Harold Jackman)

What is Africa to me:
Copper sun or scarlet sea,
Jungle star or jungle track,
Strong bronzed men, or regal black
Women from whose loins I sprang
When the birds of Eden sang?
One three centuries removed
From the scenes his fathers loved,
Spicy grove, cinnamon tree,
What is Africa to me?

So I lie, who all day long
Want no sound except the song
Sung by wild barbaric birds
Goading massive jungle herds,
Juggernauts of flesh that pass
Trampling tall defiant grass
Where young forest lovers lie,
Plighting troth beneath the sky.
So I lie, who always hear,
Though I cram against my ear
Both my thumbs, and keep them there,
Great drums throbbing through the air.
So I lie, whose fount of pride,
Dear distress, and joy allied,
Is my somber flesh and skin,
With the dark blood dammed within
Like great pulsing tides of wine
That, I fear, must burst the fine
Channels of the chafing net
Where they surge and foam and fret.

Africa? A book one thumbs
Listlessly, till slumber comes.
Unremembered are her bats
Circling through the night, her cats
Crouching in the river reeds,
Stalking gentle flesh that feeds
By the river brink; no more
Does the bugle-throated roar
Cry that monarch claws have leapt
From the scabbards where they slept.
Silver snakes that once a year
Doff the lovely coats you wear,
Seek no covert in your fear
Lest a mortal eye should see;
What's your nakedness to me?
Here no leprous flowers rear

Fierce corollas in the air;
Here no bodies sleek and wet,
Dripping mingled rain and sweat,
Tread the savage measures of
Jungle boys and girls in love.
What is last year's snow to me,
Last year's anything? The tree
Budding yearly must forget
How its past arose or set—
Bough and blossom, flower, fruit,
Even what shy bird with mute
Wonder at her travail there,
Meekly labored in its hair.
One three centuries removed
From the scenes his fathers loved,
Spicy grove, cinnamon tree,
What is Africa to me?

So I lie, who find no peace
Night or day, no slight release
From the unremittant beat
Made by cruel padded feet
Walking through my body's street.
Up and down they go, and back,
Treading out a jungle track.
So I lie, who never quite
Safely sleep from rain at night—
I can never rest at all
When the rain begins to fall;
Like a soul gone mad with pain
I must match its weird refrain;
Ever must I twist and squirm,
Writhing like a baited worm,
While its primal measures drip
Through my body, crying, "Strip!
Doff this new exuberance.
Come and dance the Lover's Dance!"

In an old remembered way
Rain works on me night and day.

Quaint, outlandish heathen gods
Black men fashion out of rods,
Clay, and brittle bits of stone,
In a likeness like their own,
My conversion came high-priced;
I belong to Jesus Christ,
Preacher of humility;
Heathen gods are naught to me.

Father, Son, and Holy Ghost,
So I make an idle boast;
Jesus of the twice-turned cheek,
Lamb of God, although I speak
With my mouth thus, in my heart
Do I play a double part.
Ever at Thy glowing altar
Must my heart grow sick and falter,
Wishing He I served were black,
Thinking then it would not lack
Precedent of pain to guide it,
Let who would or might deride it;
Surely then this flesh would know
Yours had borne a kindred woe.
Lord, I fashion dark gods, too,
Daring even to give You
Dark despairing features where,
Crowned with dark rebellious hair,
Patience wavers just so much as
Mortal grief compels, while touches
Quick and hot, of anger, rise
To smitten cheek and weary eyes.
Lord, forgive me if my need
Sometimes shapes a human creed.
All day long and all night through,

One thing only must I do:
Quench my pride and cool my blood,
Lest I perish in the flood.
Lest a hidden ember set
Timber that I thought was wet
Burning like the dryest flax,
Melting like the merest wax,
Lest the grave restore its dead.
Not yet has my heart or head
In the least way realized
They and I are civilized.

LANGSTON HUGHES

Laughers

Dream singers,
Story tellers,
Dancers,
Loud laughers in the hands of Fate—
  My people.
Dish-washers,
Elevator-boys,
Ladies' maids,
Crap-shooters,
Cooks,
Waiters,
Jazzers,
Nurses of babies,
Loaders of ships,
Rounders,
Number writers,
Comedians in vaudeville
And band-men in circuses—
Dream-singers all,—
  My people.
Story-tellers all,—
  My people.
  Dancers—
God! What dancers!
  Singers—
God! What singers!
Singers and dancers.
Dancers and laughers.
  Laughers?
Yes, laughters . . . laughers . . . laughers—
Loud-mouthed laughers in the hands
  Of Fate.

When Sue Wears Red

When Susanna Jones wears red
Her face is like an ancient cameo
Turned brown by the ages.

Come with a blast of trumpets,
    Jesus!

When Susanna Jones wears red
A queen from some time-dead Egyptian night
Walks once again.

Blow trumpets, Jesus!

And the beauty of Susanna Jones in red
Burns in my heart a love-fire sharp like pain.

Sweet silver trumpets,
    Jesus!

Mother to Son

Well, son, I'll tell you:
Life for me ain't been no crystal stair.
It's had tacks in it,
And splinters,
And boards torn up,
And places with no carpet on the floor—
Bare.
But all the time

I'se been a-climbin' on,
And reachin' landin's,
And turnin' corners,
And sometimes goin' in the dark
Where there ain't been no light.
So boy, don't you turn back.
Don't you set down on the steps
'Cause you finds it's kinder hard.
Don't you fall now—
For I'se still goin', honey,
I'se still climbin',
And life for me ain't been no crystal stair.

Song for a Banjo Dance

Shake your brown feet, honey,
Shake your brown feet, chile,
Shake your brown feet, honey,
Shake 'em swift and wil'—
   Get way back, honey,
   Do that low-down step.
   Walk on over, darling,
     Now! Come out
     With your left.
Shake your brown feet, honey,
Shake 'em, honey chile.

Sun's going down this evening—
Might never rise no mo'.
The sun's going down this very night—
Might never rise no mo'—
So dance with swift feet, honey,
   (The banjo's sobbing low)
Dance with swift feet, honey—
   Might never dance no mo'.

Shake your brown feet, Liza,
Shake 'em, Liza, chile,
Shake you brown feet, Liza,
    (The music's soft and wil')
Shake your brown feet, Liza,
    (The banjo's sobbing low)
The sun's going down this very night—
    Might never rise no mo'.

Jazzonia

Oh, silver tree!
Oh, shining rivers of the soul!

In a Harlem cabaret
Six long-headed jazzers play.
A dancing girl whose eyes are bold
Lifts high a dress of silken gold.

Oh, singing tree!
Oh, shining rivers of the soul!

Were Eve's eyes
In the first garden
Just a bit too bold?
Was Cleopatra gorgeous
In a gown of gold?

Oh, shining tree!
Oh, silver rivers of the soul!

In a whirling cabaret
Six long-headed jazzers play.

The Negro Speaks of Rivers

(To W. E. B. Du Bois)

I've known rivers:
I've known rivers ancient as the world and older than the
  flow of human blood in human veins.

My soul has grown deep like the rivers.

I bathed in the Euphrates when dawns were young.
I built my hut near the Congo and it lulled me to sleep.
I looked upon the Nile and raised the pyramids above it.
I heard the singing of the Mississippi when Abe Lincoln
  went down to New Orleans, and I've seen its muddy
  bosom turn all golden in the sunset.

I've known rivers:
Ancient, dusky rivers.

My soul has grown deep like the rivers.

STERLING A. BROWN

Cabaret

Rich, flashy, puffy-faced,
Hebrew and Anglo-Saxon,
The overlords sprawl here with their glittering darlings.
The smoke curls thick, in the dimmed light
Surreptitiously, deaf-mute waiters
Flatter the grandees,
Going easily over the rich carpets,
Wary lest they kick over the bottles
Under the tables.

The jazzband unleashes its frenzy.

> *Now, now,*
> *To it, Roger; that's a nice doggie,*
> *Show your tricks to the gentlemen.*

The trombone belches, and the saxophone
Wails curdlingly, the cymbals clash,
The drummer twitches in an epileptic fit

> Muddy water
> Round my feet
> Muddy water

The chorus sways in.
The "Creole Beauties from New Orleans"
(By way of Atlanta, Louisville, Washington, Yonkers,
With stop-overs they've used nearly all their lives)
Their creamy skin flushing rose warm,
O, le bal des belles quarteronnes!
Their shapely bodies naked save

For tattered pink silk bodices, short velvet tights,
And shining silver-buckled boots;
Red bandannas on their sleek and close-clipped hair;
To bring to mind (aided by the bottles under the tables)
Life upon the river—

      Muddy water, river sweet

(Lafitte the pirate, instead,
And his doughty diggers of gold)

      There's peace and happiness there
      I declare

(In Arkansas,
Poor half-naked fools, tagged with identification numbers,
Worn out upon the levees,
Are carted back to the serfdom
They had never left before
And may never leave again)

      Bee—dap—ee—DOOP, dee—ba—dee—BOOP

The girls wiggle and twist

    Oh you too,
    Proud high-stepping beauties,
    Show your paces to the gentlemen.
    A prime filly, seh.
    What am I offered, gentlemen, gentlemen. . . .

    I've been away a year today
    To wander and roam
    I don't care if it's muddy there

(Now that the floods recede,
What is there left the miserable folk?

Oh time in abundance to count their losses,
There is so little else to count.)

        Still it's my home, sweet home

From the lovely throats
Moans and deep cries for home:
Nashville, Toledo, Spout Springs, Boston,
Creoles from Germantown;—
The bodies twist and rock;
The glasses are filled up again. . . .

(In Mississippi
The black folk huddle, mute, uncomprehending,
Wondering "how come the good Lord
Could treat them this a way")

        shelter
      Down in the Delta

(Along the Yazoo
The buzzards fly over, over, low,
Glutted, but with their scrawny necks stretching,
Peering still.)

       I've got my toes turned Dixie ways
       Round that Delta let me laze

The band goes mad, the drummer throws his sticks
At the moon, a *papier-mâché* moon,
The chorus leaps into weird posturings,
The firm-fleshed arms plucking at grapes to stain
Their coralled mouths; seductive bodies weaving
Bending, writhing, turning

       My heart cries out for
       M U D D Y   W A T E R

(Down in the valleys
The stench of the drying mud
Is a bitter reminder of death.)

Dee da dee D A A A A H

Maumee Ruth

Might as well bury her
   And bury her deep,
Might as well put her
   Where she can sleep.

Might as well lay her
   Out in her shiny black;
And for the love of God
   Not wish her back.

Maum Sal may miss her—
   Maum Sal, she only—
With no one now to scoff,
   Sal may be lonely. . . .

Nobody else there is
   Who will be caring
How rocky was the road
   For her wayfaring;

Nobody be heeding in
   Cabin, or town,
That she is lying here
   In her best gown.

Boy that she suckled—
   How should he know,

Hiding in city holes,
   Sniffing the "snow"?

And how should the news
   Pierce Harlem's din,
To reach her baby gal,
   Sodden with gin?

To cut her withered heart
   They cannot come again,
Preach her the lies about
   Jordan, and then

Might as well drop her
   Deep in the ground,
Might as well pray for her,
   That she sleep sound. . . .

Ma Rainey

1

When Ma Rainey
Comes to town,
Folks from anyplace
Miles aroun',
From Cape Girardeau,
Poplar Bluff,
Flocks in to hear
Ma do her stuff;
Comes flivverin' in,
Or ridin' mules,
Or packed in trains,
Picknickin' fools. . . .
That's what it's like,
Fo' miles on down,

To New Orleans delta
An' Mobile town,
When Ma hits
Anywheres aroun'.

2

Dey comes to hear Ma Rainey from de little river settlements,
From blackbottom cornrows and from lumber camps;
Dey stumble in de hall, jes' a-laughin' an' a-cacklin',
Cheerin' lak roarin' water, lak wind in river swamps.

An' some jokers keeps deir laughs a-goin' in de crowded
   aisles,
An' some folks sits dere waitin' wid deir aches an' miseries,
Till Ma comes out before dem, a-smilin' gold-toofed smiles
An' Long Boy ripples minors on de black an' yellow keys.

3

O Ma Rainey,
Sing yo' song;
Now you's back
Whah you belong,
Git way inside us,
Keep us strong. . . .
O Ma Rainey,
Li'l an' low;
Sing us 'bout de hard luck   .
Roun' our do';
Sing us 'bout de lonesome road
We mus' go. . . .

4

I talked to a fellow, an' the fellow say,
"She jes' catch hold of us, somekindaway.
She sang Backwater Blues one day:
   'It rained fo' days an' de skies was dark as night,
   Trouble taken place in de lowlands at night.

'*Thundered an' lightened an' the storm begin to roll*
Thousan's of people ain't got no place to go.

'*Den I went an' stood upon some high ol' lonesome hill,*
An' looked down on the place where I used to live.'

An' den de folks, dey natchally bowed dey heads an' cried,
Bowed dey heavy heads, shet dey moufs up tight an' cried,
An' Ma lef' de stage, an' followed some de folks outside."

Dere wasn't much more de fellow say:
She jes' gits hold of us dataway.

Slim Greer

Listen to the tale
Of Ole Slim Greer,
Waitines' devil
Waitin' here;

      Talkinges' guy
      An' biggest liar,
      With always a new lie
      On the fire.

Tells a tale
Of Arkansaw
That keeps the kitchen
In a roar;

      Tells in a long-drawled
      Careless tone,
      As solemn as a Baptist
      Parson's moan.

How he in Arkansaw
Passed for white,
An' he no lighter
Than a dark midnight.

Found a nice white woman
At a dance,
Thought he was from Spain
Or else from France;

Nobody suspicioned
Ole Slim Greer's race
But a Hill Billy, always
Roun' the place,

Who called one day
On the trustful dame
An' found Slim comfy
When he came.

The whites lef' the parlor
All to Slim
Which didn't cut
No ice with him,

An' he started a-tinklin'
Some mo'nful blues,
An' a-pattin' the time
With No. Fourteen shoes.

The cracker listened
An' then he spat
An' said, "No white man
Could play like that. . . ."

The white jane ordered
The tattler out

Then, female like
Began to doubt.

Crept into the parlor
Soft as you please,
Where Slim was agitatin'
The ivories.

Heard Slim's music—
An' then, hot damn!
Shouted sharp—"Nigger!"
An' Slim said, "Ma'am?"

She screamed and the crackers
Swarmed up soon,
But found only echoes
Of his tune;

'Cause Slim had sold out
With lightnin' speed;
"Hope I may die, sir—
Yes, indeed. . . ."

Slim in Hell

I
Slim Greer went to heaven;
   St. Peter said, "Slim,
You been a right good boy."
   An' he winked at him.

"You been a travelin' rascal
   In yo' day.
You kin roam once mo';
   Den you comes to stay.

"Put dese wings on yo' shoulders,
    An' save yo' feet."
Slim grin, and he speak up,
    "Thankye, Pete."

            Den Peter say, "Go
                To Hell an' see
            All dat is doing, and
                Report to me.

"Be sure to remember
    How everything go."
Slim say, "I be seein' yuh
    On de late watch, bo."

            Slim got to cavortin'
                Swell as you choose,
            Like Lindy in de Spirit
                Of St. Louis Blues.

He flew an' he flew,
    Till at last he hit
A hangar wid de sign readin'
    DIS IS IT.

            Den he parked his wings,
              ˙ An' strolled aroun',
            Gittin' used to his feet
                On de solid ground.

II
Big bloodhound came aroarin'
    Like Niagry Falls,
Sicked on by white devils
    In overhalls.

Now Slim warn't scared,
    Cross my heart, it's a fac',

And de dog went on a bayin'
Some po' devil's track.

Den Slim saw a mansion
An' walked right in;
De Devil looked up
Wid a sickly grin.

"Suttinly didn't look
Fo' you, Mr. Greer,
How it happen you comes
To visit here?"

Slim say—"Oh, jes' thought
I'd drop by a spell."
"Feel at home, seh, an' here's
De keys to hell."

Den he took Slim around
An' showed him people
Rasin' hell as high as
De First Church Steeple.

Lots of folks fightin'
At de roulette wheel,
Like old Rampart Street,
Or leastwise Beale.

Showed him bawdy houses
An' cabarets,
Slim thought of New Orleans
An' Memphis days.

Each devil was busy
Wid a devilish broad,
An' Slim cried, "Lawdy,
Lawd, Lawd, Lawd."

Took him in a room
  Where Slim see
De preacher wid a brownskin
  On each knee.

    Showed him giant stills,
      Going everywhere,
    Wid a passel of devils
      Stretched dead drunk there.

Den he took him to de furnace
  Dat some devils was firing,
Hot as hell, an' Slim start
  A mean presspirin'.

    White devils wid pitchforks
      Threw black devils on,
    Slim thought he'd better
      Be gittin' along.

An' he say—"Dis makes
  Me think of home—
Vicksburg, Little Rock, Jackson,
  Waco and Rome."

    Den de devil gave Slim
      De big Ha-Ha;
    An' turned into a cracker,
      Wid a sheriff's star.

Slim ran fo' his wings,
  Lit out from de groun'
Hauled it back to St. Peter,
  Safety boun'.

    III
    St. Peter said, "Well,

You got back quick.
How's de devil? An' what's
His latest trick?"

An' Slim say, "Peter,
  I really cain't tell,
The place was Dixie
  That I took for hell."

Then Peter say, "You must
  Be crazy, I vow,
Where'n hell dja think Hell *was*,
  Anyhow?

"Git on back to de yearth,
  Cause I got de fear,
You'se a leetle too dumb,
  Fo' to stay up here . . ."

Children's Children

When they hear
These songs, born of the travail of their sires,
Diamonds of song, deep buried beneath the weight
Of dark and heavy years;
They laugh.

When they hear
Saccharine melodies of loving and its fevers,
Soft-flowing lies of love everlasting;
Conjuring divinity out of gross flesh itch;
They sigh
And look goggle-eyed
At one another.

They have forgotten, they have never known,
Long days beneath the torrid Dixie sun
In miasma'd riceswamps;
The chopping of dried grass, on the third go round
In strangling cotton;
Wintry nights in mud-daubed makeshift huts,
With these songs, sole comfort.

They have forgotten
What had to be endured—

That they, babbling young ones,
With their paled faces, coppered lips,
And sleek hair cajoled to Caucasian straightness,
Might drown the quiet voice of beauty
With sensuous stridency;

And might, on hearing these memoirs of their sires,
Giggle,
And nudge each other's satin clad
Sleek sides. . . .

FRANK MARSHALL DAVIS

Jazz Band

Play that thing, you jazz mad fools!
Boil a skyscraper with a jungle
Dish it to 'em sweet and hot—
Ahhhhhhhhh
Rip it open then sew it up, jazz band!

Thick bass notes from a moon faced drum
Saxophones moan, banjo strings hum
High thin notes from the cornet's throat
Trombone snorting, bass horn snorting
Short tan notes from the piano
And the short tan notes from the piano

Plink plank plunk a plunk
Plink plank plunk a plunk
Chopin gone screwy, Wagner with the blues
Plink plank plunk a plunk
Got a date with Satan—ain't no time to lose
Plink plank plunk a plunk
Strut it in Harlem, let Fifth Avenue shake it slow
Plink plank plunk a plunk
Ain't goin' to heaven nohow—
    crowd up there's too slow . . .
Plink plank plunk a plunk
Plink plank plunk a plunk
Plunk

Do that thing, jazz band!

Whip it to a jelly

Sock it, rock it; heat it, beat it; then fling it at 'em

Let the jazz stuff fall like hail on king and truck driver, queen
and laundress, lord and laborer, banker and bum

Let it fall in London, Moscow, Paris, Hongkong, Cairo,
Buenos Aires, Chicago, Sydney

Let it rub hard thighs, let it be molten fire in the veins of
dancers

Make 'em shout a crazy jargon of hot hosannas to a fiddle-
faced jazz god

Send Dios, Jehovah, Gott, Allah, Buddha past in a high
stepping cake walk
Do that thing, jazz band!

Your music's been drinking hard liquor
Got shanghaied and it's fightin' mad
Stripped to the waist feedin' ocean liner bellies
Big burly bibulous brute
Poet hands and bone crusher shoulders—
Black sheep or white?

Hey, Hey!
Pick it, papa!
Twee twa twee twa twa
Step on it, black boy
Do re mi fa sol la ti do
Boomp boomp
Play that thing, you jazz mad fools!

Roosevelt Smith

You ask what happened to Roosevelt Smith

Well . . .

Conscience and the critics got him

Roosevelt Smith was the only dusky child born and bred
in the village of Pine City, Nebraska

At college they worshipped the novelty of a black poet and
predicted fame

At twenty-three he published his first book . . . the critics
said he imitated Carl Sandburg, Edgar Lee Masters and
Vachel Lindsay . . . they raved about a wealth of racial
material and the charm of darky dialect

So for two years Roosevelt worked and observed in Dixie

At twenty-five a second book . . . Negroes complained about
plantation scenes and said he dragged Aframerica's good
name in the mire for gold . . . "Europe," they said, "hon-
ors Dunbar for his 'Ships That Pass In The Night' and
not for his dialect which they don't understand"

For another two years Roosevelt strove for a different me-
dium of expression

At twenty-seven a third book . . . the critics said the density
of Gertrude Stein or T. S. Eliot hardly fitted the simple
material to which a Negro had access

For another two years Roosevelt worked

[*146*]

At twenty-nine his fourth book . . . the critics said a Negro
had no business imitating the classic forms of Keats,
Browning and Shakespeare . . . "Roosevelt Smith," they
announced, "has nothing original and is merely a black-
face white. His African heritage is a rich source should he
use it"

So for another two years Roosevelt went into the interior of
Africa

At thirty-one his fifth book . . . interesting enough, the
critics said, but since it followed nothing done by any
white poet it was probably just a new kind of prose

Day after the reviews came out Roosevelt traded conscience
and critics for the leather pouch and bunions of a mail
carrier and read in the papers until his death how little
the American Negro had contributed to his nation's litera-
ture . . .

MELVIN B. TOLSON

Lambda

From the mouth of the Harlem Gallery
came a voice like a
ferry horn in a river of fog:

"Hey, man, when you gonna close this dump?
Fetch highbrow stuff for the middlebrows who
don't give a damn and the lowbrows who ain't hip!
Think you're a little high-yellow Jesus?"

No longer was I a boxer with a brain bruised
against its walls by Tyche's fists,
as I welcomed Hideho Heights,
the vagabond bard of Lenox Avenue,
whose satyric legends adhered like beggar's-lice.

"Sorry, Curator, I got here late:
my black ma birthed me in the Whites' bottom drawer,
and the Reds forgot to fish me out!"

His belly laughed and quaked
the Blakean tigers and lambs on the walls.
Haw-Haw's whale of a forefinger mocked
Max Donachie's revolutionary hero, Crispus Attucks,
in the Harlem Gallery and on Boston Commons.
"In the beginning was the Word,"
he challenged, "not the Brush!"
The scorn in the eyes that raked the gallery
was the scorn of an Ozymandias.

The metal smelted from the ore of ideas,
his grin revealed all the gold he had stored away.

"Just came from a jam session
at the Daddy-O Club," he said.
"I'm just one step from heaven
with the blues a-percolating in my head.
You should've heard old Satchmo blow his horn!
The Lord God A'mighty made no mistake
the day that cat was born!"

Like a bridegroom unloosing a virgin knot,
from an inner pocket he coaxed a manuscript.
"Just given Satchmo a one-way ticket
to Immortality," he said. "Pure inspiration!"
His lips folded about the neck of a whiskey bottle
whose label belied its white-heat hooch.
I heard a gurgle, a gurgle—a death rattle.
His eyes as bright as a parachute light,
he began to rhetorize in the grand style
of a Doctor Faustus in the dilapidated Harlem Opera House:

King Oliver of New Orleans
has kicked the bucket, but he left behind
old Satchmo with his red-hot horn
to syncopate the heart and mind.
The honky-tonks in Storyville
have turned to ashes, have turned to dust,
but old Satchmo is still around
like Uncle Sam's IN GOD WE TRUST.

Where, oh, where is Bessie Smith
with her heart as big as the blues of truth?
Where, oh, where is Mister Jelly Roll
with his Cadillac and diamond tooth?
Where, oh, where is Papa Handy
with his blue notes a-dragging from bar to bar?
Where, oh, where is bulletproof Leadbelly
with his tall tales and 12-string guitar?

Old Hip Cats,
when you sang and played the blues
the night Satchmo was born,
did you know hypodermic needles in Rome
couldn't hoodoo him away from his horn?
Wyatt Earp's legend, John Henry's, too,
is a dare and a bet to old Satchmo
when his groovy blues put headlines in the news
from the Gold Coast to cold Moscow.

Old Satchmo's
gravelly voice and tapping foot and crazy notes
set my soul on fire.
If I climbed
the seventy-seven steps of the Seventh
Heaven, Satchmo's high C would carry me higher!
Are you hip to this, Harlem? Are you hip?
On Judgment Day, Gabriel will say
after he blows his horn:
"I'd be the greatest trumpeter in the Universe,
if old Satchmo had never been born!"

ROBERT HAYDEN

Witch Doctor

I.

He dines alone surrounded by reflections
of himself. Then after sleep and benzedrine
descends the Cinquecento stair his magic
wrought from hypochondria of the well-
to-do and nagging deathwish of the poor;
swirls on smiling genuflections of
his liveried chauffeur into a crested
lilac limousine, the cynosure
of mousey neighbors tittering behind
Venetian blinds and half afraid of him
and half admiring his outrageous flair.

II.

Meanwhile his mother, priestess in gold lamé,
precedes him to the quondam theater
now Israel Temple of the Highest Alpha,
where the bored, the sick, the alien, the tired
await euphoria. With deadly vigor
she prepares the way for mystery
and lucre. Shouts in blues-contralto, "He's
God's dictaphone of all-redeeming truth.
Oh he's the holyweight champeen who's come
to give the knockout lick to your bad luck;
say he's the holyweight champeen who's here
to deal a knockout punch to your hard luck."

III.

Reposing on cushions of black leopard skin,
he telephones instructions for a long
slow drive across the park that burgeons now
with spring and sailors. Peers questingly

into the green fountainous twilight, sighs
and turns the gold-plate dial to Music For
Your Dining-Dancing Pleasure. Smoking Egyptian
cigarettes rehearses in his mind
a new device that he must use tonight.

IV.
Approaching Israel Temple, mask in place,
he hears ragtime allegros of a "Song
of Zion" that becomes when he appears
a hallelujah wave for him to walk.
His mother and a rainbow-surpliced cordon
conduct him choiring to the altar-stage,
and there he kneels and seems to pray before
a lighted Jesus painted sealskin-brown.
Then with a glittering flourish he arises,
turns, gracefully extends his draperied arms:
"Israelites, true Jews, O found lost tribe
of Israel, receive my blessing now.
Selah, selah." He feels them yearn toward him
as toward a lover, exults before the image
of himself their trust gives back. Stands as though
in meditation, letting their eyes caress
his garments jewelled and chatoyant, cut
to fall, to flow from his tall figure
dramatically just so. Then all at once
he sways, quivers, gesticulates as if
to ward off blows or kisses, and when he speaks
again he utters wildering vocables,
hypnotic no-words planned (and never failing)
to enmesh his flock in theopathic tension.
Cries of eudaemonic pain attest
his artistry. Behind the mask he smiles.
And now in subtly altering light he chants
and sinuously trembles, chants and trembles
while convulsive energies of eager faith
surcharge the theater with power of

their own, a power he has counted on
and for a space allows to carry him.
Dishevelled antiphons proclaim the moment
his followers all have hungered for,
but which is his alone.
He signals: tambourines begin, frenetic
drumbeat and glissando. He dances from the altar,
robes hissing, flaring, shimmering; down aisles
where mantled guardsmen intercept wild hands
that arduously strain to clutch his vestments,
he dances, dances, ensorcelled and aloof,
the fervid juba of God as lover, healer,
conjurer. And of him as God.

Mourning Poem for the Queen of Sunday

Lord's lost Him His mockingbird,
His fancy warbler;
Satan sweet-talked her,
four bullets hushed her.
Who would have thought
she'd end that way?

Four bullets hushed her. And the world a-clang with evil.
Who's going to make old hardened sinner men tremble now
and the righteous rock?
Oh who and oh who will sing Jesus down
to help with struggling and doing without and being colored
all through blue Monday?
Till way next Sunday?

All those angels
in their cretonne clouds and finery
the true believer saw

when she rared back her head and sang,
all those angels are surely weeping.
Who would have thought
she'd end that way?

Four holes in her heart. The gold works wrecked.
But she looks so natural in her big bronze coffin
among the Broken Hearts and Gates-Ajar,
it's as if any moment she'd lift her head
from its pillow of chill gardenias
and turn this quiet into shouting Sunday
and make folks forget what she did on Monday.

Oh, Satan sweet-talked her,
and four bullets hushed her.
Lord's lost Him His diva,
His fancy warbler's gone.
Who would have thought,
who would have thought she'd end that way?

The Ballad of Nat Turner

Then fled, O brethren, the wicked juba
    and wandered wandered far
from curfew joys in the Dismal's night.
    Fool of St. Elmo's fire.

In scary night I wandered, praying,
    Lord God my harshener,
speak to me now or let me die;
    speak, Lord, to this mourner.

And came at length to livid trees
    where Ibo warriors

hung shadowless, turning in wind
    that moaned like Africa,

Their belltongue bodies dead, their eyes
    alive with the anger deep
in my own heart. Is this the sign,
    the sign forepromised me?

The spirits vanished. Afraid and lonely
    I wandered on in blackness.
Speak to me now or let me die.
    Die, whispered the blackness.

And wild things gasped and scuffled in
    the night; seething shapes
of evil frolicked upon the air.
    I reeled with fear, I prayed.

Sudden brightness clove the preying
    darkness, brightness that was
itself a golden darkness, brightness
    so bright that it was darkness.

And there were angels, their faces hidden
    from me, angels at war
with one another, angels in dazzling
    combat. And oh the splendor,

The fearful splendor of that warring.
    Hide me, I cried to rock and bramble.
Hide me, the rock, the bramble cried. . . .
    How tell you of that holy battle?

The shock of wing on wing and sword
    on sword was the tumult of
a taken city burning. I cannot
    say how long they strove,

For the wheel in a turning wheel which is time
    in eternity had ceased
its whirling, and owl and moccasin,
    panther and nameless beast

And I were held like creatures fixed
    in flaming, in fiery amber.
But I saw I saw oh many of
    those mighty beings waver,

Waver and fall, go streaking down
    into swamp water, and the water
hissed and steamed and bubbled and locked
    shuddering shuddering over

The fallen and soon was motionless.
    Then that massive light
began a-folding slowly in
    upon itself, and I

Beheld the conqueror faces and, lo,
    they were like mine, I saw
they were like mine and in joy and terror
    wept, praising praising Jehovah.

Oh praised my honer, harshener
    till a sleep came over me,
a sleep heavy as death. And when
    I awoke at last free

And purified, I rose and prayed
    and returned after a time
to the blazing fields, to the humbleness.
    And bided my time.

Runagate Runagate

Runs falls rises stumbles on from darkness into darkness
and the darkness thicketed with shapes of terror
and the hunters pursuing and the hounds pursuing
and the night cold and the night long and the river
to cross and the jack-muh-lanterns beckoning beckoning
and blackness ahead and when shall I reach that somewhere
morning and keep on going and never turn back and keep on
    going

            Runagate
                  Runagate
                        Runagate

Many thousands rise and go
many thousands crossing over

                          O mythic North
                  O star-shaped yonder Bible city

Some go weeping and some rejoicing
some in coffins and some in carriages
some in silks and some in shackles

        Rise and go or fare you well

No more action block for me
no more driver's lash for me

      If you see my Pompey, 30 yrs of age,
      new breeches, plain stockings, negro shoes;
      if you see my Anna, likely young mulatto
      branded E on the right cheek, R on the left,

catch them if you can and notify subscriber.
Catch them if you can, but it won't be easy.
They'll dart underground when you try to catch them,
plunge into quicksand, whirlpools, mazes,
turn into scorpions when you try to catch them.

And before I'll be a slave
I'll be buried in my grave

North star and bonanza gold
I'm bound for the freedom, freedom-bound
and oh Susyanna don't you cry for me

Runagate

Runagate

II.
Rises from their anguish and their power,

Harriet Tubman,

woman of earth, whipscarred,
a summoning, a shining

Mean to be free

And this was the way of it, brethren brethren,
way we journeyed from Can't to Can.
Moon so bright and no place to hide,
the cry up and the patterollers riding,
hound dogs belling in bladed air.
And fear starts a-murbling, Never make it,
we'll never make it. *Hush that now,*
and she's turned upon us, levelled pistol
glinting in the moonlight:
Dead folks can't jaybird-talk, she says;
you keep on going now or die, she says.

Wanted   Harriet Tubman   alias The General
alias Moses   Stealer of Slaves

In league with Garrison   Alcott   Emerson
Garrett   Douglass   Thoreau   John Brown

Armed and known to be Dangerous

Wanted   Reward   Dead or Alive

    Tell me, Ezekiel, oh tell me do you see
    mailed Jehovah coming to deliver me?

Hoot-owl calling in the ghosted air,
five times calling to the hants in the air.
Shadow of a face in the scary leaves,
shadow of a voice in the talking leaves

    Come ride-a my train

    Oh that train, ghost-story train
    through swamp and savanna movering movering,
    over trestles of dew, through caves of the wish,
    Midnight Special on a sabre track movering movering,
    first stop Mercy and the last Hallelujah.

    Come ride-a my train

    Mean mean mean to be free.

Frederick Douglass

When it is finally ours, this freedom, this liberty, this
    beautiful
and terrible thing, needful to man as air,
usable as earth; when it belongs at last to all,

when it is truly instinct, brain matter, diastole, systole,
reflex action; when it is finally won; when it is more
than the gaudy mumbo jumbo of politicians:
this man, this Douglass, this former slave, this Negro
beaten to his knees, exiled, visioning a world
where none is lonely, none hunted, alien,
this man, superb in love and logic, this man
shall be remembered. Oh, not with statues' rhetoric,
not with legends and poems and wreaths of bronze alone,
but with the lives grown out of his life, the lives
fleshing his dream of the beautiful, needful thing.

MARGARET WALKER

Ballad of the Hoppy-Toad

Ain't been on Market Street for nothing
With my regular washing load
When the Saturday crowd went stomping
Down the Johnny-jumping road,

Seen Sally Jones come running
With a razor at her throat,
Seen Deacon's daughter lurching
Like a drunken alley goat.

But the biggest for my money,
And the saddest for my throw
Was the night I seen the goopher man
Throw dust around my door.

Come sneaking round my doorway
In a stovepipe hat and coat;
Come sneaking round my doorway
To drop the evil note.

I run down to Sis Avery's
And told her what I seen
"Root-worker's out to git me
What you reckon that there mean?"

Sis Avery she done told me,
"Now honey go on back
I knows just what will hex him
And that old goopher sack."

Now I done burned the candles
Till I seen the face of Jim

And I done been to Church and prayed
But can't git rid of him.

Don't want to burn his picture
Don't want to dig his grave
Just want to have my peace of mind
And make that dog behave.

Was running through the fields one day
Sis Avery's chopping corn
Big horse come stomping after me
I knowed then I was gone.

Sis Avery grabbed that horse's mane
And not one minute late
Cause trembling down behind her
I seen my ugly fate.

She hollered to that horse to "Whoa!
I gotcha hoppy-toad."
And yonder come the goopher man
A-running down the road.

She hollered to that horse to "Whoa"
And what you wanta think?
Great-God-a-mighty, that there horse
Begun to sweat and shrink.

He shrunk up to a teeny horse
He shrunk up to a toad
And yonder come the goopher man
Still running down the road.

She hollered to that horse to "Whoa"
She said, "I'm killing him.
Now you just watch this hoppy-toad
And you'll be rid of Jim."

The goopher man was hollering
"Don't kill that hoppy-toad."
Sis Avery she said "Honey,
You bout to lose your load."

That hoppy-toad was dying
Right there in the road
And goopher man was screaming
"Don't kill that hoppy-toad."

The hoppy-toad shook one more time
And then he up and died
Old goopher man fell dying, too.
"O hoppy-toad," he cried.

For My People

For my people everywhere singing their slave songs repeat-
     edly: their dirges and their ditties and their blues
     and jubilees, praying their prayers nightly to an un-
     known god, bending their knees humbly to an un-
     seen power;

For my people lending their strength to the years, to the
     gone years and the now years and the maybe years,
     washing ironing cooking scrubbing sewing mending
     hoeing plowing digging planting pruning patching
     dragging along never gaining never reaping never
     knowing and never understanding;

For my playmates in the clay and dust and sand of Alabama
     backyards playing baptizing and preaching and doc-
     tor and jail and soldier and school and mama and
     cooking and playhouse and concert and store and
     hair and Miss Choomby and company;

For the cramped bewildered years we went to school to learn
to know the reasons why and the answers to and the
people who and the places where and the days when,
in memory of the bitter hours when we discovered
we were black and poor and small and different and
nobody cared and nobody wondered and nobody
understood;

For the boys and girls who grew in spite of these things to be
man and woman, to laugh and dance and sing and
play and drink their wine and religion and success,
to marry their playmates and bear children and then
die of consumption and anemia and lynching;

For my people thronging 47th Street in Chicago and Lenox
Avenue in New York and Rampart Street in New
Orleans, lost disinherited dispossessed and happy
people filling the cabarets and taverns and other
people's pockets needing bread and shoes and milk
and land and money and something—something all
our own;

For my people walking blindly spreading joy, losing time
being lazy, sleeping when hungry, shouting when
burdened, drinking when hopeless, tied and shackled
and tangled among ourselves by the unseen creatures
who tower over us omnisciently and laugh;

For my people blundering and groping and floundering in
the dark of churches and schools and clubs and
societies, associations and councils and committees
and conventions, distressed and disturbed and de-
ceived and devoured by money-hungry glory-craving
leeches, preyed on by facile force of state and fad and
novelty, by false prophet and holy believer;

For my people standing staring trying to fashion a better
way from confusion, from hypocrisy and misunder-

standing, trying to fashion a world that will hold all
the people, all the faces, all the adams and eves and
their countless generations;

Let a new earth rise. Let another world be born. Let a bloody
peace be written in the sky. Let a second generation
full of courage issue forth; let a people loving free-
dom come to growth. Let a beauty full of healing
and a strength of final clenching be the pulsing in
our spirits and our blood. Let the martial songs be
written, let the dirges disappear. Let a race of men
now rise and take control.

For Malcolm X

All you violated ones with gentle hearts;
You violent dreamers whose cries shout heartbreak;
Whose voices echo clamors of our cool capers,
And whose black faces have hollowed pits for eyes.
All you gambling sons and hooked children and bowery bums
Hating white devils and black bourgeoisie,
Thumbing your noses at your burning red suns,
Gather round this coffin and mourn your dying swan.

Snow-white moslem head-dress around a dead black face!
Beautiful were your sand-papering words against our skins!
Our blood and water pour from your flowing wounds.
You have cut open our breasts and dug scalpels in our brains.
When and Where will another come to take your holy place?
Old man mumbling in his dotage, or crying child, unborn?

Micah
(In Memory of Medgar Evers of Mississippi)

Micah was a young man of the people
Who came up from the streets of Mississippi
And cried out his Vision to his people;
Who stood fearless before the waiting throng
Like an astronaut shooting into space.
Micah was a man who spoke against Oppression
Crying: Woe to you Workers of iniquity!
Crying: Woe to you doers of violence!
Crying: Woe to you breakers of the peace!
Crying: Woe to you, my enemy!
For when I fall I shall rise in deathless dedication.
When I stagger under the wound of your paid assassins
I shall be whole again in deathless triumph!
For your rich men are full of violence
And your mayors of your cities speak lies.
They are full of deceit.
We do not fear them.
They shall not enter the City of good-will.
We shall dwell under our own vine and fig tree in peace.
And they shall not be remembered in the Book of Life.
Micah was a Man.

The Ballad of the Free

Bold Nat Turner by the blood of God
Rose up preaching on Virginia's sod;
Smote the land with his passionate plea
Time's done come to set my people free.

The serpent is loosed and the hour is come
The last shall be first and the first shall be none
The serpent is loosed and the hour is come

Gabriel Prosser looked at the sun,
Said, "Sun, stand still till the work is done.
The world is wide and the time is long
And man must meet the avenging wrong."

The serpent is loosed and the hour is come
The last shall be first and the first shall be none
The serpent is loosed and the hour is come

Denmark Vesey led his band
Across the hot Carolina land.
The plot was foiled, the brave men killed,
But Freedom's cry was never stilled.

The serpent is loosed and the hour is come
The last shall be first and the first shall be none
The serpent is loosed and the hour is come

Toussaint L'Ouverture won
All his battles in the tropic sun,
Hero of the black man's pride
Among those hundred who fought and died.

The serpent is loosed and the hour is come
The last shall be first and the first shall be none
The serpent is loosed and the hour is come

Brave John Brown was killed but he
Became a martyr of the free,
For he declared that blood would run
Before the slaves their freedom won.

The serpent is loosed and the hour is come

The last shall be first and the first shall be none
The serpent is loosed and the hour is come

Wars and Rumors of Wars have gone,
But Freedom's army marches on.
The heroes' list of dead is long,
And Freedom still is for the strong.

The serpent is loosed and the hour is come
The last shall be first and the first shall be none
The serpent is loosed and the hour is come

GWENDOLYN BROOKS

The Preacher: Ruminates Behind the Sermon

I think it must be lonely to be God.
Nobody loves a master. No. Despite
The bright hosannas, bright dear-Lords, and bright
Determined reverence of Sunday eyes.

Picture Jehovah striding through the hall
Of His importance, creatures running out
From servant-corners to acclaim, to shout
Appreciation of His merit's glare.

But who walks with Him?—dares to take His arm,
To slap Him on the shoulder, tweak His ear,
Buy Him a Coca-Cola or a beer,
Pooh-pooh His politics, call Him a fool?

Perhaps—who knows?—He tires of looking down.
Those eyes are never lifted. Never straight.
Perhaps sometimes He tires of being great
In solitude. Without a hand to hold.

The Sundays of Satin-Legs Smith

Inamoratas, with an approbation,
Bestowed his title. Blessed his inclination.

He wakes, unwinds, elaborately: a cat
Tawny, reluctant, royal. He is fat
And fine this morning. Definite. Reimbursed.

He waits a moment, he designs his reign,
That no performance may be plain or vain.
Then rises in a clear delirium.

He sheds, with his pajamas, shabby days.
And his desertedness, his intricate fear, the
Postponed resentments and the prim precautions.

Now, at his bath, would you deny him lavender
Or take away the power of his pine?
What smelly substitute, heady as wine,
Would you provide? life must be aromatic.
There must be scent, somehow there must be some.
Would you have flowers in his life? suggest
Asters? a Really Good geranium?
A white carnation? would you prescribe a Show
With the cold lilies, formal chrysanthemum
Magnificence, poinsettias, and emphatic
Red of prize roses? might his happiest
Alternative (you muse) be, after all,
A bit of gentle garden in the best
Of taste and straight tradition? Maybe so.
But you forget, or did you ever know,
His heritage of cabbage and pigtails,
Old intimacy with alleys, garbage pails,
Down in the deep (but always beautiful) South
Where roses blush their blithest (it is said)
And sweet magnolias put Chanel to shame.

No! He has not a flower to his name.
Except a feather one, for his lapel.
Apart from that, if he should think of flowers
It is in terms of dandelions or death.
Ah, there is little hope. You might as well—
Unless you care to set the world a-boil
And do a lot of equalizing things,
Remove a little ermine, say, from kings,

Shake hands with paupers and appoint them men,
For instance—certainly you might as well
Leave him his lotion, lavender and oil.

Let us proceed. Let us inspect, together
With his meticulous and serious love,
The innards of this closet. Which is a vault
Whose glory is not diamonds, not pearls,
Not silver plate with just enough dull shine.
But wonder-suits in yellow and in wine,
Sarcastic green and zebra-striped cobalt.
With shoulder padding that is wide
And cocky and determined as his pride;
Ballooning pants that taper off to ends
Scheduled to choke precisely.

                              Here are hats
Like bright umbrellas; and hysterical ties
Like narrow banners for some gathering war.

People are so in need, in need of help.
People want so much that they do not know.

Below the tinkling trade of little coins
The gold impulse not possible to show
Or spend. Promise piled over and betrayed.

These kneaded limbs receive the kiss of silk.
Then they receive the brave and beautiful
Embrace of some of that equivocal wool.
He looks into his mirror, loves himself—
The neat curve here; the angularity
That is appropriate at just its place;
The technique of a variegated grace.

Here is all his sculpture and his art
And all his architectural design.

Perhaps you would prefer to this a fine
Value of marble, complicated stone.
Would have him think with horror of baroque,
Rococo. You forget and you forget.

He dances down the hotel steps that keep
Remnants of last night's high life and distress.
As spat-out purchased kisses and spilled beer.
He swallows sunshine with a secret yelp.
Passes to coffee and a roll or two.
Has breakfasted.

                Out. Sounds about him smear,
Become a unit. He hears and does not hear
The alarm clock meddling in somebody's sleep;
Children's governed Sunday happiness;
The dry tone of a plane; a woman's oath;
Consumption's spiritless expectoration;
An indignant robin's resolute donation
Pinching a track through apathy and din;
Restaurant vendors weeping; and the L
That comes on like a slightly horrible thought.

Pictures, too, as usual, are blurred.
He sees and does not see the broken windows
Hiding their shame with newsprint; little girl
With ribbons decking wornness, little boy
Wearing the trousers with the decentest patch,
To honor Sunday; women on their way
From "service," temperate holiness arranged
Ably on asking faces; men estranged
From music and from wonder and from joy
But far familiar with the guiding awe
Of foodlessness.
           He loiters.
                   Restaurant vendors
Weep, or out of them rolls a restless glee.

The Lonesome Blues, the Long-lost Blues, I Want A
Big Fat Mama. Down these sore avenues
Comes no Saint-Saëns, no piquant elusive Grieg,
And not Tschaikovsky's wayward eloquence
And not the shapely tender drift of Brahms.
But could he love them? Since a man must bring
To music what his mother spanked him for
When he was two: bits of forgotten hate,
Devotion: whether or not his mattress hurts:
The little dream his father humored: the thing
His sister did for money: what he ate
For breakfast—and for dinner twenty years
Ago last autumn: all his skipped desserts.

The pasts of his ancestors lean against
Him. Crowd him. Fog out his identity.
Hundreds of hungers mingle with his own,
Hundreds of voices advise so dexterously
He quite considers his reactions his,
Judges he walks most powerfully alone,
That everything is—simply what it is.

But movie-time approaches, time to boo
The hero's kiss, and boo the heroine
Whose ivory and yellow it is sin
For his eye to eat of. The Mickey Mouse,
However, is for everyone in the house.

Squires his lady to dinner at Joe's Eats.
His lady alters as to leg and eye,
Thickness and height, such minor points as these,
From Sunday to Sunday. But no matter what
Her name or body positively she's
In Queen Lace stockings with ambitious heels
That strain to kiss the calves, and vivid shoes
Frontless and backless, Chinese fingernails,
Earrings, three layers of lipstick, intense hat

Dripping with the most voluble of veils.
Her affable extremes are like sweet bombs
About him, whom no middle grace or good
Could gratify. He had no education
In quiet arts of compromise. He would
Not understand your counsels on control, nor
Thank you for your late trouble.

                                    At Joe's Eats
You get your fish or chicken on meat platters.
With coleslaw, macaroni, candied sweets,
Coffee and apple pie. You go out full.
(The end is—isn't it?—all that really matters.)

                    And even and intrepid come
                    The tender boots of night to home.

                    Her body is like new brown bread
                    Under the Woolworth mignonette.

                    Her body is a honey bowl
                    Whose waiting honey is deep and hot.
                    Her body is like summer earth,
                    Receptive, soft, and absolute . . .

I Love Those Little Booths at Benvenuti's

They get to Benvenuti's. There are booths
To hide in while observing tropical truths
About this—dusky folk, so clamorous!
So colorfully incorrect,
So amorous,
So flatly brave!
Boothed-in, one can detect,
Dissect.

One knows and scarcely knows what to expect.

What antics, knives, what lurching dirt; what ditty—
Dirty, rich, carmine, hot, not bottled up,
Straining in sexual soprano, cut
And praying in the bass, partial, unpretty.

They sit, sup,
(Whose friends, if not themselves, arrange
To rent in Venice "a very large cabana,
Small palace," and eat mostly what is strange.)
They sit, they settle; presently are met
By the light heat, the lazy upward whine
And lazy croaky downward drawl of "Tanya."
And their interiors sweat.
They lean back in the half-light, stab their stares
At: walls, panels of imitation oak
With would-be marbly look; linoleum squares
Of dusty rose and brown with little white splashes,
White curls; a vendor tidily encased;
Young yellow waiter moving with straight haste,
Old oaken waiter, lolling and amused;
Some paper napkins in a water glass;
Table, initialed, rubbed, as a desk in school.

They stare. They tire. They feel refused,
Feel overwhelmed by subtle treasons!
Nobody here will take the part of jester.

The absolute stutters, and the rationale
Stoops off in astonishment.
But not gaily
And not with their consent.

They play "They All Say I'm The Biggest Fool"
And "Voo Me On The Vot Nay" and "New Lester
Leaps In" and "For Sentimental Reasons."

But how shall they tell people they have been
Out Bronzeville way? For all the nickels in
Have not bought savagery or defined a "folk."

The colored people will not "clown."

The colored people arrive, sit firmly down,
Eat their Express Spaghetti, their T-bone steak,
Handling their steel and crockery with no clatter,
Laugh punily, rise, go firmly out of the door.

We Real Cool

              The Pool Players.
              Seven at the Golden Shovel.

We real cool. We
Left school. We

Lurk late. We
Strike straight. We

Sing sin. We
Thin gin. We

Jazz June. We
Die soon.

OWEN DODSON

Black Mother Praying

My great God, You been a tenderness to me,
Through the thick and through the thin;
You been a pilla to my soul;
You been like the shinin light a mornin in the black dark,
A elevator to my spirit.

Now there's a fire in this land like a last judgment,
And I done sat down by the rivers of Babylon
And wept deep when I remembered Zion,
Seein the water that can't quench fire
And the fire that burn up rivers.
Lord, I'm gonna say my say real quick and simple:

You know bout this war that's bitin the skies and gougin
     out the earth.
Last month, Lord, I bid my last boy away to fight.
I got all my boys fightin now for they country.
Didn't think bout it cept it were for freedom;
Didn't think cause they was black they wasn't American;
Didn't think a thing cept that they was my only sons,
And there was mothers all over the world
Sacrificin they sons like You let Yours be nailed
To the wood for men to behold the right.

Now I'm a black mother, Lord, I knows that now,
Black and burnin in these burnin times.
I can't hold my peace cause peace ain't fit to mention
When they's fightin right here in our streets
Like dogs—mongrel dogs and hill cats.
White is fightin black right here where hate abides like a
     cancer wound

And Freedom is writ big and crossed out:
Where, bless God, they's draggin us outta cars
In Texas and California, in Newark, Detroit.

Blood on the darkness, Lord, blood on the pavement,
Leavin us moanin and afraid.
What has we done?
Where and when has we done?
They's plantin the seeds of hate down in our bone marrow
When we don't want to hate.

We don't speak much in the street where I live, my God,
Nobody speak much, but we thinkin deep
Of the black sons in lands far as the wind can go,
Black boys fightin this war with them.

We thinkin deep bout they sisters stitchin airplane canvas,
And they old fathers plowin for wheat,
And they mothers bendin over washtubs,
They brothers at the factory wheels:
They all is bein body beat and spirit beat and heart sore
    and wonderin.

Listen, Lord, they ain't nowhere for black mothers to turn.
Won't You plant Your Son's goodness in this land
Before it too late?
Set Your stars of sweetness twinklin over us like winda lamps
Before it too late?
Help these men to see they losin while they winnin
Long as they allow theyselves to lynch in the city streets and
    on country roads?

When can I pray again,
View peace in my own parlor again?
When my sons come home
How can I show em my broken hands?
How can I show em they sister's twisted back?

How can I present they land to them?
How, when they been battlin in far places for freedom?
Better let em die in the desert drinkin sand
Or holdin onto water and shippin into death
Than they come back an see they sufferin for vain.

I done seen a man runnin for his life,
Runnin like the wind from a mob, to no shelter.
Where were a hidin place for him?
Saw a dark girl nine years old
Cryin cause her father done had
The light scratched from his eyes in the month of June.
Where the seein place for him?
A black boy lyin with his arms huggin the pavement in pain.
What he starin at?
Good people hands up, searched for guns and razors
    and pipes.
When they gonna pray again?

How, precious God, can I watch my sons' eyes
When they hear this terrible?
How can I pray again when my tongue
Is near cleavin to the roof of my mouth?
Tell me, Lord, how?

Every time they strike us, they strikin Your Son;
Every time they shove us in, they cornerin they own children.
I'm gonna scream before I hope again.
I ain't never gonna hush my mouth or lay down this heavy,
    black, weary, terrible load
Until I fights to stamp my feet with my black sons
On a freedom solid rock and stand there peaceful
And look out into the star wilderness of the sky
And the land lyin about clean, and secure land,
And people not afraid again.

Lord, let us all see the golden wheat together,

Harvest the harvest together,
Touch the fulness and the hallelujah together.
                                    Amen.

Countee Cullen

Now begins the sleep, my friend:
Where the cold dirt blanket is, you will be warm,
Where seeds begin to root, you will flower.
The dilapidation of our earth is left for us to order.
Your heart that was strong will help us carry
Whatever trouble springs to hunch our backs,
Whatever anger grows to sty our eyelids,
Whatever unexpected happiness comes like hope to smile
    our lips
—We would be ugly now except for hope.

Now begins the sleep, my friend:
You showed us that men could see
Deep into the cause of Lazarus,
Believe in resurrection.
You come back to us
Not unwinding a shroud and blinking at known light
But singing like all the famed birds,
Nightingale, lark and nightjar.
You come back to us with the truth
Of your indignation, protest and irony.
Also in your brave and tender singing
We hear all mankind yearning
For a new year without hemlock in our glasses.

Section III:

The New Black Consciousness,
The Same Difference

III
These are the words of lovers.
Of dancers, of dynamite singers
These are songs if you have the
music

Imamu Amiri Baraka (LeRoi Jones),
Three Movements and a Coda

Despite its variety the poetry of the sixties is informed and unified by the new consciousness of Blackness. As this consciousness shifted from Civil Rights to Black Power to Black Nationalism to Revolutionary Pan-Africanism, the poets changed too. Sometimes they were instrumental in the change. Some changed with greater grace and effectiveness than others. Some retained the ideas and imagery and sentiments of earlier stages; some stopped writing or publishing altogether; some reaffirmed the validity of their personal view of Blackness. Still others began the painful task of self-examination and self-purgation as prelude to the construction of a Black Aesthetic, a Black value system, a Black Nation.

All of these—in one form or another—already exist. The question is therefore that of unity and institutionalization. These are by no means new, either in a political, social or cultural sense for North American Blacks. What is new, however, is the widespread sophistication regarding means as well as ends. What is new is the large numbers of people who have become aware of the international dimensions of the Black Struggle through the work of Black artists, especially of Black poets. What is new is the serious search for effective public vehicles. What is new is the radicalization of Roots, the Black rediscovery of the revolutionary potential in Blackness itself. The various writers reflect aspects of the process in different stages of transformation. Historically, therefore, they are all important; but the Black Struggle is not amorphous:

it has movement, it has contour, it has direction, it has goals.

Any single writer in this section embodies the movement to some degree. Each reacts to the Soul-Field, in his own way, in his own time. Chronological age is not too important. The crucial thing is Spirit/Soul/Vision and revolutionary perspective. Thus in addition to his mastery of the dozens and adapting them to political uses, one finds Rap Brown quoting (*Die Nigger Die!* pp. 133, 134) with impassioned approval a poem by Georgia Douglass Johnson, a poet of the Harlem Renaissance who is hardly a revolutionary poet, either in theme or in technique. And in the seventies we find writers who belong to the Post-Renaissance generation—poets like Gwendolyn Brooks and Samuel Allen sharpening their focus and clarifying their objectives and inspiring the young. For these two, at least, there has never been any doubt about their commitment.

Other formal poets have also sensed the change, the breakthrough to Black sensibility—the awareness that Black Sensibility itself may be a powerful political catalyst. So there is a lucid, confident strength in James Emanuel and a fiery elegance in Mari Evans, as the former updates his technique and the latter shifts from personal to public voice.

In the college poets—the *Dasein* Group and the *Ex Umbra* Group—one sees again this breakthrough into a radicalizing Blackness. The neglected *Dasein* poets wrote in the late fifties and early sixties. Their sense of history, their precise knowledge of the importance of Black culture, their absorption of modern scientific thought into the fabric of their poetry stands in contrast to the parochialism of some more recent writers. Although the influence of the Beat movement upon them is obvious, what is less obvious in the case of Percy Johnston, for example, is the way the *Dasein* poets embody and amplify the Black influence upon the Beat movement itself. This influence, of course, is epitomized in the presence of Bob Kaufman.

The Southern college poets—with the exception of Walter Dancy and "Dante"—are more lyrical, less cerebral, responding directly to the immediate impress of events. They are generally about ten years younger on the average than the poets of the *Dasein* Group and attracted attention around 1967. Because of their largely rural backgrounds they document an important part of the shift in consciousness of the decade. These poets and others at Southern schools were further inspired in the last years of the decade by their first personal contact with professional Black poets, when Julia Fields, Audre Lorde, A. B. Spellman, Larry Neal, Margaret Danner, Samuel Allen, Mari Evans, Keorapetse Kgositsile, Lebert Bethune, and Jay Wright toured a number of Black colleges in the region. A few were later named poet-in-residence, a new and important opportunity, which is continuing, and which has already produced voices like Arthur Pfister and Karl Carter.

Other professional poets have also played a significant role in stimulating young talent. Foremost among these is Don L. Lee, who is more widely imitated than any other Black poet with the exception of Imamu Baraka (LeRoi Jones). His unique delivery has given him a popular appeal which is tantamount to stardom. His influence is enormous, and is still growing. A similar popular status has been achieved by Nikki Giovanni. Other poets have more specialized reputations.

And there are too, aside from the Southern colleges, other regional groupings on the West Coast represented here by Sarah Webster Fabio; the Midwest—represented here by the OBAC writers, Ebon, Don L. Lee, Carolyn Rodgers, and Johari Amini; also by

Detroit poets Dudley Randall, Margaret Danner, Ahmed Alhamisi, and Leo J. Mason; Indiana poets, Mari Evans and Etheridge Knight; and by the largest group of all, the East Coast poets, Imamu Baraka (Le-Roi Jones), Larry Neal, Jay Wright, and others. But too much stress should not be placed on regional origin, although there are traces of regionalism, for what joins them together is the startling awareness that Black people are poems, that all Black people are Africans, and that the ultimate poem is the literal transfiguration of Africa and her peoples—socially, politically, morally, and spiritually. That great potential lies in the dynamics of the Black Experience, and the poet who has dramatized this fact for the present generation is Imamu Baraka (LeRoi Jones). In him the poet and the politic man, the seeker after wisdom and the prophet are one. In the evolution of his thought and craft, in the magic words "Black Arts," the trajectory is clear.

H. RAP BROWN

Rap's Poem

Signifying is more humane. Instead of coming down on somebody's mother, you come down on them. But, before you can signify you got to be able to rap. A session would start maybe by a brother saying, "Man, before you mess with me you'd rather run rabbits, eat shit, and bark at the moon." Then, if he was talking to me, I'd tell him:

Man, you must don't know who I am.
I'm sweet peeter jeeter the womb beater
The baby maker the cradle shaker
The deerslayer the buckbinder the women finder
Known from the Gold Coast to the rocky shores of Maine
Rap is my name and love is my game.
I'm the bed tucker the cock plucker the motherfucker
The milkshaker the record breaker the population maker
The gun slinger the baby bringer
The hum-dinger the pussy ringer
The man with the terrible middle finger.
The hard hitter the bullshitter the polynussy getter
The beast from the East the Judge the sludge
The women's pet the men's fret and the punks' pin-up boy.
They call me Rap the dicker the ass kicker
The cherry picker the city slicker the titty licker
And I ain't giving nothing but bubble gum and hard times
　　and I'm fresh out of bubble gum.
I'm giving up wooden nickels 'cause I know they won't spend
And I got a pocketful of splinter change.
I'm a member of the bathtub club: I'm seeing a whole lot of
　　ass but I ain't taking no shit.
I'm the man who walked the water and tied the whale's tail
　　in a knot

Taught the little fishes how to swim
Crossed the burning sands and shook the devil's hand
Rode around the world on the back of a snail carrying a sack
saying AIR MAIL.
Walked 49 miles of barbwire and used a Cobra snake for a
necktie
And got a brand new home on the roadside made from a
cracker's hide,
Got a brand new chimney setting on top made from the
cracker's skull
Took a hammer and nail and built the world and called it
"THE BUCKET OF BLOOD"
Yes, I'm hemp the demp the women's pimp
Women fight for my delight.
I'm a bad motherfucker. Rap the rip-saw the devil's brother
'n law.
I roam the world I'm known to wander and this .45 is where
I get my thunder.
I'm the only man in the world who knows why white milk
makes yellow butter.
I know where the lights go when you cut the switch off.
I might not be the best in the world, but I'm in the top two
and my brother's getting old.
And ain't nothing bad 'bout you but your breath.

Now, if the brother couldn't come back behind that, I
usually cut him some slack (depending on time, place, and
his attitude). We learned what the white folks call verbal
skills. We learned how to throw them words together.
[H. Rap Brown, *Die Nigger Die!*]

REGINALD BUTLER

Something to Think About and Dig Jazz

To Be Left Alone

Life is wonderful with it big summer green trees
but the best thrill yet is to do as one please
Like take the one who have love for pot
should death be ones down fall or not
Like why does life have to all ways win
Like the same for boys why become men
Like men you go your way I go mine just remember
I want to be left alone

Really in the Swing

If life to you seem to be hard
Dont just smile and take it
Like talk as one please and damn it
The world dont allways agree
How you live and that also goes for me
Like man forget the square world
Be like the bell and ring
And like you will really be in the swing

Friendship

You set in your pad or gallows   Like your skins in your
hand and you wail   The sound is so unearthy uncanny
Like so penalizing that you zoom into an intoxacated won-
derland and like dad you like it   Like you are group with
some kats some honorable horrify cool screeming kats that
dig you   Like like hypnosis hysteria   Like imbibe
Like boss man cool screeming   Like mad mad   Like
real mad

Drum Story

Boom Boom   Boom Boom Boom Boom Boom Boom
Boom Boom   Boom Boom   Boom Boom Boom Boom
Boom Boom   Boom boom   Boom Boom   Boom
Boom Boom Boom Boom Boom Boom Boom Boom Boom
Boom Tap Tap Tap   Boom Boom Boom Tap Tap Tap
Tap   Tap Tap Tap Tap Tap tap tap tap tap tap
tap   Tap

PERCY E. JOHNSTON

Number Five Cooper Square
For Mike Winston & Harvey Hanson

Six serapes shouldered by a
Villa Cuna moon, and man! A
Memphis boy is cooking Blakey style—
Wham! Scit! Wham! Scit!
I remember Clifford tossing
Bubbles, Scit! Whoom!, from an
Ante-bellum moon. Scit! And
Killer Joe's golden chain, Scit!
While Ornette gives a lecture on
A Sanskrit theme with Bachian
Footnotes, scit. Take a jet for
Monterey, scit! The hour of glory
Is on the Bowery bossed, scit, by
Flugelhorns, doom! I remember
Clifford and those uptown blues.
Scit! Two cats out of New Laredo, scit!
Hobble to a fractured dream, scit!
Like cadavers rinsed of feed back
Reside, scit! The feline sadist
On a double-brass shoom!

Apology to Leopold Sedar Senghor

But it **was** my black hand which
Mashed the crimson trigger which
Launched the urban renewal of
Europe, and ultimately assured

The slavery continuum in your
Continent by descendants of cavemen.

There were no thoughts of Congo or
Kenya or any other part of the
Old Country in my mind when I was
Jaweh's thunderbolt striking the
Architecture of the Orient. My
Communique belonged to December.

My nocturnal efforts have produced
Only ferment, a low watt sky, and
The bird's theme is a twelve bar blues.

Leopold, brother in negritude, I sing
Of He showers and uranous rain, and
Promenading women who search for narcotics
And search for tricks, while I carried
The bloodstained sword of Western enlightenment.

'Round 'Bout Midnight, Opus 17

The night is dark
Mortician like
The night is dark
Mortician like

And dues are piled up
Barstool high,
Barstool high—

Animated lights, fluorescent
Warnings
That somebody's
Really

Into something;
Sidemen bare their souls
With funky blues
And midnight calls for dues.

Let's blow
A chorus all 'bout
Cabbage and yams,
Let's blow
A chorus all 'bout
Cornbread and fish,
With brush or pen or horn or
Just your voice
Just as long as someone's
Blowing blues.

You can't dig this song
We play at midnight
Unless
Life's feces
Have bathed your face,
Going to the Apollo or the Howard
Midnight show
Won't help you dig this tune.
You can't be a member
Just because you sleep with
        our sisters.
So keep your nickel
You walking Brylcreem ad!

Animated lights
Incandescent swinging
Nude above some pig's feet
Keeping time for Monk's tune,
Now we float away upon
        a bluegray cloud
And midnight costs five cents.

LE ROY STONE

Flamenco Sketches
(To Miles Davis)

ouvert

Blue Milan
New York red in weeping
Black-draped Chicago mourning
Tinted all in Spanish suggestions
Flamenco episodes

selim

Comment
blue utterance
uttering in mutes a passion

whisper
intoned in fifths
slivered through Davis durations

furtive chuckle
on many passing tones
of multi-colored n-dimension shadings

cannons

Dissonant nostalgia of one kiss
Penance to a Spanish maid
She was his Flamenco cadence—
three-four time

Leave him pay these awesome dues
In splashes of Flamenco blues

[*194*]

Should one make a full confession?—
still in three-four

Need he confess necessary slavery
to hot breath "en extase"
or incredibly disturbing breasts?—
out

enart

Repay with Kansas City cadences
Repay in Atlanta nuances
Repay with crescents from the Orient

Pointed turns
from female urns,
that seemed like evergreen ferns

And with the scars paint flamenco sketches
And through the tears look to New Orleans
And in a heavy twelve-bar mist we sing

bill

Comment
on a cloud of oriental ninths
comment!

OSWALD GOVAN

The Lynching

In the ends of the year
when the ice rained remorselessly
over the garbage ragged and hound scrounged
alleys, in the tar backed humps
of tenements and the seed beds of babies,
a black man knelt on the stones of the year
and baring there the ashes and bricks
that ringed his heart cold, burst his mind
from the tiding of the dark whip crack.

He wept, he moaned, he cried;
deliver him from the whip and the rope
that gnashed him raw round
his seething heart.

Lift him all up in pride, he cried,
that his heart may dance joyous
in the racial tide
hymned and wedded among ages and men.

The dark door of his home glided wide
and the white robed vultures rode near.
Nigger! they cried, Nigger! they gnashed,
Nigger! their foul jaws clacked in degenerate pride

In the poles of the year
the serpent rope slithered hissing
in the dawn air.

And coiling there on his drawn shoulders
he was jerked sprawling and trembling
in the dark earth.

[*196*]

He saw the pit of his death gliding wide
and his body descending to be enfolded
in the engulfing tide of the dark inhuman bride
in the center of wanton oblivion.

Two by two they carried him twisting and howling
down the hills of the far night.
"Fear not the evil for though they destroy the body
they have no power over the spirit."
the voice in him rang clear.
and he lay still, his death accepted.

For he had walked the wild earth
in the youth of his years
and hailed his people in the birth
of their new spring tide.

"For I will bring forth clad in shining armour
those who were born in darkness."
And the sons of darkness roared
at his dark pride.

His people wept and hailed him wide
and hymned his name on their silent lips
and feared in their hearts.

He was soaked in oil and the match thrown
He screamed, he cried, he moaned,
he crackled in his fiery inhuman dance.

In the acid poles of the year
the pit of his death yawned wide
and the body descended in the cool dawn air
to be hymned and wedded in the dark tide.

A spear burns
in the cool dark earth.
A spear burns
and a tide descends.

LANCE JEFFERS

My Blackness Is the Beauty of This Land

My blackness is the beauty of this land,
my blackness,
tender and strong, wounded and wise,
my blackness:
I, drawling black grandmother, smile muscular and sweet,
unstraightened white hair soon to grow in earth,
work-thickened hand thoughtful and gentle on grandson's
          head,
my heart is bloody-razored by a million memories' thrall:

          remembering the crook-necked cracker who spat
              on my naked body,
          remembering the splintering of my son's spirit
              because he remembered to be proud
          remembering the tragic eyes in my daughter's
              dark face when she learned her color's
              meaning,

and my own dark rage a rusty knife with teeth to gnaw
          my bowels,
my agony ripped loose by anguished shouts in Sunday's
          humble church,
my agony rainbowed to ecstasy when my feet oversoared
          Montgomery's slime,

ah, this hurt, this hate, this ecstasy before I die,
and all my love a strong cathedral!
My blackness is the beauty of this land!

Lay this against my whiteness, this land!
Lay me, young Brutus stamping hard on the cat's tail,

gutting the Indian, gouging the nigger,
booting Little Rock's Minniejean Brown in the buttocks and
      boast,
    my sharp white teeth derision-bared as I the
      conqueror crush!
Skyscraper-I, white hands burying God's human clouds
      beneath the dust!
Skyscraper-I, slim blond young Empire
      thrusting up my loveless bayonet to rape the sky,
then shrink all my long body with filth and in the gutter lie
as lie I will to perfume this armpit garbage,
While I here standing black beside
wrench tears from which the lies would suck the salt
to make me more American than America . . .
But yet my love and yet my hate shall civilize this land,
this land's salvation.

Black Soul of the Land

I saw an old black man walk down the road,
a Georgia country road.
I stopped and asked where the nearest town might lie
where I could find a meal.
I might have driven on then to the town nearby
but I stayed to talk to the old black man
and read the future in his eyes.

His face was leathered, lean, and strong,
gashed with struggle scars.
His eyes were piercing, weary, red,
but in the old grief-soul that stared
through his eyes at me
and in the humble frame bent with humiliation and age,
there stood a secret manhood tough and tall
that circumstance and crackers could not kill:

a secret spine unbent within a spine,
a secret source of steel,
a secret sturdy rugged love,
a secret crouching hate,
a secret knife within his hand,
a secret bullet in his eye.

Give me your spine, old man, old man,
give me your rugged hate,
give me your sturdy oak-tree love,
give me your source of steel.
Teach me to sing so that the song may be mine
"Keep your hands on the plow: hold on!"
One day the nation's soul shall turn black like yours
and America shall cease to be its name.

How High the Moon

(first the melody, clean and hard,
and the flat slurs are faint;
the downknotted mouth, tugged in deprecation,
is not there. But near the end of the first chorus
the slurs have come
with the street of the quiet pogrom:
the beat of the street talk flares strong,
the scornful laughter and the gestures cut the air.)

"BLOW! BLOW!" the side-men cry,

and the thin black young man with an old man's face
lungs up
the tissue of a trumpet from his deep-cancered corners,
racks out a high and searing curse!
    Full from the sullen grace of his street it sprouts:
        NEVER YOUR CAPTIVE!

Breath in My Nostrils

Breath in my nostrils this breasty spring day
shouts a jubilee
like one of my old sweaty fathers
in the surge of song and
sweetness of green trees and
the steamy blacky earth,
he lifted his head to a wildhorse tilt
and forgot that he was a slave!

I Spread These Flaps of Flesh and Fly

Lord God I spread these flaps of flesh and fly
beyond my narrow back:
I murmur song up from my loins,
my song's of my nation,
a song of unbroken dark creation:
of angel's wings no longer weighted with lead:
the brain unbroken and the sweet bird of prey,
of sobbing tigers and babies with teeth like nails,
of the woman who is pregnant with the river and the bay,
of a newfolk who will bury the jails.

WALTER DE LEGALL

Psalm for Sonny Rollins

This vibrant, all-embracing, all-pervading
Sound which bleeds from the vinylite veins
Of my record, steals into the conduits of my heart
Forces entrance into the sanctuary
Of my soul, trespasses into the temple
Of my gonads. In a lifespan-while, I am
Absorbed into the womb of the sound.
    I am in the sound
    The sound is in me.
    I am the sound.
I am your tears that you shed for forty days
And forty nights, Theodore. I am
Your pain who you accepted as
Your bedfellow. I am your hunger and
Your thirst, which purified your
Soul, Theodore. I am your sorrow that
You won in a raffle. Pick up your axe
And let us blow down the Chicago citadels
Of convention. "You just can't play like that in here."
Let us blow down the Caucasian battlements
Of bigotry. "But we don't hire Colored musicians."
Open your tenor mouth and let
Us blow into oblivion the insensible
Strongholds of morality.
"And I'm sure he's an addict."
Blow down thunder and lightning
And White People!! Blow down moons
And stars and Christs! Blow down
Rains and trees and Coltranes! Blow down
Shirleys and Star-eyes and West Coasts!

Walk naked into a 52nd street basement
And show Them the "Bird" in your thighs.
Open your Prestige mouth and let them see
The "Hawk" in your voice. Recite ten
Stanzas of blackeyed-pead Bluing. Sing
A hundred choruses of South Street
Solid. Paint a thousand canvases of Dig
For Joe White. Lead us you Harlem
Piper with a Selmer pipe. The black
Boned children of tomorrow follow
You through space and time
            Lead us to truth,
            To order, To Zen.
            Lead us to Poetry,
            To love, to God.

            Ring halleluiahs from a sombre past.
            Roll halleluiahs to a buoyant dream.
            Breathe halleluiahs for a solemn few.
            Halleluiah! Halleluiah! Halleluiah!!

NATHAN A. RICHARDS

Cranes of Wrath and Other Tragedies

Because no gild-edged machete severed
your umbilical cord at birth and no
frenzied mobs of calypso-high minstrels
ravished the icons that dominate you
even before you were yourself and no shot-
gun blasts echoed from cockpit caves;

Because your chief warriors lie limp
and aged at the steps of Valhalla and
no mother's love shrilled sorrowful
dirge to mourn the sacrificed in their
thirst to be free and neither textbooks
nor oratory warned you against swapping
john for sam bull;

Because your children have never learned
that space-time alone will neither change the colour
of their skin nor smooth the kinks from
their knappy heads nor alter the facts of
their historical misfortune nor unlock the
secrets to who they are now;

Because you and your womb-sprouts were
never seized in the vortex of passionate
surges to extirpate an abhorrent past . . .

Your suffering will be infinite as the
clamouring wings of the eagle smother
you in its penumbral clutches . . .

O hordes of sisyphean children of unre-
membered origins

who unwittingly sailed the straits of
captivity
whose finger-popping spirits buckle
under the pain of unsutured knife-wounds
whose girders tighten as the froth of hope
cleaves to the rainbow of yesterday's
windstorm;

O hordes of sisyphean children
unshafted by the cranes of wrath
to grope in the unknown abyss of desolation
while slogan-men and highbrow
patrons celebrate themselves at your
slow demise, do not despair;

Do not despair for no night-time
panic button can thwart the
timeless sway of the time machine
that ticks and ticks in your tearless eyesockets
as you watch and wait, watch and wait in the shadows
of next summer's coffin grees.

Fork-lightning will not frighten you anymore.

BOB KAUFMAN

Letter to the Chronicle

Oct. 5th, 1963
Chronicle
Letters to the Editor
5th & Mission
San Francisco, Calif.

Gentlemen:

Arriving back in San Francisco to be greeted by a blacklist and eviction, I am writing these lines to the responsible non-people. One thing is certain I am not white. Thank God for that. It makes everything else bearable.

The Loneliness of the Long Distance Runner is due to the oneliness of the Long Distance Runner, that uniqueness that is the Long Distance Runner's alone, and only his. The Loneliness of the Long Distance Runner is the only reason for the Long Distance Runner's existence. Short distance runners run, they finish neither first nor last, they finish, that is all that can be said about them, nothing can be said for them, an ordinariness that is their closest proximity to the truly unique. Men die, as all men come to know, sooner or later, at any rate either way, men die. On that all men can depend.

To answer that rarely asked question. . . . Why are all blacklists white? Perhaps because all light lists are black, the listing of all that is listed is done by who is brown, the colors of an earthquake are black, brown & beige, on the Ellington scale, such sweet thunder, there is a silent beat in between the drums.

That silent beat makes the drumbeat, it makes the drum, it makes the beat. Without it there is no drum, no beat. It is not the beat played by who is beating the drum. His is a noisy loud one, the silent beat is beaten by who is not beating on the drum, his silent beat drowns out all the noise, it comes before and after every beat, you hear it in beatween, its sound is

Bob Kaufman, Poet

I Have Folded My Sorrows

I have folded my sorrows into the mantle of summer night,
Assigning each brief storm its allotted space in time,
Quietly pursuing catastrophic histories buried in my eyes.
And yes, the world is not some unplayed Cosmic Game,
And the sun is still ninety-three million miles from me,
And in the imaginary forest, the shingled hippo becomes
    the gay unicorn.
No, my traffic is not with addled keepers of yesterday's
    disasters,
Seekers of manifest disembowelment on shafts of yesterday's
    pains.
Blues come dressed like introspective echoes of a journey.
And yes, I have searched the rooms of the moon on cold
    summer nights.
And yes, I have refought those unfinished encounters.
    Still, they remain unfinished.
And yes, I have at times wished myself something different.

The tragedies are sung nightly at the funerals of the poet;
The revisited soul is wrapped in the aura of familiarity.

O—Jazz—O

Where the string
At
Some point,
Was some umbilical jazz,
Or perhaps,
In memory,
A long lost bloody cross,
Buried in some steel calvary.
In what time
For whom do we bleed,
Lost notes, from some jazzman's
Broken needle.
Musical tears from lost
Eyes,
Broken drumsticks, why?
Pitter patter, boom dropping
Bombs in the middle
Of my emotions
My father's sound
My mother's sound,
Is love,
Is life.

Walking Parker Home

Sweet beats of jazz impaled on slivers of wind
Kansas Black Morning/ First Horn Eyes/
Historical sound pictures on New Bird wings
People shouts/ boy alto dreams/ Tomorrow's

Gold belled pipe of stops and future Blues Times
Lurking Hawkins/ shadows of Lester/ realization
Bronze fingers—brain extensions seeking trapped sounds
Ghetto thoughts/ bandstand courage/ solo flight
Nerve-wracked suspicions of newer songs and doubts
New York altar city/ black tears/ secret disciples
Hammer horn pounding soul marks on unswinging gates
Culture gods/ mob sounds/ visions of spikes
Panic excursions to tribal Jazz wombs and transfusions
Heroin nights of birth/ and soaring/ over boppy new
    ground.
Smothered rage covering pyramids of notes spontaneously
    exploding
Cool revelations/ shrill hopes/ beauty speared into
    greedy ears
Birdland nights on bop mountains, windy saxophone
    revolutions
Dayrooms of junk/ and melting walls and circling vultures/
Money cancer/ remembered pain/ terror flights/
Death and indestructible existence

In that Jazz corner of life
Wrapped in a mist of sound
His legacy, our Jazz-tinted dawn
Wailing his triumphs of oddly begotten dreams
Inviting the nerveless to feel once more
That fierce dying of humans consumed
In raging fires of Love.

Blues Note

Ray Charles is the black wind of Kilimanjaro,
Screaming up-and-down blues,
Moaning happy on all the elevators of my time.

Smiling into the camera, with an African symphony
Hidden in his throat, and (*I Got a Woman*) wails, too.

He burst from Bessie's crushed black skull
One cold night outside of Nashville, shouting,
And grows bluer from memory, glowing bluer, still.

At certain times you can see the moon
Balanced on his head.

From his mouth he hurls chunks of raw soul.
He separated the sea of polluted sounds
And led the blues into the Promised Land.

Ray Charles is a dangerous man ('way cross town),
And I love him.

for Ray Charles's birthday
N.Y.C./ 1961

IMAMU AMIRI BARAKA (LE ROI JONES)

Prettyditty

Who were the guys
who wrote, who winced around
and thought
about
things? Oh, the kind of cats, you know wobbling
through a crowd full of electric
identifications, and the blessings
of the planets? who said that, howd
you get in this bar, what are you a
smart dude, with his hair some kind
a funny way, with his hand to prop
ersition the enemies of grace amen
music drowns us sit down anyway you
louse, and you got a story, i got
one he got one, and that bitch way cross
there,
she gott
a mother
fucker.

A Poem for Black Hearts

For Malcolm's eyes, when they broke
the face of some dumb white man, For
Malcolm's hands raised to bless us
all black and strong in his image
of ourselves, For Malcolm's words
fire darts, the victor's tireless

thrusts, words hung above the world
change as it may, he said it, and
for this he was killed, for saying,
and feeling, and being/ change, all
collected hot in his heart, For Malcolm's
heart, raising us above our filthy cities,
for his stride, and his beat, and his address
to the grey monsters of the world, For Malcolm's
pleas for your dignity, black men, for your life,
black man, for the filling of your minds
with righteousness, For all of him dead and
gone and vanished from us, and all of him which
clings to our speech black god of our time.
For all of him, and all of yourself, look up,
black man, quit stuttering and shuffling, look up,
black man, quit whining and stooping, for all of him,
For Great Malcolm a prince of the earth, let nothing in us
    rest
until we avenge ourselves for his death, stupid animals
that killed him, let us never breathe a pure breath if
we fail, and white men call us faggots till the end of
the earth.

SOS

Calling black people
Calling all black people, man woman child
Wherever you are, calling you, urgent, come in
Black People, come in, wherever you are, urgent, calling
you, calling all black people
calling all black people, come in, black people, come
on in.

Black Art

Poems are bullshit unless they are
teeth or trees or lemons piled
on a step. Or black ladies dying
of men leaving nickel hearts
beating them down. Fuck poems
and they are useful, wd they shoot
come at you, love what you are,
breathe like wrestlers, or shudder
strangely after pissing. We want live
words of the hip world live flesh &
coursing blood. Hearts Brains
Souls splintering fire. We want poems
like fists beating niggers out of Jocks
or dagger poems in the slimy bellies
of the owner-jews. Black poems to
smear on girdlemamma mulatto bitches
whose brains are red jelly stuck
between 'lizabeth taylor's toes. Stinking
Whores! We want "poems that kill."
Assassin poems, Poems that shoot
guns. Poems that wrestle cops into alleys
and take their weapons leaving them dead
with tongues pulled out and sent to Ireland. Knockoff
poems for dope selling wops or slick halfwhite
politicians Airplane poems, rrrrrrrrrrrrrrr
rrrrrrrrrrrrrrr . . . tuhtuhtuhtuhtuhtuhtuhtuhtuh
. . . rrrrrrrrrrrrrrrr . . . Setting fire and death to
whities ass. Look at the Liberal
Spokesman for the jews clutch his throat
& puke himself into eternity . . . rrrrrrrr
There's a negroleader pinned to

a bar stool in Sardi's eyeballs melting
in hot flame Another negroleader
on the steps of the white house one
kneeling between the sheriff's thighs
negotiating coolly for his people.
Agggh . . . stumbles across the room . . .
Put it on him, poem. Strip him naked
to the world! Another bad poem cracking
steel knuckles in a jewlady's mouth
Poem scream poison gas on beasts in green berets
Clean out the world for virtue and love,
Let there be no love poems written
until love can exist freely and
cleanly. Let Black People understand
that they are the lovers and the sons
of lovers and warriors and sons
of warriors Are poems & poets &
all the loveliness here in the world

We want a black poem. And a
Black World.
Let the world be a Black Poem
And Let All Black People Speak This Poem
Silently
or LOUD

Three Movements and a Coda

THE QUALITY OF NIGHT THAT YOU HATE MOST
IS ITS BLACK AND ITS STARTEETH EYES, AND
STICKS ITS STICKY FINGERS IN YOUR EARS.
RED NIGGER EYES LOOKING UP FROM A
BLACK HOLE. RED NIGGER LIPS TURNING
KILLER GEOMETRY, LIKE HIS EYES ROLL

[*214*]

UP LIKE HE THOUGHT RELIGION WAS BEBOP.
LIKE HE THOUGHT RELIGION WAS
BEBOP . . . SIXTEEN KILLERS ON A
LIVE MAN'S CHEST . . .
                          THE LONE RANGER
IS DEAD.
THE SHADOW
IS DEAD.
ALL YOUR HEROES ARE DYING.
J. EDGAR HOOVER WILL SOON BE DEAD.
YOUR MOTHER WILL DIE. LYNDON JOHNSON,
                          these are natural
                          things. No one is
                          threatening anybody
                          thats just the way life
                          is,
                          boss.

Red Spick talking to you from a foxhole very close to the
Vampire Nazis' lines. I can see a few Vampire Nazis
moving very quickly back and forth under the heavy
smoke. I hear, and perhaps you do, in the back ground,
the steady deadly cough of mortars, and the light shatter
of machine guns.

BANZAI!! BANZAI!! BANZAI!!
BANZAI!! BANZAI!!

Came running out of the drugstore window with
an electric alarm clock, and then dropped the motherfucker
and broke it. Go get somethin' else. Take everything
in there. Look in the cashregister. TAKE THE MONEY.
TAKE THE MONEY. YEH. TAKE IT ALL.
YOU DONT HAVE TO CLOSE THE DRAWER.
COME ON MAN, I SAW A TAPE RECORDER
BACK THERE.

These are the words of lovers.
Of dancers, of dynamite singers
These are songs if you have the
music

I Am Speaking of Future Good-ness
and Social Philosophy

I.
When musicians say Cookin
it is food for the soul
that is being prepared, food
for the mad rain makers, black witches
good nature, whether rain everyday, or the
brightest of suns, every day, in our meat and
tubes, the newness and deadness of the central character.
Man is essential
to my philosophy,
man.

II.
The weather in spain could ride
in a train. Of generals and bishops
their assholes reamed with malice, the mountains
more beautiful than they,
though they be men. As the white man
is a man, no less his disqualification,
and subsequent reappearance as the beast
of the age. Men, no less. Though we must
finally kill them, rid the earth of them,
because they are a diseased species, but
recognized as God Fearing

So we must become Gods.
Gigantic black ones.
And scare them back into the dirt.

With the heat of our words, and
burning stares. With the heat of
our holy passion.

And then, with steel
              with bricks
              with garbage
              dogs, purposes,
              madness, tranquility,
              weakness, strength,
              deadness, vitality,
              youth and infirmity,
              with knives and razors
              and plans,

                              III.
                              (these ain't
                              clams

you eatin,
an ol' nigger
say, overhearing
this poem in my bowels,
                    ain't clams
                    dad.)

In short, everything that is magical, will respond, in men,
if we have the code
to their hearts.
Men are no more than
ourselves, other
places.
We should not despise our selves
but we must,
but never our brothers who are closer
to us than any
self,
      ours
      included.

We want to make things right.
We want to disappear except for our essence, which
is rightness.
We want to be nature and a natural thing.

Prepare for perfection.
All men who need it.
Prepare right positions.
All who deserve them.
Prepare for the real work of everybody.
Prepare for every real thing.
The mountains of dead will be sign of the times, invisible
suddenly, due to some beautiful tech
nology. Dead heaps of white ash, vanished, and the sun
allowed to shine. At the front door, baby, at the front
door, or any door, on anything, wail sun, beat on
everybody good.

Study Peace

Out of the shadow, I am come in to you whole a Black holy
    man
whole of heaven in my hand in my head look out two yeas
    to ice
what does not belong in the universe of humanity and love.
    I am
the Black magician you have heard of, you knew was on you
    in you now
my whole self, which is the star beneath the knower's arc,
    when the star it
self rose and its light illuminated the first prophet, the five
    pointed being
of love.
I have come through my senses

The five the six the fourteen
of them. And I am a fourteen point star
of the cosmic stage, spinning in my appointed orbit
giving orders to my dreams, ordering my imagination
that the world it gives birth to is the beautiful quranic vision

We are phantoms and visions, ourselves
Some star's projections, some sun's growth beneath that holy
    star
And all the other worlds there are exist alive beneath their
    own beautiful fires
real and alive, just as we are
beings of the star's mind
images cast against the eternally shifting
heavens.

TED JOANS

S. C. Threw S. C. into the Railroad Yard
to Stokely who threw it away on that day

It is crystal clear
He threw it away   He shoved it into the sky He tossed it
    away
like an old dry piece of shit
He pushed it up   high   into the space thrust it up there
    with the strength of a million winged black bird
He got rid of it   He lost it from his neck for ever He shed it
    in the filthy Chalk air over the boring Dialectic farm
He made it go far away he caused the distance to grow as it
    soared
It is gone it is dead it is no more   the sky trap has claimed it
He has got his own
from his own sent to him by his own   He is longer alone or
    wearing borrowed bits
He has a gri-gri of his own   It has freed him from
    St Christopher's medal
He is no longer under the spell of false god/A white man's
    medal-god worn also by the three astronauts who fried in
    Florida's famous event
The medal no longer hangs from his black neck
He has a gri-gri of his own   made of spiritual materials
    living elements
Gri-gri from Africa   black magic to do great harm to his
    oppressors
gri-gri to give him strength and wisdom   Growing stronger
    encircling his
body   just around his neck   below his handsome black head
His Bambara face   His Nilotic frame   His Ashanti majesty
    His Hipness of Harlem
He has thrown the white medal of St Christopher away

He is now free   from the money Man's bit   He no longer
   sucks Holy Mary's tit
He has a gri-gri of his own
A black gri-gri
a grinning cunt shaped cowrie shell gri-gri
a brown black blue leather breathing amulet gri-gri
brought from the black sorceror
across the Sahara   across the Atlantic and Mediterranean
from black Africa   by me

Jazz Must Be a Woman
to all the jazzmen that I fail to include

Jazz must be a woman because its the only thing that
Albert Ayler Albert Ammons Albert Nichols Gene Ammons
Cat Anderson Louis Armstrong Buddy Bolden Ornette
Coleman Buster Bailey Ben Bailey Benny Harris Ben
Webster Beaver Harris Alan Shorter Coleman Hawkins
Count Basie Dave Bailey Dexter Gordon Danny Barker
Wayne Shorter Duke Ellington Jay Macshann Earl Hines
Tiny Grimes Barney Bigard Sahib Shihab Sid Catlett Jelly
Roll Morton Nat King Cole Johnny Coles Lee Collins
John Collins Sonny Rollins Pete Brown Jay Jay Johnson
Dickie Wells Vic Dickenson Ray Nance Junior Mance
Sonny Parker Charlie Parker Leo Parker Lee Morgan Mal
Waldron Ramsey Lewis John Lewis George Lewis Pops
Foster Curtiss Fuller Jimmie Cleveland Billy Higgins John
Coltrane Cozy Cole Bill Coleman Idries Sulimann Hank
Mobley Charlie Mingus Dizzy Gillespie Lester Young Harney
Carney Cecil Payne Sonny Payne Roy Haynes Max Roach
Thelonious Monk Wes Montgomery Johnny Dodds
Johnny Hodges Kenny Drew Kenny Durham Ernie Wilkins
Royal Babs Gonzales McCoy Tyner Clifford Brown
Shadow Wilson Teddy Wilson Gerald Wilson Wynton

Kelly Huddie Leadbelly Big Bill Bronzy Cannonball
Adderly Bobbie Timmons Sidney Bechet Sonny Criss Sonny
Stitt Fats Navarro Ray Charles Benny Carter Lawrence
Brown Ray Brown Charlie Moffett Sonny Murray Milt
Buckner Milt Jackson Miles Davis Horace Silver Bud Powell
Kenny Burrell Teddy Bunn Teddy Buckner King Oliver
Oliver Nelson Tricky Sam Nanton Buber Miley Freddy
Webster Freddy Redd Benny Green Jackie Maclean Art
Simmins Art Blakey Art Taylor Cecil Taylor Billy Taylor
Gene Taylor Clark Terry Don Cherry Sonny Terry Joe
Turner Joe Thomas Fay Bryant Freddie Greene Freddie
Hubbard Donald Byrd Roland Kirk Carl Perkins Morris
Lane Harry Edison Percey Heath Jimmy Heath Jimmy Smith
Willie Smith Buster Smith Floyd Smith Johnny Smith
Pinetop Smith Stuff Smith Tab Smith Willie 'the Lion'
Smith Roy Eldridge Charlie Shavers Eddie South Les Spann
Les Macann Speckled Red Eddie Vinson Mr. Cleanhead
Rex Stewart Slam Stewart Art Tatum Erskine Hawkins
Cootie Williams Lionel Hampton Ted Curson John
Tchicai Joe Thomas Lucky Thompson Sir Charles
Thompson T-Bone Walker Fats Waller Julius Watkins
Doug Watkins Muddy Waters Washboard Sam Memphis
Slim Leo Watson Chick Webb Frank Wess Denzil
Best Randy Weston Clarence Williams Joe Williams
Rubberlegs Williams Spencer Williams Sonnyboy Williams
Tampa Red Jimmy Witherspoon Britt Woodman Leo
Wright Jimmy Yancey Trummy Young Snooky Young
James P Johnson Bunk Johnson Budd Johnson Red
Garland Erroll Garner Jimmy Garrison Matthew Gee
Cecil Gant Walter Fuller Roosevelt Skyes Slim Gaillard
Harold Land Pete Laroca Yusef Lateef Billy Kyle John
Kirby Al Killian Andy Kirk Freddie Keppard Taft Jordan
Duke Jordon Louis Jordan Cliff Jordan Scott Joplin Willie
Jones Wallace Jones Sam Jones Rejnald Jones Quincy Jones
Philly Jo Jones Jimmy Jones Hank Jones Elvin Jones Ed
Jones Claude Jones Rufus Jones Curtiss Jones Richard
Jones Wilore "slick" Jones Thad Jones and of course me. . . .

TED JONES/yes JAZZ must be a WOMAN because it's
the only thing that we Jazzmen want to . . . . . B L O W ! !

Santa Claws

IF THAT WHITE MOTHER HUBBARD COMES
DOWN MY BLACK CHIMNEY DRAGGING HIS
PLAYFUL BAG
IF THAT RED SUITED FAGGOT STARTS HO HO
HOING ON MY ROOFTOP
IF THAT OLD FAT CRACKER CREEPS INTO MY
HOUSE
IF THAT ANTIQUE REINDEER RAPER RACES
ACROSS MY LAWN
IF THAT OLD TIME NIGGER KNOCKER FILLS MY
WIFE'S STOCKING
IF THAT HAINT WHO THINKS HE'S A SAINT
COMES SLED FLYING ACROSS MY HOME
IF THAT OLD CON MAN COMES ON WITH HIS TOY-
FUL JIVE
IF THAT OVER STUFFED GUT BUSTING GANG-
STER SHOWS UP TONIGHT
HE AND ME SHOW GONNA HAVE A BATTLING
XMAS AND IT SHOW AINT GONNA BE WHITE!

The Nice Colored Man

Nice Nigger Educated Nigger Never Nigger Southern Nigger
Clever Nigger Northern Nigger Nasty Nigger Unforgivable
Nigger Unforgettable Nigger Unspeakable Nigger Rude &
Uncouth Nigger Mean & Vicious Nigger Smart Black Nigger
Smart Black Nigger Smart Black Nigger Smart Black Nigger

Smart Black Nigger Smart Black Nigger Smart Black
Nigger Smart Black Nigger Knife Carrying Nigger Gun
Toting Nigger Military Nigger Clock Watching Nigger Food
Poisoning Nigger Disgusting Nigger Black Ass Nigger
Black Ass Nigger Black Ass Nigger Black Ass Nigger Half
White Nigger Big Stupid Nigger Big Dick Nigger Jive Ass
Nigger Wrong Nigger Naughty Nigger Uppity Nigger
Middleclass Nigger Government Nigger Sneaky Nigger
Houndog Nigger Grease Head Nigger Nappy Head Nigger
Cut Throat Nigger Dangerous Nigger Sharp Nigger Rich
Nigger Poor Nigger Begging Nigger Hustling Nigger
Whoring Nigger Pimping Nigger No Good Nigger Dirty
Nigger Unhappy Nigger Explosive Nigger Godamn Nigger
Godamnigger Godamnigger Godamnigger Godamnigger
Godamnigger Godamn Nigger Godamnigger Godamnigger
Godamnigger Godamnigger Godamnigger
                        Neat Nigger Progressive
Nigger Nextdoor Nigger Classmate Nigger Roomate Nigger
Laymate Nigger Weekend Date Nigger Dancing Nigger
Smiling Nigger Ageless Nigger Old Tired Nigger Silly Nigger
Hippy Nigger White Folks Nigger Integrated Nigger
Non-Violent Nigger Demonstrating Nigger Cooperative
Nigger Peaceful Nigger American Nigger Uneducated
Nigger Under Rated Nigger Bad Nigger Sad Nigger Slum
Nigger Jailhouse Nigger Stealing Nigger Robbing Nigger
Raping Nigger
                        Lonely Nigger Blues Singing Nigger Dues
Paying Nigger Unemployed Nigger Unwanted Nigger
Impossible Nigger Cunning Nigger Running Nigger Cruel
Nigger Well Known Nigger Individual Nigger Purple Nigger
Beige Nigger Bronze Nigger Brown Nigger Red Nigger Bed
Nigger Yellow Nigger Tan Nigger Mulatto Nigger Creole
Nigger Inevitable Nigger Mixed Up Nigger Slave Nigger
Unfree Nigger Savage Nigger Jazz Nigger Musical Nigger
Godamnigger Godamnigger Godamnigger Godamnigger
Godamnigger Godamnigger Jesus Loves Us Nigger
Preaching Nigger We Shall Overcome Nigger Someday

[*224*]

Nigger Militant Nigger Real Nigger Brave Nigger Real
Nigger Violent Nigger Real Nigger Intelligent Nigger Real
Nigger Active Nigger Real Nigger Wise Nigger Real Nigger
Deceitful Nigger Real Nigger Courageous Nigger Real
Nigger Cool Nigger Real Nigger Hip Nigger Real Nigger
Hot Nigger Real Nigger Funky Nigger Real Nigger (I Can't
Figger This Nigger He's Too Much This Nigger! He's All
Over Us This Nigger I Dont Trust This Nigger He's Far
Too Much He's Everywhere . . . This Nigger!)
Eeny Meeny Minee Mo
Catch Whitey By His Throat
If He Says—Nigger C U T   I T ! !

SAMUEL ALLEN (PAUL VESEY)

To Satch

Sometimes I feel I will *never* stop
Just go on forever
Till one fine mornin
I'm gonna reach up and grab me a handfulla stars
Swing out my long lean leg
And whip three hot strikes burnin down the heavens
And look over at God and say
How about that!

In My Father's House: A Reverie

In my father's house when dusk had fallen
I was alone on the dim first floor
I knew there was someone some power desirous
Of forcing the outer door.

How shall I explain—

I bolted it securely
And was locking the inner when
Somehow I was constrained to turn
To see it silently again.

Transfixed before the panther night
My heart gave one tremendous bound
Paralyzed, my feet refused
The intervening ground.

How shall I say—

I was in the house and dusk had fallen
I was alone on the earthen floor
I knew there was a power
Lurking beyond the door.

I bolted the outside door
And was closing the inner when
I noticed the first had swung open again
My heart bound and I knew it would be upon me
                        I rushed to the door
It came on me out of the night and I rushed to the yard
If I could throw the ball the stone the spear in my hand
Against the wall my father would be warned but now
Their hands had fallen on me and they had taken me and
                        I tried
To cry out but O I could not cry out and the cold gray waves
Came over me O stifling me and drowning me . . .

Ivory Tusks

Pale and uncertain
lost in the distance
the ivory tusks they do not want.
The bleached sands sweep my eyelids,
heavy with revolving doors
I turn and reeling, turn again
but I am yet not comforted.

I seek the solace of the circling fangs
but I cannot be comforted
I drink huge vats of blood
I devour houses gleaming in the sun
twining green with vine
and I am yet not comforted.

Inconsolable inconsolable
all that matters lost
ice ages of days
and I will not be comforted.

Springtime, Ghetto, USA

Two pairs of eyes peered face to face
    in the soft moonlight.
The Ides had passed, again the Spring had come
The lucent shaft glowed through the window
Etching dimly the quiet room
    in the moon's light.

Outside, beyond, the April winds
Pillaged the frail clouds
Slashing them about
Stirring the window boxes
Now urging lovers toward each other
    on the grasses
        in the soft light.

Inside the shadowed tenement
One pair of eyes looked up
The rodent's down
    into the crib
        in the moon's light.

MARGARET DANNER

Garnishing the Aviary
"are you beautiful still?"

Our moulting days are in their twilight stage.
These lengthy dreaded suns of draggling plumes.
These days of moods that swiftly alternate between

the former preen and a downcast rage
or crest-fallen lag, are fading out. The initial bloom;
exotic, dazzling in its indigo, tangerine

splendor; this rare, conflicting coat had to be shed.
Our drooping feathers turn all shades. We spew
this unamicable aviary, gag upon the worm, and fling

our loosening quills. We make a riotous spread
upon the dust and mire that beds us. We do not shoo
so quickly; but the shades of the pinfeathers resulting

from this chaotic push, though still exotic,
blend in more easily with those on the wings
of the birds surrounding them; garnishing
the aviary, burnishing this zoo.

The Slave and the Iron Lace

The craving of Samuel Rouse for clearance to create
was surely as hot as the iron that buffeted him. His passion
for freedom so strong that it molded the smouldering fashions
he laced, for how also could a slave plot
or counterplot such incomparable shapes,

form or reform, for house after house,
the intricate Patio pattern, the delicate
Rose and Lyre, the Debutante Settee,
the complex but famous Grape; frame the classic vein
in an iron bench?

How could he turn an iron Venetian urn, wind the Grape
    Vine, chain
the trunk of a pine with a Round-the-Tree-settee,
mold a Floating Flower tray, a French chair—create all this
in such exquisite fairyland taste, that he'd be freed
and his skill would still resound a hundred years after?

And I wonder if I, with this thick asbestos glove of an
attitude could lace, forge and bend this ton of lead-chained
    spleen surrounding me?
Could I manifest and sustain it into a new free-form screen
of, not necessarily love, but (at the very least, for all
    concerned) grace.

This Is an African Worm

This is an African worm
but then a worm in any land
is still a worm.

It will not stride, run, stand up
before the butterflies, who
have passed their worm-like state.

It must keep low, not lift its head.
I've had the dread experience, I know.
A worm can do no thing but crawl.

Crawl, and wait.

Passive Resistance

And to this Man who turned the other cheek,
this Man who murmured not a word,
or fought at persecutors,
remained meek under it all,
I crawl, in wonder.

For as the evil tongues begin to turn on me
I want to fight, strike back,
and see them quail
in some rat-ridden jail,
or suffering for
the suffering they've caused.
I want no more of this humility.
But I must bow,
bow low before it now,
and love the evil ones,
as You did.   Yet, I am sure
it was much easier for
God's son.

My Birthright, Too

What, I wonder, but not for long,

is wrong with you

who came by your volition

from that same fatherland

from which I was torn

    I have the legitimate right to
    ENJOY THIS INCREDIBLY CARVED AFRICAN
       MASQUE
    and so I lovingly do enjoy
    ENJOY THIS INCREDIBLY CARVED AFRICAN
       MASQUE

It is the glorious part of my past too

a past that has its part-time file of inglory

DUDLEY RANDALL

Ballad of Birmingham

"Mother dear, may I go downtown
instead of out to play,
and march the streets of Birmingham
in a freedom march today?"

"No, baby, no, you may not go,
for the dogs are fierce and wild,
and clubs and hoses, guns and jails
aren't good for a little child."

"But, mother, I won't be alone.
Other children will go with me,
and march the streets of Birmingham
to make our country free."

"No, baby, no, you may not go,
for I fear those guns will fire.
But you may go to church instead,
and sing in the children's choir."

She has combed and brushed her nightdark hair,
and bathed rose petal sweet,
and drawn white gloves on her small brown hands,
and white shoes on her feet.

The mother smiled to know her child
was in the sacred place,
but that smile was the last smile
to come upon her face.

For when she heard the explosion,
her eyes grew wet and wild.

She raced through the streets of Birmingham
calling for her child.

She clawed through bits of glass and brick,
then lifted out a shoe.
"O, here's the shoe my baby wore,
but, baby, where are you?"

Black Poet, White Critic

A critic advises
not to write on controversial subjects
like freedom or murder,
but to treat universal themes
and timeless symbols
like the white unicorn.

A white unicorn?

JAMES A. EMANUEL

For Malcolm, U. S. A.

Thin, black javelin
Flying low.
Heads up!
Hear Malcolm go!

Cheekless tiger
On the prowl.
Breathlessly:
Hear Malcolm growl.

Lightning, lightning
Shot the sky.
Silently:
Did Malcolm die?

Brother, brother,
Hold my hand.
Malcolm was
My native land.

Emmett Till

I hear a whistling
Through the water.
Little Emmett
Won't be still.
He keeps floating
Round the darkness,
Edging through

The silent chill.
Tell me, please,
That bedtime story
Of the fairy
River Boy
Who swims forever,
Deep in treasures,
Necklaced in
A coral toy.

To a Negro Preacher

Lightning grows old,
Red-ribboned in a luminous page,
Hung down in rage
Rehearsed and kindly sold.
And thunder trickles into song
The pew-line hums along.

Long years of tambourines
Have shaken out unburied cries,
And plates of weary-knuckled coins
Have pyramided to the skies
One callous-handed prayer:
Oh, stricken Christ, be there!

Unhook us, Old Man.
Relax this page before our eyes.
This holy word will keep, will rise
Upon our shoulders African
Before the beast, before the spear.
The jungle test is here.

The benediction of your heart,
The strong brown of your hand

We claim for banners as we start
The Golgotha to free our land.
Help man us on the streets of clay:
We demonstrate today.

Freedom Rider: Washout

The first blow hurt.
(God is love, is love.)
My blood spit into the dirt.
(Sustain my love, oh, Lord above!)
Curses circled one another.
(They were angry with their brother.)

I was too weak
For this holy game.
A single freckled fist
Knocked out the memory of His name.
Bloody, I heard a long, black moan,
Like waves from slave ships long ago.
With Gabriel Prosser's dogged knuckles
I struck an ancient blow.

MICHAEL HARPER

Dear John, Dear Coltrane

> *a love supreme, a love supreme*
> *a love supreme, a love supreme*

Sex fingers toes
in the marketplace
near your father's church
in Hamlet, North Carolina—
witness to this love
in this calm fallow
of these minds,
there is no substitute for pain:
genitals gone or going,
seed burned out,
you tuck the roots in the earth,
turn back, and move
by river through the swamps,
singing: *a love supreme, a love supreme;*
what does it all mean?
Loss, so great each black
woman expects your failure
in mute change, the seed gone.
You plod up into the electric city—
your song now crystal and
the blues. You pick up the horn
with some will and blow
into the freezing night:
a love supreme, a love supreme—

Dawn comes and you cook
up the thick sin 'tween
impotence and death, fuel

the tenor sax cannibal
heart, genitals and sweat
that makes you clean—
a love supreme, a love supreme—

Why you so black?
cause I am
why you so funky?
cause I am
why you so black?
cause I am
why you so sweet?
cause I am
why you so black?
cause I am
a love supreme, a love supreme:

So sick
you couldn't play *Naima,*
so flat we ached
for song you'd concealed
with your own blood,
your diseased liver gave
out its purity,
the inflated heart
pumps out, the tenor kiss,
tenor love:
a love supreme, a love supreme—
a love supreme, a love supreme—

To James Brown

Little brother, little brother,
put your feet on the floor.

You've asked for Jimmy Brown,
beautiful cat, the wrong man.

Little brother, don't nobody know
your name, feet off the floor,

movin' again. Black Brother!
Somebody tell little brother

'bout James Brown:
please, please, please,

please, please, please.

SARAH WEBSTER FABIO

Evil Is No Black Thing

I
Ahab's gaily clad fisherfriends,
questing under the blue skies after
the albino prize, find the green sea
cold and dark at its deep center,
but calm—unperturbed by the fates
of men and whales.

Rowing shoreward, with wet and empty
hands, their sun-rich smiles fuzz
with bafflement as the frothing
surf buckles underneath and their
sea-scarred craft is dashed to pieces
near the shore; glancing backward,
the spiraling waves are white-capped.

II
Evil is no black thing: black
the rain clouds attending a storm
but the fury of it neither begins
nor ends there. Weeping tear-clear
rain, trying to contain the hoarse
blue-throated thunder and the fierce
quick-silver tongue of lightning, bands
of clouds wring their hands.

Once I saw dark clouds in Texas
stand by idly while a Northeaster
screamed its icy puffs, ringtailing
raindrops, rolling them into baseballs

of hail, then descending upon the
tin-roofed houses unrelentingly
battering them down.

III
And the night is blackest where
gay throated cuckoos sing among the
dense firs of the Black Forest, where
terrible flurries of snow are blinding
bright: somewhere, concealed here deeply,
lies a high-walled town, whitewashed.

Seen at sunset, only the gaping ditch
and overhanging, crooked tree are painted
pitch to match the night: but I've seen
a dying beam of light reach through
the barred windows of a shower chamber,
illuminating its blood-scratched walls.

IV
Evil is no black thing: black
may be the undertaker's hearse
and so many of the civil trappings
of death, but not its essence:
the riderless horse, the armbands
and veils of mourning, the grave shine
darkly; but these are the rituals
of the living.

One day I found its meaning as I
rushed breathless through a wind-parched
field, stumbling unaware: suddenly there
it was, lying at my feet, hidden
beneath towering goldenrods,
a criss-crossed pile of
sun-bleached bones.

Tribute to Duke

Rhythm and Blues
sired you; gospel's
your mother tongue:
that of a MAN
praying in the
miraculous language
of song—soul
communion with
his maker,
a sacred offering
from the
God-in-man
to the
God-of-man.

You reigned King
of Jazz before
Whiteman imitations
of "Black-Brown and
Beige" became the
order of the day.
Here, now, we but add
one star more to
your two-grand
jewel-studded crown
for that many tunes
you turned the world
onto in your
half-centuried
creative fever riffed
in scales of color

Ohh, Ooh, Oh,
moaning low,
I got
the blues.

Sometimes I'm
up; sometimes
I'm down.

Sometimes I'm
down; sometimes
I'm up

Oh happy day
When Jesus washed
my sin away.
(musical background
with a medly of
tunes)

Boss, boss
tunes in
technicolor
SOUL—
Black-
Brown-
Beige-
Creole-

Black

from "Black Beauty"
to "Creole Rhapsody"
and "Black and Tan
   Fantasy."
All praises
to Duke,
King of Jazz

To run it down
for you. That
fever that came on
with that "Uptown Beat"
caused Cotton when
he came to Harlem
that first time to
do a "Sugar Hill
Shim Sham."

When things got down
and funky
you bit into the blues
and blew into the air,
"I Got It Bad and
That Ain't Good,"
And from deep
down into your
"Solitude," you
touched both
"Satin Doll" and
"Sophisticated Lady"
wrapped them in
"Mood Indigo" and made
each moment
"A Prelude
to a kiss."

Way back then, Man,

[244]

and

Tan

is

the color
of my fantasy.
When things
got down
and really
funky
fever, fever,
light
my fire.

Down,
down
down
Nee-eev-eer
treat me
kind
and gentle—
BLOW
(music in the
background)
the way you
should
BLOW, MAN
Ain't
I
Got
it
Bad.

Break it down.

you were doing
your thing.
Blowing minds with
riffs capping
whimsical whiffs of
lush melody—
changing minds
with moods and
modulations,
changing minds,
changing faces,
changing tunes,

changing changes,
tripping out with
Billy to "Take the
A Train," making it
your theme—
your heat—
coming on strong
with bold dissonance
and fast, fast, beat
of the early, late
sound of our time.

"Harlem Airshaft"
"Rent Party Blues"
jangling jazzed tone
portraits of life
in the streets.
"Harlem"—a symphony
of cacaphonous sound,
bristling rhythms,
haunting laments
trumpeting into the air
defiant blasts blown solo
to fully orchestrated

Break
it down
Right on down
   to
    the
   Real
   nitty gritty.
  ("Solitude"
   as background
   sound)
Blow,
  blow,

   blow

Do your thing.

Change, change, change
your 'chine
and Take
  The
   A Train.

Ain't
got no
  money
Ain't got no bread.
Ain't got
no place
to lay my Afro head.
 I got
  those low down
  blues.
Chorus: Hot-and-Cold-
Running- Harlem

folk chorus.
World Ambassador,
translating Life
into lyric; voice
into song; pulse
into beat
the beat, the beat,
a beat, a beat, a beat,
beat, beat, beat, beat
Do it now.
Get down.
"A Drum Is a Woman,"
and what more
language does
a sweetback need
to trip out to
"Mood Indigo,"

Right on, Duke
Do your thing,
your own thing.
And, Man,
the word's out
when you
get down
Bad
it's good,
Real good,

And as you
go
know
you're tops,
and whatever
you do,
"We love you
madly."

[246]

"Rent Party Blues."

Break it down,
down
  down
   down
Right on down
to the
  Real
  nitty gritty.
  drums in the
  background become
   drum solo)

(Theme song)

Take

The
A
Train.

Right on.

Right
on
out
of
this
funky
world.

MARI EVANS

Vive Noir!

i
am going to rise
en masse
from Inner City

    sick
     of newyork ghettos
     chicago tenements
     l a's slums
weary
  of exhausted lands
  sagging privies
  saying yessuh yessah
  yes SIR
  in an assortment
  of geographical dialects i
have seen my last
broken down plantation
even from a
distance
    i
will load all my goods
in '50 Chevy pickups '53
Fords fly United and '66
caddys i
  have packed in
  the old man and the old lady and
  wiped the children's noses
    I'm tired
     of hand me downs
      shut me ups
       pin me ins

                    keep me outs
                        messing me over have
                    just had it
                baby
            from
        you . . .
i'm
gonna spread out
over America
            intrude
my proud blackness
all
    over the place
                i have wrested wheat fields
                from the forests
                turned rivers
                from their courses
                leveled mountains
                at a word
                festooned the land with
                brides
                            gemlike
                    on filaments of steel
                            moved
                glistening towers of Babel in place.

                sweated a whole
                civilization
                    now
                            i'm
                gonna breathe fire
                through flaming nostrils BURN
                    a place for

                    me

                in the skyscrapers and the
                schoolrooms on the green

               lawns and the white
               beaches
                              i'm
               gonna wear the robes and
               sit on the benches
               make the rules and make
               the arrests say
               who can and who
               can't
                       baby you don't stand
                       a
                       chance
i'm
       gonna put black angels
       in all the books and a black
       Christchild in Mary's arms i'm
       gonna make black bunnies black
       fairies black santas black
       nursery rhymes and
                              black
       ice cream
                       i'm
gonna make it a
       crime
               to be anything BUT   black
gonna make white
a twenty-four hour
lifetime
J.O.B.

Black jam for dr. negro

Pullin me in off the corner to wash my face an
cut my afro turn
my collar
down
when that aint my
thang I
walk heels first
nose round an tilted
up my ancient
eyes
see your thang
baby
an it aint
shit
your thang
puts my eyes out baby
turns my seeking fingers
   into splintering fists
messes up my head
an I scream you out
your thang
is whats wrong
   an you keep
   pilin it on rubbin it
   in
   smoothly
   doin it
   to death

what you sweatin
baby
         your

puked an rotten guts
waiting
to be defended

To Mother and Steve

All I wanted
was your
love

when I roiled down
Brewster blew
soft pot clouds on
subs when
I lay in nameless rooms
cold-sweating
horse in nameless rooms
crawled
thru white hell owning
no one no one no one save
one purple-bruised soul
pawned
in exchange for
oblivion
   all I wanted
was
your love

not twice but
constantly
I tried
to free you
it was all
such cold shit

then
the last day
of the
last year
of my raw-edged anguish
I was able wearily
at last—
to roll.

(all I wanted
was
your love)
I bought this final
battered gift

(do not refuse—for it
was all
I had)

with my back supported
by the tolerant
arms
of a picket fence and my
legs crumpled crazily in front
and love fell
soft and cold and
covered me in
blanket
like
the one you
tucked around me
centuries
ago and like that
later
gently pulled
across my face
and in this season

of peace and
goodwill and the smell
of cedar
remembered
thru warm yellow
windows—
   all I wanted
and it was more than
I could stand and
more than a thousand passions and
I could not
mainline it
away

   was your
   love

Speak the Truth to the People

Speak the truth to the people
Talk sense to the people
Free them with reason
Free them with honesty
Free the people with Love and Courage and Care for
   their Being
Spare them the fantasy
Fantasy enslaves
A slave is enslaved
Can be enslaved by unwisdom
Can be enslaved by black unwisdom
Can be re-enslaved while in flight from the enemy
Can be enslaved by his brother whom he loves
His brother whom he trusts
His brother with the loud voice

And the unwisdom
Speak the truth to the people
It is not necessary to green the heart
Only to identify the enemy
It is not necessary to blow the mind
Only to free the mind
To identify the enemy is to free the mind
A free mind has no need to scream
A free mind is ready for other things

To BUILD black schools
To BUILD black children
To BUILD black minds
To BUILD black love
To BUILD black impregnability
To BUILD a strong black nation
To BUILD.

Speak the truth to the people.
Spare them the opium of devil-hate.
They need no trips on honky-chants.
Move them instead to a BLACK ONENESS.
A black strength which will defend its own
Needing no cacophony of screams for activation
A black strength which attacks the laws
exposes the lies disassembles the structure
and ravages the very foundation of evil.

Speak the truth to the people
To identify the enemy is to free the mind
Free the mind of the people
Speak to the mind of the people
Speak Truth.

CONRAD KENT RIVERS

In Defense of Black Poets

(for Hoyt)

The critics cry unfair
    yet the poem is born.
Some black emancipated baby
    will scratch his head
wondering why you felt compelled
    to say whatever you said

A black poet must bear in mind
    the misery.
The color-seekers fear poems
    they can't buy for a ten-dollar
bill or with a clever contract.
    Some black kid is bound to read you.

A black poet must remember the horrors.
    The good jobs can't last forever.
It shall come to pass that the fury
    of a token revolution will fade
into the bank accounts of countless blacks
    and freedom-loving whites.

The brilliant novels shall pass
    into the archives of a "keep cool
we've done enough for you" generation:
    the movement organizations already
await their monthly checks from Downtown
    and

only the forgotten wails of a few black
    poets and artists

shall survive the then of then,
   the now of now.

Watts

Must I shoot the
white man dead
to free the nigger
in his head?

A Mourning Letter from Paris
(for Richard Wright)

All night I walked among your spirits, Richard:
the Paris you adored is most politely dead.

I found French-speaking bigots and some sterile blacks,
bright African boys forgetting their ancestral robes,
a few men of color seeking the same French girl.

Polished Americans watched the stark reality
of mass integration, pretending not to look homeward
where the high ground smelled of their daughters' death.

I searched for the skin of your bones, Richard.
Mississippi called you back to her genuine hard clay,
but here one finds a groove, adapts, then lingers on.

For me, my good dead friend of searing words
and thirsty truth, the road to Paris leads back home:
one gets to miss the stir of Harlem's honeyed voice,
or one forgets the joy to which we were born.

Underground
(black cat)

Under bright city lights
I swing on rusty water pipes
like a wolf running wacky
across high circus wires.

I frequent basement parlors
where jazz freaks a blonde
drunk on black jazzmen blowing
sartonian melodies.

In air-cooled clean apartments where
dim darkness is defined powerless
by a parted sun patently and
niggardly going berserk, baby,
in the first person singular
I swing through the city full of blues.

For All Things Black and Beautiful
(for Langston Hughes)

For all things black and beautiful,
The brown faces you loved so well and long,
the endless roads leading back to Harlem.
   For all things black and beautiful
   The seeking and the labor always waiting and coming
   Until you began to dream of Nubian queens
   And black kings shifting the dust of eternity
   Before the white man brought his shame and God.

For all things black and beautiful
It took a lot of stones from little white boys
To produce the poem and quench the first desire to taste
Their nectar and the black wine of black empires
Flowing through your black bursting bewildered body.

For all things black and beautiful
And your Indian grandmother weaving tragic tales
Until the sea consumed you and the world you had loved
In ports and places few of your black brothers knew.

For all things black and beautiful
And the strange house in Taos and your white old man
Under a yellow Mexican sun dying black and moaning
Those weary blues until you came home to Harlem seeking
A way and worship and luster in the jive and the jazz
Once chained to the bottom of slave ships and whipped
In the public squares of our most democratic colorful cities.

For all things black and beautiful
The white savior and the black Christ dreaming dreams
While a black brother hangs from an oak without branches.

For all things black and beautiful
And big black Bessie doing her solo thrice times
Until Louie saves her by blasting his golden horn
And the whites shout and the blacks dance and night cries
Coming with her bullets in our bodies and death in our
    brains
But we cry out and finance our misery until our guts
Belong to the holy holy company and they laugh and eat well
While we die young and strong though tired of time
    payments.

For all things black and beautiful
Your poetry's a monument to our violated homes without
    hope

As we go weeping behind your box wanting to hear your
    tunes.
But if our poet is dead and Simple no longer sips divinity
Then we have not heard it in the breeze that blows our
    music
And our song into the vespers and the dens of white
    America
When our very faces are not wanted somehow we do exist
    there.

For all things black and beautiful
The music you heard in the hallways and hid in the noun
The street woman you loved and saved with a sober ballad
The urban holocaust that swept you through the ghetto-
    ghetto land
The barbeque and sweet potatoes too many nights you went
    without
The sounds you heard in your head like dripping meal from
    cornbread
The dishwater like blood on your hands and filth on your
    heart
The Renaissance and Du Bois and Roberson and Carl and
    Arna and Zora
All gone like a Russian moon passes through the bight of
    Benin.

For all things black and beautiful
And Mali rising again and Timbuktu spreading culture
    across the land
And Yardbird smoking and cleansing this roomy world of
    dry ashes
Until Sweet Sue understands the beauty of her black sunset
    silk skin
And the glory of her carmelite brown brighter than a blue
    red sun
Echoing the ancient truths of her own black culture and
    being.

For all things black and beautiful seen through your eyes:
Willie Mays doing his ballet in centerfield and Lady Day
   praying
And Harlem The Black Mother weeping and my own wet
   eyes, Langston
Feeling the darkness and the decline of the kingdom and
   glory of all
Things you made so black and beautiful in your fashion and
   way.
Africa is in your grave and may all the elements find peace
   with you.

A. B. SPELLMAN

Did John's Music Kill Him?

in the morning part
of evening he would stand
before his crowd. the voice
would call his name &
redlight fell around him.
jimmy'd bow a quarter hour
till Mccoy fed block chords
to his stroke. elvin's thunder
roll & eric's scream. then john.

then john. *little old lady*
had a nasty mouth. *summertime*
when the war is. *africa* ululating
a line bunched up like itself
into knots paints beauty black.

trane's horn had words in it
i know when i sleep sober & dream
those dreams i duck in the world
of sun & shadow. yet even in the day john
& a little grass put them on me clear
as tomorrow in a glass enclosure.

kill me john my life eats
life. the thing that beats out of
me happens in a vat enclosed
& fermenting & wanting to explode
like your song.

     so beat john's death words down
     on me in the darker part
     of evening. the black light issued

from him in the pit he made
around us. worms came clear
to me where i thought i had been
brilliant. o john death will
not contain you death
will not contain you

Untitled

in orangeburg my brothers did
the african twist around a bonfire they'd built
at the gate to keep the hunkies out. the day
before they'd caught one shooting up
the campus like the white hunter
he was. but a bonfire? only conjures
up the devil. up popped the devil from behind a bush
the brothers danced the fire
danced the bullets cut their flesh
like bullets. black death
black death black death black
brothers black sisters black me with no white blood on my
    hands
we are so beautiful
we study our history backwards
& that must be the beast's most fatal message
that we die to learn it well.

The Joel Blues
after and for him

i know your door baby
better than i know my own.
i know your door baby
better than i know my own.

it's been so long since i seen you
i'm sure you done up and gone.

in the morning, in the evening
in the daytime & the nighttime too:
in the morning, in the evening
in the daytime & the nighttime too:
    it don't matter what i'm doing
    all i got to think about is you.

well the sun froze to the river
& the wind was freezing to the ground.
o the sun froze to the river
& the wind was freezing to the ground.
    if you hadn't heard me calling
    i don't think i ever could been found.

o i ain't no deacon baby,
i ain't never been a praying man.
o i ain't no deacon baby,
i ain't never been a praying man.
    but i had to call to someone
    you the only one was close to hand.

i'm a easy riding papa,
i'm your everloving so & so.
i'm a easy riding papa,
i'm your everloving so & so.
    don't think i don't hear you calling
    cause i'm coming when you want to go.

it's a pity pretty mama
that i go to look for you at all.
it's a pity pretty mama
that i go to look for you at all.
    but if it wasn't for the looking
    i'd be climbing up & down the wall.

DAVID HENDERSON

Elvin Jones Gretsch Freak
(Coltrane at the Half-Note)

> To Elvin Jones/tub man of
> the John Coltrane Quartet.
> GRETSCH is outstanding on
> his bass drum that faces the
> audience at the Half-Note,
> Spring Street, New York City.

gretsch love
gretsch hate
gretsch mother   father fuck
fuck gretsch

> The Halfnote should be
> a basement cafe like the "A" train
> Jazz/drums of gretsch
> on the fastest and least stopping
> transportation scene in NYC
> subways are for gretsch
> "A" train long as a long city block
> the tenements of the underground rails
> west 4th
> 34th   42nd   125th
> farther down in the reverse

                          local at west 4th
      waterfront   warehouse   truck/produce   vacant
      the halfnote

                  our city fathers keep us on the right track
zones/   ozone

                  fumes of tracks   /smokestacks
The Halfnote
westside truck exhaust and spent breath

of Holland Tunnel   exhaust   soot darkness jazz
speeding cars   noisy/   noiseless
speeding gretsch   tremulous gretsch
Elvin Jones the man behind the pussy
four men love on a stage
the loud orgy
gretsch trembles and titters
                    gretsch is love
                    gretsch is love
                    gretsch is love

Elvin's drum ensemble the aggressive cunt
the feminine mystique
cymbals tinny clitorous   resounding
lips snares flanked/   encircling
thumping foot drum peter rabbit the fuck   take
this   and take   that
elvin behind the uterus of his sticks
the mad embryo
panting sweat-dripping embryo
misshapen/   hunched
Coltrane sane/ cock   the forceps
the fox and the hare
the chase
screaming and thumping
traffic of music on Spring Street
'Trane says to young apprentice Ron Ferral "Fill in the
solids, get it while it's hot and comely; Elvin fucks almost
as good as his Mama."

The Halfnote is as packed as   rush hour on 42nd & 8th
"A" train territory
coltrane is off with a hoot
directed supine
nowhere in generalness
into the din and the death
between   bar and tables   reds silver glass molten mass shout

tobacco fumes across the boardwalk
                    (coney island is the "D" train change
                    at west 4th if you want it)
Coltrane steps the catwalk
                    elvin jones drums gretsch
                    gretsch shimmy and shout
elvin drums a 1939 ford
99 pushing miles per hour/   shoving barefoot driver
                    in the heats
Coltrane/ Jones
riffing   face to face
instrument charge
        stools to kneecap
many faceted rhythm structure   to   tomahawk
gretsch rocks 'n rolls   gretsch rattles
fuck gretsch/
                    we know so well strident drums
                    children singing death songs /war
                    tenor and soprano   high
tenor soar/   flux of drums   chasing
        keen inviolate   blue
the model "T" ford & air hammer
                    Holland tunnel
                    "Avenue of the Americas"
                    cobbled stones/   din   of rubber
                    of tin
to the truck graveyard
line-up of Boston Blackie nights/   deserted
right here model "T" & tomahawk
                    sometimes late in silent din of night
                    I hear
                    bagpipes/   death march
                        music of ago/   kennedy

gretsch   gretsch tune optical color-jumping gretsch
    Elvin's F-86 Sabre jet/ remember Korea/ Horace Silver
    the fine smooth jackets the colored boys brought back
                blazing the back   —a forgotten flame

[266]

from the far east with 'U.S. Air Force'   a map of Japan
        blazing the back   —a forgotten flame
Elvin tom-tomming
bassing the chest   "E/ gretsch   "J"/ gretsch
                       clashing metal mad
                       tin frantic road of roaring/   gretsch
                       roar

peck morrison
the *bass* player
told me once about a drum set
with a central anchor/   every drum connected
        unable to jump or sway
        drums like the cockpit of a TXF spy plane
        ejaculator seat and all
                              (call up brubecks joe dodge,
                                        al hirt
                    Lester Lanin et al)

pilot conflict
and the man elvin behind the baptismal tubs
that leap like cannons   to the slashing sound of knives
black elvin knows so well
the knives the Daily News displays along with the photo
of a grinning award-winning cop
the kind of knives elvin talks about
downtown by the water
and uptown
near the park.

Pentecostal Sunday
A Song of Power

            (*It aint the father*
            It aint the son
            Its the holy ghost
            yall)

they boys from philadelphia
calling
      our lady St. Guadalupe
      Saint Martin
      Saint Expedite
           do it now!

he was cripple in the aisle
walking with a cane
the preacher broke his cane
the preacher spit fire on the man
the man burn up
the sisters sang
the music played
the man danced in the aisle
                HOW MANY PEOPLE HERE
                SAW GOD!
                LIFT THIS MAN UP OFF HIS
                CANE!

PENTECOSTAL Sunday
north africa to rome
en route a donkey and a coffin
within
the original christian church
the original
christian ritual
the holy ghost
the holy spirit
        within the spirit in the dance
        within the spirit in the dance
        in the getting of the spirit
        in the body of the dancer
        in the sweat gyrations head falling off
        heat body sweat power of the atom
        grows a breast back in Spanish Harlem
power to drink blood and whiskey mixed
power to handle snakes

power to be what you want to be
the spirit on the temple floor
writhing and screaming
jumping and shouting
getting happy
the spirits have come
doing the jackleo and the boogaloo

fear no fear in memphis
fear no fear in dallas
fear no fear in atlanta
fear no fear in the original christian church
north africa and reverend ike
glory glory
        he say
             put your hand on the radio
               repeat after me

    it cost money to be on the air
    but everybody got something
    and it took sacrifice to get it

yusef rahman say /"yeah them preachers talking bout the
                  real thing when Rev. Ike say put God on
                  the spot when you in trouble he's saying
                  put yourself yusef on the spot. Put God
                  on the spot, he'll surely get you out.
                  Can't run away. Got to deal with it. Let
                  God get you
                  out. Put God on the spot for you."

the ritual is black
the ritual is in the storefront temple
on the corner
the drum and organ the guitar and tambourine
glory glory glory

bid the preacher to teach
cause the shit is deep

baptist preacher
man of god
strong man of the tongue and heart
ptah of egypt lay source to osiris
the corn in earth heart
next to the water
the river spirits/ good people
the crossing over
a wash basin and wooden raft
take me over
dance upon Nile Delta
isis mourning.

SONIA SANCHEZ

poem at thirty

it is midnight
no magical bewitching
hour for me
i know only that
i am here waiting
remembering that
once as a child
i walked two
miles in my sleep.
did i know
then where i
was going?
traveling. i'm
always traveling.
i want to tell
you about me
about nights on a
brown couch when
i wrapped my
bones in lint and
refused to move.
no one touches
me anymore.
father do not
send me out
among strangers.
you you black man
stretching scraping
the mold from your body.
here is my hand.
i am not afraid
of the night.

to Blk/record/buyers

don't play me no
righteous bros.
           white people
ain't rt bout nothing
no mo.
       don't tell me bout
foreign dudes
         cuz no blk/
people are grooving on a
sunday afternoon.
           they either
making out/
       signifying/
          drinking/
making molotov cocktails/
           stealing
or rather more taking their goods
from the honky thieves who
ain't hung up
       on no pacifist/jesus/
         cross/   but.
play blk/songs
      to drown out the
shit/screams of honkies.   AAAH.
AAAH. AAAH. yeah.   brothers.
   andmanymoretogo.

to CHucK

i'm gonna write me
  a poem like
         e. e.
    cum
       mings to
         day. a
bout you
        mov
ing iNsIdE
       me touc
hing my vis
      cera un
    til i turn
in
  side out. i'
       m
go
  n n
    a sc
    rew
  u on   pap   er
cuz u
    3
    0
    0
    0
  mi
    awayfromme
my   MAN
   ca
   re
   ss my br

                    ea
            sts   my
                bl
                    ack

ass
    rul
            ED   on   these
lin
    es.   they
                        yours
yeah.
        imgonnawritemea
pOeM
            like
                    e.
E.   cu
            MmIn
        gS   to
                    day   cuz
heknewallabout
                scr
                    EW
ing
on   WH
                    ite   pa   per.

a/coltrane/poem

            my favorite things
                        is u/blowen
                                    yo/favorite/things.
            stretchen the mind
                        till it bursts past the con/fines of
            solo/en melodies.

[*274*]

                              to the manv solos
        of the
              mind/spirit.
                              are u sleepen   (to be
                              are u sleepen   sung
                              brotha john   softly)
                              brotha john
                                    where u have gone to.
                              no mornin bells
                              are ringen here. only the quiet
        aftermath of assassinations.
                              but i saw yo/murder/
        the massacre
                      of all blk/musicians. planned
        in advance.
                      yrs befo u blew away our passsst
            and showed us our futureeeeee
        screech   screeech   screeeeech   screeech
        a/love/supreme. alovesupreme a lovesupreme.
        A LOVE SUPREME
scrEEEccCHHHHH screeeeEEECHHHHHHH
        sCReeeEEECHHHHHH SCREEEECCCCHHHH
        SCREEEEEEEECCCHHHHHHHHHHHH
        a lovesupremealovesupremealovesupreme for our blk
        people.
              BRING IN THE WITE/MOTHA/fuckas
              ALL THE MILLIONAIRES/BANKERS/ol
        MAIN/LINE/ASS/RISTOCRATS (ALL
        THEM SO-CALLED BEAUTIFUL
        PEOPLE)
              WHO HAVE KILLED
        WILL CONTINUE TO
                      KILL US WITH
        THEY CAPITALISM/18% OWNERSHIP
        OF THE WORLD.
                      YEH. U RIGHT
        THERE. U ROCKEFELLERS. MELLONS

VANDERBILTS
            FORDS.
                    yeh.
GITem.
      PUSHem/PUNCHem/STOMPem. THEN
LIGHT A FIRE TO
                THEY pilgrim asses.
TEAROUT THEY eyes.
                    STRETCH they necks
till no mo
            raunchy sounds of MURDER/
POVERTY/STARVATION
                        come from they
throats.
screeeeeeeeeeeeeeeeeCHHHHHHHHHHH
SCREEEEEEEEEEEEEEECHHHHHHHHHH
screeEEEEEEEEEEEEEEEEEEEEEEEE
EECCCCHHHHHHH
SCREEEEEEEEEEEEEEEEEEEEEEEEEEEEEEE
      EEEEEECHHHHHHHHHH
BRING IN THE WITE/LIBERALS ON THE SOLO
SOUND OF YO/FIGHT IS MY FIGHT
                        SAXOPHONE.
                            TORTURE
THEM FIRST AS THEY HAVE
                    TORTURED US WITH
PROMISES/
        PROMISES. IN WITE/AMURICA. WHEN
ALL THEY WUZ DOEN
                WAS HAVEN FUN WITH THEY
ORGIASTIC DREAMS OF BLKNESS.
                        (JUST SOME MO
CRACKERS FUCKEN OVER OUR MINDS.)
                        MAKE THEM
SCREEEEEEAM
            FORGIVE ME.   IN SWAHILI.
DON'T ACCEPT NO MEA CULPAS.

                              DON'T WANT TO
                              HEAR
BOUT NO EUROPEAN FOR/GIVE/NESS.
DEADDYINDEADDYINDEADDYINWITEWESTERN
                    SHITTTTTT

(softly   da-dum-da da da da da da da da da/da-dum-da
till it   da da da da da da da da da
builds   da-dum- da da da
up)   da-dum. da. da. da. this is a part of my
             favorite things.
             da dum da da da da da da
             da da da da
             da dum da da da da da da
             da da da da
                 da dum da da da da
                 da dum da da da da — — — — —
(to be   rise up blk/people
sung   de dum da da da da
slowly   move straight in yo/blkness
to tune   da dum da da da da
of my   step over the wite/ness
favorite   that is yesssss terrrrrr day
things.)   weeeeeeee are toooooooday.
(f   da dum
a   da da da (stomp, stomp) da da da
s   da dum
t   da da da (stomp, stomp) da da da
e   da dum
r)   da da da (stomp)   da da da dum (stomp)
             weeeeeeeee (stomp)
                 areeeeeeeee (stomp)
                         areeeeeeeee (stomp, stomp)
             tooooooday   (stomp.
                 day   stomp.
                 day   stomp.
                 day   stomp.
                 day   stomp!)

                                              [277]

(soft   rise up blk/people. rise up blk/people
chant)   RISE. & BE. what u can.
           MUST BE.BE.BE.BE.BE.BE.BE-E-E-E-
                      BE-E-E-E-E-
                  yeh. john coltrane.
my favorite things is u.
                          showen us life/
                                    liven.
a love supreme.
                 for each
           other
         if we just
      lissssssSSSTEN.

NIKKI GIOVANNI

Reflections on April 4, 1968

What can I, a poor Black woman, do to destroy america?
This is a question, with appropriate variations, being asked
in every Black heart. There is one answer—I can kill. There
is one compromise—I can protect those who kill. There is
one cop-out—I can encourage others to kill. There are no
other ways.

The assassination of Martin Luther King is an act of war.
President johnson, your friendly uncandidate, has declared
war on Black people. He is not making any distinction be-
tween us and negroes. The question—does it have rhythm?
The answer—yes. The response—kill it. They have been
known to shoot at the wind and violate the earth's gravity
for these very reasons.

Obviously the first step toward peace is the removal of at
least two fingers, and most probably three, from both hands
of all white people. Fingers that are not controlled must be
removed. This is the first step toward a true and lasting
peace. We would also suggest blinding or the removal of
at least two eyes from one of the heads of all albino freaks.

And some honkie asked about the reaction? What do you
people want? Isn't it enough that you killed him? You want
to tell me how to mourn? You want to determine and qualify
how I, a lover, should respond to the death of my beloved?

May he rest in peace. May his blood choke the life from
ten hundred million whites. May the warriors in the streets
go ever forth into the stores for guns and tv's, for whatever
makes them happy (for only a happy people make successful
Revolution) and this day begin the Black Revolution.

[279]

How can one hundred and fifty policemen allow a man to be shot? Police were seen coming from the direction of the shots. And there was no conspiracy? Just as there was no violent reaction to his death. And no city official regretted his death but only that it occurred in Memphis. We heard similar statements from Dallas—this country has too many large Southern cities.

Do not be fooled, Black people. Johnson's footprints are the footprints of death. He came in on a death, he is presiding over a death and his own death should take him out. Let us pray for the whole state of Christ's church.

Zeus has wrestled the Black Madonna and he is down for the count. Intonations to nadinolia gods and a slain honkie will not overcome. Let america's baptism be the fire this time. Any comic book can tell you if you fill a room with combustible materials then close it up tight it will catch fire. This is a thirsty fire they have created. It will not be squelched until it destroys them. Such is the nature of revolution.

America has called itself the promised land—and themselves God's chosen people. This is where we come in, Black people. God's chosen people have always had to suffer—to endure—to overcome. We have suffered and america has been rewarded. This is a foul equation. We must now seek our reward. God will not love us unless we share with others our suffering. Precious Lord—Take Our Hands—Lead Us On.

Revolutionary Music

you've just got to dig sly
and the family stone
damn the words
you gonna be dancing to the music

james brown can go to
viet nam
or sing about whatever he
has to
since he already told
the honkie
"although you happy you better try
to get along
money won't change you
but time is taking you on"
not to mention
doing a whole
song they can't even snap
their fingers to
"good god! ugh!"
talking bout
"i got the feeling baby i got the feeling"
and "hey everybody let me tell you the news"
martha and the vandellas dancing in the streets
while shorty long is functioning at that junction
yeah we hip to that
aretha said they better
think
but she already said
"ain't no way to love you"
(and you know she wasn't talking to us)
and dig the o'jays asking "must i always be a stand in
for love"
i mean they say "i'm a fool for being myself"

While the mighty mighty impressions have told the
world
for once and for all
"We're a Winner"
even our names—le roi has said—are together
impressions
temptations
supremes

delfonics
miracles
intruders (i mean intruders?)
not beatles and animals and white bad things like
young rascals and shit
we be digging all
our revolutionary music consciously or un
cause sam cooke said "a change is gonna come"

AUDRE LORDE

Naturally

Since Naturally Black is Naturally Beautiful
I must be proud
And, naturally
Black and
Beautiful
Who always was a trifle
Yellow
And plain, though proud,
Before.

Now I've given up pomades
Having spent the summer sunning
And feeling naturally free
   (if I die of skin cancer
   oh well—one less
   black and beautiful me)
Yet no agency spends millions
To prevent my summer tanning
And who trembles nightly
With the fear of their lily cities being swallowed
By a summer ocean of naturally woolly hair?

But I've bought my can of
Natural Hair Spray
Made and marketed in Watts
Still thinking more
Proud beautiful Black women
Could better make and use
Black bread.

Coal

Is the total black, being spoken
From the earth's inside.
There are many kinds of open.
How a diamond comes into a knot of flame
How a sound comes into a word, colored
By who pays what for speaking.

Some words are open
Like a diamond on glass windows
Singing out within the crash of passing sun
Then there are words like stapled wagers
In a perforated book—buy and sign and tear apart—
And come whatever wills all chances
The stub remains
An ill-pulled tooth with a ragged edge.
Some words live in my throat
Breeding like adders. Others know sun
Seeking like gypsies over my tongue
To explode through my lips
Like young sparrows bursting from shell.
Some words
Bedevil me.

Love is a word another kind of open—
As a diamond comes into a knot of flame
I am black because I come from the earth's inside
Take my word for jewel in your open light.

Father Son and Holy Ghost

I have not ever seen my father's grave.
Not that his judgment eyes have been forgotten
Nor his great hands print
On our evening doorknobs
One half turn each night and he would come
Misty from the world's business
Massive and silent as the whole day's wish, ready
To re-define each of our shapes—
But that now the evening doorknobs
Wait, and do not recognize us as we pass.

Each week a different woman
Regular as his one quick glass each evening—
Pulls up the grass his stillness grows
Calling it weed. Each week
A different woman has my mother's face
And he, who time has
Changeless
Must be amazed, who knew and loved but one.

My father died in silence, loving creation
And well-defined response.
He lived still judgments on familiar things
And died, knowing a January fifteenth that year me.

Lest I go into dust
I have not ever seen my father's grave.

JAY WRIGHT

Death as History

I

They are all dying,
all the ones who make
living worth the price,
and there is hardly time
to lament the passing
of their historical necessity.
Young poets sit in their rooms
like perverted Penelopes,
unraveling everything,
kicking the threads
into the wind,
and I stop,
woolly-eyed,
trying to record
this peculiar American game.
But they are dying,
the living ones,
and I am sapped of all resolve,
fleeced, finally, of the skill
to live among these others.
To be charged with so much living
is such an improbability,
to be improbable about living
is such a charge to hold
against oneself,
against those who are dying.

II

Dropping his history books,
a young man, lined against the horizon

like an exclamation point with nothing to assert,
stumbles into the dance.
The dancers go round and round
like drones on an unhappy flight.
They look to him for another possibility.
They hum.
They plead.
They circle him with outstretched hands.
They offer him their own salvation.
And he moves forward with a rose.
All that long search
to bring back death.
Who wants that old mystery?

III

But still there is the probable.
And even in Madrid
the golden ages settle
in their sturdy coffins.
Oh, you can say that there
where the olive trees burst up
through the asphalt cells,
where well-endowed bulls butt
the tail-end of tame Sundays,
and coquettish river flings
its hips at the cattle-mouthed mountains.
Everything there is an imitation.
The girls always advance on the square,
repeating the vital moments,
needing no bookish priests
to redeem that dance.
And it is always the credible dance.

IV

It is always like the beginning.
It is always having the egg
and seven circles,

always casting about in the wind
on that particular spot;
it is that African myth
we use to challenge death.
What we learn is that
death is not complete in itself,
only the final going from self to self.

V

And death is the reason
to begin again, without letting go.
And who can lament
such historical necessity?
If they are all dying,
the living ones,
they charge us with the improbable.

A Plea for the Politic Man
(For Malcolm)

Here is what you saw,
all this distended grief,
the world split up and curved
back on its boweled order,
an impolitic people gnawing
its grizzled skulls,
all these poets rummaging
through their own discontent.
Senators gag and girdle
the devastating ghettos.
Old oppressions come back as law.
Governors pop up in the debris,
new heroes flying at their sides,
to deal with the politic demands.

Unskilled, unslung,
I run from the city I love
like a particle knocking
in a familiar chamber.
I wanted something to discover.
But what is here?

We turn back to create
what we have never really known,
what we fear we may not learn,
feeling safe in the human ignorance
of all that's human,
uncertain, even, of the symbols
of our making,
not caring to acknowledge our politic grace.

The frenzied, idiotic world
will nourish our laments,
and you will turn there, sadly,
to face your politic death.

LARRY NEAL

Don't Say Goodbye to the Pork-Pie Hat
(For Langston Hughes)

Don't say goodbye to the pork-pie hat that rolled along on
  padded shoulders,
                    that swang be-hop phrases
                    in Minton's jelly-roll dreams.
don't say goodbye to hip hats tilted in the style of a soulful era,
the pork-pie hat that Lester dug,
swirling in the sound of sun saxes,
repeating phrase on phrase, repeating bluely
as hi-hat cymbals crash and trumpets scream while
musicians move in and out of this gloom; the pork-pie hat
  reigns supreme,
the elegance of style
gleaned from the city's underbelly.
                    tonal memories
                    tonal memories
of salt-peanuts and hot house birds. the pork-pie hat
                              sees.
And who was the musician who
                blew Bird way by accident, then died, obscure,
an obscene riff repeating lynch scenes?
repeating weird changes. The chorus repeats itself also, the
  horns slide
from note to note in blue, in blue streaks of mad wisdom;
blues notes
coiling around
the pork-pie hat and the drum-dancing hips defying the
  sanctity of white
America.
and who was the trumpet player in that small town in Kansas
  who

begged to sit in,
blew a chorus, then fainted dead on the bandstand?
blew you away.
that same musician resurrected himself in Philly at the Blue
    Note Cafe
                        Ridge Avenue and 16th St.
after the third set, had him an old horn and was wearing the
    pork-pie
                        hat.
    asn't he familiar? didn't you think that you were seeing a
    ghost?
and didn't the pork-pie hat leave Minton's
                        for 52nd St?
and didn't it later make it to Paris where they dug him too?
and didn't the pork-pie buy Bird a meal in '35
when said musician was kicked out of the High-Hat (18th &
    South)
                                        for blowing
strange changes?

I saw the pork-pie hat skimming the horizon
                    flashing bluegreenyellowlights
he was blowing black stars
and
weird looneymoon changes and chords were wrapped around
    him
                                        and he was flying
fast, zipping past note, past sound into cosmic silence.
Caresses flowed from the voice in the horn in the blue
of the yellow whiskey room where hustlers
with big coats and fly sisters moved; finger popping while
                    tearing at chicken and waffles—
the pork-pie hat loomed specter like, a vision for the world,
dressed in a camel hair coat, shiny knob toe shoes, sporting
a hip pin stripe suit with pants pressed razor sharp, caressing
    his horn
            baby-like.

And who was the bitch in the bar in Boston who kept trying
    to make it
with the pork-pie hat while it fingered for the changes
on Dewey Square? She almost make you blow your cool.
you did blow your cool, 'cause on the side I got you hollered
shut-up across that slick white boy's
tape recorder. Yeah the one who copped your music & made
some fat money after you died. didn't you
                        blow your cool?
and didn't you almost lose your pork-pie hat behind all that
    shit?
Who was the ofay chick that followed the group
                        from Boston to Philly
                        from New York to Washington
                        from Chicago to Kansas City
                        was that Backstage Sally?
or was Backstage Sally a blue-voiced soul sister who lived
                        on Brown street in Philly.
who dug you, who fed you cold nights with soul food
and soul-body. was that Backstage Sally?
Sounds drift above the cities of Black America;
all over America black musicians are putting
on the pork-pie hat again, picking up their axes,
preparing to blow away the white dream. you can
hear them screeching love in rolling sheets of sound;
with movement and rhythm recreating themselves and the
    world;
sounds splintering the deepest regions of the spiritual
    universe—
crisp and moaning voices leaping in the horns of destruction,
blowing doom and death to all who have no use for the Spirit.
don't say goodbye to the pork-pie hat, it lives. Yeah . . .

Lester lives and leaps
Delancey's dilemma is over
Bird lives
Lady lives

Eric stands next to me
while I finger the afro-horn
Bird lives
Lady lives
Lester leaps in every night
Tad's delight
is mine now
Dinah knows
Fats and Wardell blow fours
Dinah knows
Richie knows
that Bud is Buddha
that Bird is Shango
that Jelly Roll dug ju-ju
and Lester lives
in Ornette's leaping
the blues live
we live. live
spirit lives. the sound
lives bluebirdlives
lives and leaps. dig
the bluevoices
dig the pork pie dig
the spirit in Sun Ra's sound. dig
spirit lives in sound
lives sound spirit
sound lives in spirit
spirit lives in sound. blow.
spirit lives
spirit lives
spirit lives
SPIRIT . . . . . ! ! ! ! . . . . . SWHEEEEEET ! ! ! !
   Take it
      again, this time from the chorus

Kuntu

I am descended from Drum
I am descended from Drum
from that which first formed
from that which first formed
descended from Drum.
The First that formed
The First that formed
am from the first that formed
the pulse that formed
the pulse that formed
the pulse that formed the Word
the pulse that formed the Word
and the Word informing the Universe
and the Word informing the Universe
and the Word informing the pulse
Word and pulse and Universe
Word and pulse and Universe
The First that formed to link, to link
Word and Act
to link Word and Substance
to link Word and desire.

II
Word, Act, and Universe
the First form out of the Earth
Drum's Earth and Black Earth Faces
Drum's Song and Black Earth Song
Drum's first Song in the Black of Olorun—the Universe.
in Olorum the Universe, I formed
the Word and the Earth and linked them in the Dance.
the first form was formless sound

the first Word was Drum's word
am descended from Drum
The Drum's words informed us, giving us flesh,
and flesh shaped the Word; I say and flesh
shaped the Word, linked the Song, linked the Earth to Sky.

No wonder we float so lightly in Summer
we float high, drifting on the rhythms of Drum,
do air-dances O so lightly,
the Drum informing our lives, our wars.

III
Drum was there on the Armistad.
Drum was there in Jamestown.
Drum was there in Watts.
Drum was there in Newark.
Drum was there in Detroit
behind the crackle of ghetto fires,
He informed the flames
pushing the rhythms,
sending us back into our own time, our most powerful time
our time
our time
our time
back into most powerful time
Drum running down some mean shit
to all the Brothers and Sisters
all the Brothers and Sisters
listening to Drum, my Old Man.

Morning Raga for Malcolm

I

O Allah . . . receive him, a morning god
bursting springly in ascendant
colors of the sun—a crescent sword slices
the shrill morning raga; in the place
of his hajih the voice tears at blood
streaked faces. dispossessed eyes flash at
the truth brilliantly black.
a gnawing, pounding skin ripping voice
that does not back down—O Allah, great Spirit One
receive the gritting teeth, the bursting balls,
mangled bodies, ripped out guts spewed from piss pot
to armchair deaths. . . .
receive the unfulfilled, the unavenged; these hordes.
one expanded nigger face explodes in time, screaming
ghostly scorching everything in sight—Great Spirit One.

II

I awake to see my ears and arms flying into space
to feel my legs violently crack as I stretch
for another planet: blue free voice. see free voices
    spin bluely.
spin bluely spin. spin blood hopes spin. spin resurrected
    god.

I now calm airily float
lift my spirit—Allah you
am me. space undulates.
under me, space, to my sides
and under me nothing
I now calm airily float

LEBERT BETHUNE

A Juju of My Own

To make a Juju of my own
For I was tired of strange ghosts
Whose cool bones
Lived on the green furnace of my blood
Was always my destiny
So she warned me—my grandmother,
And now and now
When I kindle again her small eyes with their quick
   lights
Darting ancient love into my infancy
And when I break through to her easy voice
That voice like the pliant red clay she baked
She sings the only lullaby she sang me

"Me no care fe Bakra whip
Me no care fe fum-fum
Come Juju come"

So I am fashioning this thing
My own Juju
Out of her life and our desire
Out of an old black love
I am baking my destiny to a lullaby—

"Me no care fe Bakra whip
Me no care fe fum-fum
Come Juju come . . ."

Black Fire

Because your slender rhythms
Which I love to sing
Float from the well of blood that holds our time
Because your touch can touch my own cry
Where the black jewel of my need is locked away
alone
Because you move as you move to the pulse
Of my swift trembling dance
I want to turn my love into a burning spear
And mark the world
With black fire.

The Nature of . . .

Black is my color . . .
The gleaming song of ebony and blood
That warms the rivers of the universe
Belongs to me

Black is my color . . .
Those cries,
The agony of thunder, the joy-scream
At the black sight beyond sight
Belongs to me

Black is my color . . .
The force that swarms the sky
At the apogee of a strange night

Engulfing the white moon
Belongs to me

Black is my color . . .
The tone within the deepest reaches of the sea
That feeds the light that frees the light
Belongs to me . . .

And
At the shuddering axis of my love
The point of life and life
Black is the color of reality
Black is my color.

WALTER DANCY

Chinese River Prophet Song

Over the Yellow River and Canton
and the muddy Ganges
Times will like Gandhi's be gone over to
ideas with condition red

ideas live
echoing for centuries
now they too are subject to sudden death

Religion will swell the awing waters
of the world when only one nation
rules
When only one nation can be right and
white
then the world will glow with atomic
light to make bright the genocidal night
to teach those once and for all in darkness

Frail we cringe before Dante's Italic vision
its cineramic focus and panavision scale
swells brain-mind to deluxe colored
shell of skull holding vision and
an incision in our dreams heal
not with the words of the drunk
surgeon leader
dipping and ripping brains bathed in
the gun fluids of war

Not ready for peace
the lump of mud in our souls
resists reason competing with screaming howls

a monkey in tuxedo with tails
without a tail
we tear ourselves away from ideals
slobbering spit-mouths of threats

Like ocean spray mist flying our
hope on the wind blowing from the sea side
at high tide all is muggy and hot with fear
are we ill?

Or is the pride of reckoning for ourselves real?

The sun set sinking in the old man's eyes
the yellow burns with a tinge of sun-red glow

The child smiles before the coming locusts
seventeen years hungry
thinking them pretty in
the wild swaying wheat

Metaphors devour reality making real the unseen
but dimly felt-making felt in full the threshold
touch the floor never permanent the volcano's
rumbling unceasing

Dante raves under our quivering minds
China's earth is yellow underfoot.

The Metaphorical Egress

The metaphor writhes and twists seeking some meaning
in its dance around the mind
and we find hanging loose
the choices to choose or lose the pungency
of the words or fall

fumbling
after
connotations
and bruise our ankles on denotations
only
to lose the piont
as our hearts become simply
blood pumps and our brains cushions
to protect our skulls from content
a metaphor is writhing struggling to be born
foetal, kicking and wanting to break the sac
wanting to breathe
into the world
a wail
singing:

Tired am I from struggle's womb
gloom dooms me to cool tears
filling the pools of my sorrow
tomorrow is the year of my sun
today is the year peace flew away in the beak of an eagle
yesterday my existence was a rehearsal of a dream
waking my sorrow gains my vision of joy
weeds choke the meadowlark destroying my youth.

This the Poet as I See

A poet is a mind sailor soul dweller and teller of heartbeats.
The infinite is the galaxies of his pulse and his soul is a
chamber orchestra of endless incantations. He is a voyager on
an endless journey as far as the mind can race on the arrows
of light and the soul can feel like morning glories greeting
the rising sun. The poet is a man of all life like the timeless
Llama of Legend Tibet, he is a listener of voices, a reader of

lips and a vocalist of myriad dreams. He is colors spread like light through a prism and like sand transmuted to silicone glinting of glass. He is a searcher in the mystic deep, an author of the commonplace, an explorer of dim unrealized feeling. This is the way I see the sea and the way to see I with eye beyond infra-red and we all cyclic part of life, life from the widow's kiss to the electron quiver colorless but for the perishing and change. Black is beautiful true like all shades of Nature with potential beauty when the snow-blind melt from our eyes. A verse framer or rime dodger when the subject calls for blank conversing he is a maker of soul magic and a stroker of the mysterious cat who lives in our dreamy dark called living. A poet I see must be the me in all of we and nature and life eternal screaming and praying and saying-tell it like it is.

ASKIA MUHAMMAD TOURÉ

Extension
(for Imam El Hajj Heshaam Jabeer *
and LeRoi Jones)

We must live again—in our minds.
You know, shed the white plaster of our "negroness"
and let the free licorice oil flow through.
Then we won't need to cloak our poor sterility
with Marxism's dead, jewish robes.
No, BLACKISM: communalism soulism UJAMAA
and all those Ancestral things.
A Blackness so deep that its message lights
the universe with hot vibrations jarring
the minds of men, making them turn back
to the Root, the Primeval things before the West
raised its blue eyes from the Cave.
Brothers and Sisters—Yellow, Brown, and Black—
in robes, with drums and Wisdom, Knowledge and Freedom
Science and Beauty, Love and Truth.
I call them now: AFRICA! INDIA! CHINA! ARABIA!
shed your image of starving masses, sunken eyes,
bloated bellies, skinny limbs.
Take up the call of your Ancestors; FEEL
their cries within your bones, your blood,
within your hearts.
Smash the blue eyes in your brains, the white plaster
clogging your mental pores.
Let the Oil of Spirit, Ancient Spirit, flow
over Europe over America over Canada over Australia
over South Africa, let it flow—the Spirit flow;

* Sheik Imam Hajj Heshaam Jabeer, brilliant young spiritual leader and advisor to LeRoi Jones, who also preached the funeral of El Hajj Malik El Shabbazz (Br. Malcolm X).

[*304*]

light the Oil, watch it burn the cities down.
BROTHERS: Fools, you can't beat the Devil at his game.
You are men of the Spirit—earth-gods;
reclaim your thrones!
Let Eternal Spirit live again!
Let it grab the mechanical brains, jerk out computer wires,
short-circuit early-warning systems, resurrect
the Living God within the heart.
We in the West—a Lost Nation—are the Seers
of the earth.
S O U L a living Force as Nommo, the Living Word,
feeds us all.
The planet is ours for the taking—Now.
But not on his terms, with his methods; no not
carbon-copy devils: Capitalists, Marxists, Christians,
Materialists, etc.
But a New Thing that's the Oldest Wisdom in the Universe.
A New Thing bursting out of Black saxaphones like
Coltrane, Sun Ra, Pharoah, and all Black spiritual men.
RESURRECT REBIRTH REVERT EVOL-UTION is the
    key
as well as REVOL-UTION, remember this.

And our Sons and Daughters will bless us
and praise our names to Eternal Heaven after
the closing of our eyes.
And the Men of Tomorrow will sing of our exploits
in the Golden Ages yet to come:
The Epic of Man, Earth-god, come again.
*Khalifa * of the planet—Red and Yellow,*
Brown and Black—filled with Righteousness,
Truth and Love (a Love so deep it sweeps, like a
Moorish scimitar † through blue-eyed decadence,
slitting evil throats   taking heads, pale devils
dying everywhere—Rosemary's Baby the first to go!)

* "Khalifa," Arabic for Caliph or Supreme Ruler.
† "Scimitar," a short, curved sword used by Muslims.

When we release the Black Spiritual Oil within our Minds,
Rome will fall—burning Rome: the Pope sticky in Black
Oil, Red Devil robes greasy, catching fire: a flaming
scarecrow beneath the Crescent Moon.

And all around us singing—the whole Earth singing
BROTHERS, it is our Ancestors singing:
All the raped millions, all the plundered virgins—
Red, Yellow, Brown, Black—all the tortured mothers,
fallen warriors, singing through the Earth,
blessing our feet.
The Black Earth singing as flowers burst into bloom,
and unpolluted streams gurgle sweetly again, while God
reigns within our righteous hearts.
The TRUTH the TRUTH: Islam in our women's eyes,
in their sweet souls, flowing robes—and the Earth
one large community with open doors open minds open
hearts: Souls stretching forth into the Universe.
I S L A M:
This is my Vision, my Song of Man;
this is my legacy for Tariq, my son, and
'Roi's Obaligi, Joe's Abina, Max's Nefertiti—
I S L A M in all our children and people:
our Seed and Bloodlines flowing down the River of Time.

Let the Ritual begin:
Sun Ra, Pharoah, Coltrane, Milford tune up your Afro-horns;
let the Song begin, the Wild Song of the Black Heart:
E X T E N S I O N over the crumbling ghettoes, riding
the deep, ominous night—the Crescent Moon, Evening Star;
the crumbling ghettoes exploding exploding: BAROOM,
    BAROOM!
(A Nation rising in Midnight Robes; let it rise, *Let the
Black Nation Rise!*) E X T E N S I O N let the music flow
E X T E N S I O N and ten thousand Muslim Angels shall
light our way through the burning, bloody Night until
the Trumpets of the Fiery Dawn. ALLHUMDULILLAH!!

W. KEORAPETSE KGOSITSILE

My Name Is Afrika

All the things come to pass
when they do, if they do
All things come to their end
when they do, as they do
so will the day of the stench of oppression
leaving nothing but the lingering
taste of particles of hatred
woven around the tropical sun
while in the belly of the night
drums roll and peal a monumental song . . .
To every birth its blood
All things come to pass
when they do
We are the gods of our day and us
Panthers with claws of fire
And songs of love for the newly born
There will be ruins in Zimbabwe for real
Didn't Rap say,
They used to call it Detroit
And now they call it Destroyed!
To every birth its pain
All else is death or life

Vector or Legacy

Some day soon, someday soon . . .
we forever say
ribs clear as guitar strings to strike the bloodsong

and the children more rib than child
ribs clear as guitar strings to strike the bloodsong
their smiles butchered to death long
before they meander out of their mother's womb
keep glistening in the sun with sweat
of hopeless search for crumbs
any minute and every minute
they scramble for orange peel
from garbage pail or sometimes
a whole rotten banana from some
fat-bellied bastard's trash can
every minute and any minute they are here
swayed by hunger pangs from garbage pail
to garbage pail defying death by malnutrition
they are here the unnourished ones
to nourish your desire
the pangs in fleshless ribs
clearer than glib verse or song ask now
do you still say some day . . .

Origins (for melba)

deep in your cheeks
your specific laughter owns
all things south of the ghosts
we once were.   straight ahead
the memory beckons from the future
You and I a tribe of colors
this song that dance
godlike rhythms to birth
footsteps of memory
the very soul aspires to.   songs
of origins songs of constant beginnings
what is this thing called
love

BETTY GATES

Mamma Settles the Dropout Problem

Lawd, Son, whut um go do with you?
You makes me so mad
I don' know whut to do!
You thinks you's a man
And I hope one day you'll be,
But you got 'bout enuff
Sense to stuff a skinny flea!
Done worked myself until
Um nelly 'bout dead
So as you can go to school
An' git sumthin in yo head,
An' you come tellin me
That you gon' quit
Cause they aint got
Whut you wanna git.
Well, they sho is got
Much mo'n you
An' if you don' git it
Dis whut um go do:
Um goin' up side yo head
Wit my big fiss
An' when I swings
I don' aim to miss!
I done talked an' talked
Tell my face is blue,
Still I cain' talk
No sense in you.
Talkin' bout you
So proud you black,
If you wuz you'd
Know how to ack!

A heap a folks
Done went through hell,
Marchin' in the streets
An' goin' to jail;
An' some mighty good folks
Is laying up dead
Jes so you can
Fill yo empty head.
Now, you gon' stop
Yo ackin lak a fool!
You git yo books
An' you git back to school!

KARL CARTER

Heroes

Sometimes I sit up at night
Listening to myself cry
My sobs for those we lost
In the battle with the beast,
And thoughts flash my mind
Realizing that I am somewhere between battles
Counting those we lost;
> Rap five years in the internal concentration
> camps,
> Cleve five years in the belly of the beast,
> Stokely silenced by the belchings of racism,
> Dan Massey paralyzed by a racist cop's shot
> gun blast in the back in Nashville,
> Malcolm by an assassin's bullet
> Martin the same
Places come back like shadow figures upon a darkened
> stage and bodies lie strewn there
> soaking the ground red with their blood;
> Orangeburg, Jackson, Memphis,
> New York, Nashville,
The funeral pyres of an era breathe forth their stench
And I sit lost myself weeping inwardly
Riding somewhere in my mind with Eldridge Cleaver
Through the streets of Nashville on an April night
During a riot

Roots

The memories of my fathers
Whisper in my ears
        as the images
Of days gone before I was born
Unfold in stories told
        by my grandmother.
Songs sung on the backporch
        in the evening sun
"Lor' I'm gonna
        lay dis burdin down
        lay dis burdin down"
"Woke up dis
        mornin' wid
           Jesus
             on my min"
"Oh, yes, lor' Jesus on my min"
        "Jesus on my min"
All on the backporch somewhere
        in the summer
When I was small.

LILLIE KATE WALKER BENITEZ

Sectional Touchstone

And so they came. Hundreds and hundreds and hundreds and
        hundreds of them marching and marching,
        Mourning as they moved, mourning as they
        came.

And a threaded shrill wove the air
        "Oh mercy, mercy, take me in the stead,"
        and
        they kept marching, marching, and mourn-
        ing
        as they came.

Fearful thoughts, gruesome thoughts, thoughts of
        Purgation, desperation, and termination,
        choked them as they kept marching, march-
        ing,
        Marching and mourning as they came.

Some fell down, some died, some stopped to be carried on,
        But they kept marching, they kept marching
        and mourning as they came.

As the site drew near, the pace stunted, but they kept
        Marching and mourning as they came.
        Children were wailing, mothers were
        marching
        And mourning as they came.

Stop, children, your oral fear! Knead yourself see and feel
        This dirge that is to carry sterile to your
        Offspring. Mourning as they came.

Fabricate those men to staunch the flame and bleach their
        Bones in the savour of dead
        Mothers and children, strap them down
        To drink the smoke and march and mourn,
        march and mourn as you come, march and
        mourn as you come.

Hundreds and hundreds and hundreds and hundreds,
        Prosper my door with your entrails,
        Open up, puke every single instance of
        Your functions into the smolder of one
        man, men, one woman, women, one child,
        children.

Demurring mother cribbed her baby in her arms and
        choked it, bemourning, "This death, you
        will not give."

Lamenting woman, cut her baby into pieces and ate it,
        Wailing, "It sucked my body until it swelled
        me with writhing and burst forth from a
        vacuum as
        A rain drop pierces the surface of a spewing
        sea.
        Since that day . . . (cries out) I have been
        Hungry, hungry to this day of marching,
        mourning, marching and mourning, and
          mourning
        as they came.

Oh, God, oh dear God, can not some mirage pluck out the
        Eyes and devour the shade of blindness to
        Save this marching and mourning, march-
          ing
        and mourning, and, mourning as they came.
        Can not one more thread of mercy be
        slithered away to yoke this mourning,

marching kindling to a nemesis due to this
piteous marching and mourning, marching
and mourning, and mourning as they came.

Men, man, women, woman, children, child,
    Move into my open flame,
    Bask in its giant heat, and
    quickened singe!!

DAPHNE DIANE PAGE

Untitled

So
I've found me
at last
I'd been
looking
a long time
in mirrors.
Today by accident
I saw
A black woman in Curl-freed hair
And cameo brooch
Trapped
On the surface
of the sea.

Untitled

I take
my war machine
And fire it
at the Sun.
Everyone becomes black
and defiance ends.

GREGOR HANNIBAL

Untitled

You walk like bells
Clang!   Clang!
Demanding attention.
Clang!   Clang!   Clang!   Clang!
Your bronze dome hides
Your working parts,
And your reverberations
Hold me spellbound
C - l - a - n - g!
Your power is unbearable
Yet I can't stop paying attention,
And my head is ringing, ringing;
Higher, higher, vibrations of joy and pain . . .
C-R-A-C-K . . . !
Clop!   Clop!   Clop!

PAMELA WOODRUFF HILL

Untitled

To smell the stink of rotting
brownstones,
To hear James Brown's raspy
"Cold Sweat,"
And year
        after
               year
watch tired women
force life
        into
           already dead spirits:
Yet
   you will not begrudge me
                  one crumb.

TED HUNT

I Am a Man!

icanseefeelhealthesickandraisethedeadplayballdrinkthree
six-packsstanduplooktomyleftthentomyrightandwalkout
ofthebackdoorbutican'tgetyouwhereiwantogetyoumost.

wheniaminthisconditionyoutalkbigtalklittletalkshorttalk
andahellofalotofnonsenseallforthesakeofsayingnothing . . .
shut-up!listen!

can'tyouhearmescreamingyourname?areyoudeaf?letyour
magicentertheplayofthevalleysandthehillsofyourheart . . .
andlistentotheechoofmyvoiceiamaman.

DONALD L. GRAHAM (DANTE)

April 5th

non-violence is dead
it died last night
last night in color
i saw
Nbc tell me i saw
Abc tell me
the leader has fallen
pale newsmen cried
it seemed last night

Last night i thought
a lamb has fallen as
i heard him cry
aint gonna let no in
junction turn me round
aint gonna let no po
lice dogs turn me round
but I saw three little
girls malcolm X medgar evers
emmett till and the soft
touch I had die last night
from the corner
a white man read martin's
dream
but my sister moaned

Lord strike their ass
for they know what
they do

Poem for Eric Dolphy

Then
>   i was ten and layed in the grass
>   with mattie and let her call me
>   nasty
and snot dripped on the rag
>   then
>   12 with a sling shot for birds
>   i didnt know charlie
>   in three
>   i 15ed my way thru another year
>   chasing foxes and ragging down
>   cause that was a hip thing
and blood dripped on the sheet
>   but 17 years creased my ass before
>   i could ask who's eric

II
>   I didn't know eric
i didn't know i didn't know

you sang for black babies in apartment
buildings, drunks pissing in the halls
and black chicks doing back-bends for
pink men with slimy lips

I didn't know, i didn't know you or malcolm
or patrice or trane or me
had i known
i would have said
scream eric scream
you're a bad muthafucka

soul

coltrane must understand how
i feel when i hear
some un-sunned-be-bop-jazz-man
try

to find the cause of a man's hurt

soul aint nice it's daddy's backache
the blues my mother felt when she
bore me
in a rat-infested-harlem u.s.a.
its . . .
mammas love and daddys hate-
doing it my way
survival motion set to music

. . . We Ain't Got No Time

It finally comes down to
time and love and time and
time . . .

we say "no quick answers"
and fool ourselves with
grease-words sliding
past our inventions intentions, to-
morrows tomorrow and days after
that (we still talking
greasy.)

no tranes here just hunger
sucked faces and googogg
eyeballs swung toward
the sky dancing on
tomorrow and visions of the
promised land
rainbow dreams sparkling
like cheap multicolored jewelry under
Holy marquees and epitaphs

no trains here just
red and white writing
on a blue blackground
and they saying:
no departures from
here(on), just
stiff fingers clutching straw
tickets . . . for blue
suited conductors with
blow torches,
ice edged voices
calling so-called niggers to express cars
enroute to secret ovens and
fat cooks who specialize
in afro stew, black
butt soup and black pickled
privates for snacks
and
conversation pieces

it takes time and time
time and love

t' construct our lives
   toward living
   with each other, with the
   constant struggle for our

sanity
          though we be pushing
          each other and pulling
          grabbing, kicking stabbing
          hogging and killing
          each other
                    to be first in
                    line
                    and first in this
                    or that
it takes love and time
and time
          but.

Untitled

Remember:
          when the door closes you
          in
and I walk out to a battle that
will not bleed our spirit
          I
          wanted this/
this quickening of the heart
and sweat-palm fear
never wanted to forget
that the
          crisis is now, now,
now, now, now, now, pow
          now
          marked presently
by whip-cracks (will always
be a poet won't I) gun-shots (I know
I

wanted
this/
    cold
        death, clutched steel
   against skin
       skin against earth/
       against earth, shadow
       against earth, earth
       against breath and
I'm going out
    to embrace my dream
       I'm a lover
          always was.

ETHERIDGE KNIGHT

The Idea of Ancestry

I

Taped to the wall of my cell are 47 pictures: 47 black
faces: my father, mother, grandmothers (1 dead), grand
fathers (both dead), brothers, sisters, uncles, aunts,
cousins (1st & 2nd), nieces, and nephews. They stare
across the space at me sprawling on my bunk. I know
their dark eyes, they know mine. I know their style,
they know mine. I am all of them, they are all of me;
they are farmers, I am a thief, I am me, they are thee.

I have at one time or another been in love with my mother,
1 grandmother, 2 sisters, 2 aunts (1 went to the asylum),
and 5 cousins. I am now in love with a 7 yr old niece
(she sends me letters written in large block print, and
her picture is the only one that smiles at me).

I have the same name as 1 grandfather, 3 cousins, 3 nephews,
and 1 uncle. The uncle disappeared when he was 15, just took
off and caught a freight (they say). He's discussed each year
when the family has a reunion, he causes uneasiness in
the clan, he is an empty space. My father's mother, who is 93
and who keeps the Family Bible with everybody's birth dates
(and death dates) in it, always mentions him. There is no
place in her Bible for "whereabouts unknown."

II

Each Fall the graves of my grandfathers call me, the brown
hills and red gullies of mississippi send out their electric
messages, galvanizing my genes. Last yr/like a salmon quitting
the cold ocean—leaping and bucking up his birthstream/I
hitchhiked my way from L.A. with 16 caps in my pocket and a

monkey on my back, and I almost kicked it with the kinfolks.
I walked barefooted in my grandmother's backyard/I smelled
    the old
land and the woods/I sipped cornwhiskey from fruit jars with
    the men/
I flirted with the women/I had a ball till the caps ran out
and my habit came down. That night I looked at my grand-
    mother
and split/my guts were screaming for junk/but I was almost
contented/I had almost caught up with me.
    The next day in Memphis I cracked a croaker's crib for a
    fix.

This yr there is a gray stone wall damming my stream, and
    when
the falling leaves stir my genes, I pace my cell or flop on my
    bunk
and stare at 47 black faces across the space. I am all of them,
they are all of me, I am me, they are thee, and I have no sons
to float in the space between.

Hard Rock Returns to Prison from the Hospital for the Criminal Insane

Hard Rock was "known not to take no shit
From nobody," and he had the scars to prove it:
Split purple lips, lumped ears, welts above
His yellow eyes, and one long scar that cut
Across his temple and plowed through a thick
Canopy of kinky hair.

The WORD was that Hard Rock wasn't a mean nigger
Anymore, that the doctors had bored a hole in his head,
Cut out part of his brain, and shot electricity

Through the rest. When they brought Hard Rock back,
Handcuffed and chained, he was turned loose,
Like a freshly gelded stallion, to try his new status.
And we all waited and watched, like indians at a corral,
To see if the WORD was true.

As we waited we wrapped ourselves in the cloak
Of his exploits: "Man, the last time, it took eight
Screws to put him in the Hole." "Yeah, remember when he
Smacked the captain with his dinner tray?" "He set
The record for time in the Hole—67 straight days!"
"Ol Hard Rock! man, that's one crazy nigger."
And then the jewel of a myth that Hard Rock had once bit
A screw on the thumb and poisoned him with syphilitic spit.

The testing came, to see if Hard Rock was really tame.
A hillbilly called him a black son of a bitch
And didn't lose his teeth, a screw who knew Hard Rock
From before shook him down and barked in his face.
And Hard Rock did *nothing*. Just grinned and looked silly,
His eyes empty like knot holes in a fence.

And even after we discovered that it took Hard Rock
Exactly 3 minutes to tell you his first name,
We told ourselves that he had just wised up,
Was being cool; but we could not fool ourselves for long,
And we turned away, our eyes on the ground. Crushed.
He had been our Destroyer, the doer of things
We dreamed of doing but could not bring ourselves to do,
The fears of years, like a biting whip,
Had cut grooves too deeply across our backs.

To Dinah Washington

I have heard your voice floating, royal and real,
Across the dusky neighborhoods,
And the eyes of old men grow bright, remembering;
Children stop their play to listen,
Remembering—though they have never heard you before,
You are familiar to them:
Queen of the Blues, singing an eternal song.

In the scarred booths of Forty-Third street,
"Long Johns" suck in their bellies,
On the brass-studded leather of Elite-town,
Silk-suited Bucks raise their chins . . .

Wherever a man is without a warm woman,
Or a woman without her muscled man,
The eternal song is sung.

Some say you're sleeping.
But I say you're singing.

Unforgettable Queen.

For Langston Hughes

Gone   Gone
    Another weaver of black dreams has gone
we sat in June Bug's pad with the shades drawn
and the air thick with holy smoke, and we heard
the Lady sing Langston before we knew his name.

and when Black Bodies stopped swinging   June
Bug, TG and I went out and swung on some white cats.
now I don't think the Mythmaker meant for us to do *that*
but we didn't know what else to do.
    Gone   Gone
    Another weaver of black dreams has gone

On Universalism

I see no single thread
That binds me one to all;
Why even common dead
Men took the single fall.

No universal laws
Of human misery
Create a common cause
Or common history
That ease black people's pains
Nor break black people's chains.

Dark Prophesy
I sing of Shine

And, yeah, brothers,
while white/america sings about the unsink
able molly brown
(who was hustling the titanic
when it went down)
I sing to thee of Shine
the stoker who was hip
enough to flee the fucking ship

and let the white folks drown
with screams on their lips
(jumped his black ass into the dark sea, Shine did,
broke free from the straining steel).
Yeah, I sing of Shine
and how the millionaire banker stood on the deck
and pulled from his pocket a million dollar check
saying Shine Shine save poor me
and I'll give you all the money a black boy needs—
how Shine looked at the money and then at the sea
and said jump in muthafucka and swim like me—

Shine swam on—Shine swam on—
how the banker's daughter ran naked on the deck
with her pink tits trembling and her pants roun her neck
screaming Shine Shine save poor me
and I'll give you all the cunt a black boy needs—
how Shine said now cunt is good and that's no jive
but you got to swim not fuck to stay alive—
how Shine swam past a preacher afloat on a board
crying save me nigger Shine in the name of the Lord—
how the preacher grabbed Shine's arm and broke his stroke—
how Shine pulled his shank and cut the preacher's throat—
Shine swam on—Shine swam on—
And when the news hit shore that the titanic had sunk
Shine was up in Harlem damn near drunk—
and dancing in the streets.
damn near drunk and dancing in the streets.

DON L. LEE

Two Poems
(from "Sketches from a Black-Nappy-Headed Poet")

last week
my mother died/
& the most often asked question
at the funeral
was not of her death
or of her life before death
                                    but
why was i present
with/out
a
tie on.

i ain't seen no poems stop a .38,
i ain't seen no stanzas break a honkie's head,
i ain't seen no metaphors stop a tank,
i ain't seen no words kill
& if the word was mightier than the sword
pushkin wouldn't be fertilizing russian soil/
& until my similes can protect me from a night stick
i guess i'll keep my razor
& buy me some more bullets.

In the Interest of Black Salvation

Whom can I confess to?
The Catholics have some cat
They call father,
                        mine cutout a long time ago—
Like His did.
I tried confessing to my girl,

But she is not fast enough—except on hair styles,
                                        clothes
                                        face care and
                                        television.
if ABC, CBS, and NBC were to become educational stations
She would probably lose her cool,
                                and learn to read
Comic Books.
My neighbor, 36-19-35, volunteered to listen but
I couldn't talk—
Her numbers kept getting in the way,
Choking me.
To a Buddhist friend I went,
Listened, he didn't—
Advise, he did,
        "pray, pray, pray and keep one eye open."
I didn't pray—kept both eyes open.

Visited three comrades at Fort Hood,
There are no Cassandra cries here,
No one would hear you anyway. They didn't.
Three tried to speak, "don't want to make war."
                                        why???
When you could do countless other things like
Make life, this would be—
Useless too . . .

When I was 17,
I didn't have time to dream,
Dreams didn't exist—
Prayers did, as dreams.
I am now 17 & 8,
I still don't dream.
Father forgive us for we know what we do.
Jesus saves,
        Jesus saves,
                Jesus saves—S & H Green Stamps.

The Wall
(43rd & Langley, Chicago, Ill.)
painted by the artists and
photographers of OBAC 8/67

sending their negro
toms into the ghetto
at all hours of the day
(disguised as black people)
to dig
the wall, (the weapon)
the mighty black wall (we chase them out-kill if necessary)

whi-te people can't stand
the wall,
killed their eyes, (they cry)
black beauty hurts them—
they thought black beauty was a horse—
stupid muthafuckas, they run from
the mighty black wall

brothers & sisters screaming,
"picasso ain't got shit on us.
  send him back to art school"
we got black artists
who paint black art
the mighty black wall

negroes from south shore &
hyde park coming to check out
a black creation
black art, of the people,
for the people

art for people's sake
black people
the mighty black wall

black photographers
who take black pictures
can you dig,
                blackburn
                le roi,
                muslim sisters,
                        black on gray it's hip
they deal, black photographers deal blackness for
the mighty black wall

black artists paint,
                du bois/ garvey/ gwen brooks
                stokely/ rap/ james brown
                trane/ miracles/ ray charles
                baldwin/ killens/ muhammad ali
                alcindor/ blackness/ revolution
  our heroes, we pick them, for the wall
the mighty black wall/ about our business, blackness
                                can you dig?
if you can't you ain't black/ some other color
negro maybe??

the wall,
the mighty black wall,
"ain't the muthafucka layen there?"

Don't Cry, Scream
*(for John Coltrane/ from a black poet/
in a basement apt. crying dry tears
of "you ain't gone.")*

into the sixties
a trane
came/ out of the
fifties with a
golden boxcar
riding the rails
of novation.
  blowing
  a-melodics
  screeching,
  screaming,
  blasting—
    driving some away,
    (those paper readers who thought
    manhood was something innate)

    bring others in,
    (the few who didn't believe that the
    world existed around established whi
    teness & leonard bernstein)
music that ached.
murdered our minds (we reborn)
born into a neoteric aberration.
& suddenly
you envy the
BLIND man—
you know that he will
hear what you'll never
see.

your music is like
my head—nappy black/
a good nasty feel with
tangled songs of:
   we-eeeeeeeeeee   sing
   WE-EEEeeeeeeeeee loud &
   WE-EEEEEEEEEEEEEEEE high
              with
              feeling

a people playing
the sound of me when
i combed it. combed at
it.

i cried for billie holiday.
the blues. we ain't blue
the blues exhibited illusions of manhood.
destroyed by you. Ascension into:
   scream-eeeeeeeeeeeeee-ing sing
   SCREAM-EEEeeeeeeeeeee-ing loud &
   SCREAM-EEEEEEEEEEEEEE-ing long with
               feeling

we ain't blue, we are black.
we ain't blue, we are black.
    (all the blues did was
    make me cry)
soultrane gone on a trip
he left man images
he was a life-style of
man-makers & annihilator
of attache case carriers.

Trane done went.
(got his hat & left me one)
naw brother,

i didn't cry,
i just—   sing loud
   Scream-eeeeeeeeeeeeeeee-ed   & high
   SCREAM-EEEEEEEEEEEEEEEEEE-ED   with
    we-eeeeeeeeeeeeeeeeeeeeeeeee   feeling
    WE-EEEEEEeeeeeeeeeeEEEEEEEE   letting
    WE-EEEEEEEEEEEEEEEEEEEEEEEEE   yr/voice
    WHERE YOU DONE GONE, BROTHER? break

it hurts, brown babies
dying. born. done caught me
a trane. steel wheels broken
by popsicle sticks. i went out
& tried to buy a nickel bag
with my standard oil card.

        (swung on a faggot who politely
        scratched his ass in my presence.
        he smiled broken teeth stained from
        his over-used tongue. fisted-face.
        teeth dropped in tune with ray
        charles singing "yesterday.")

blonds had more fun—
with snagga-tooth niggers
who saved pennies & pop bottles for week-ends
to play negro & other filthy inventions.
be-bop-en to james brown's
cold sweat—these niggers didn't sweat,
they perspired. & the blond's dye came out,
i ran. she did too, with his pennies, pop bottles
& his mind. tune in next week same time same station
for anti-self in one lesson.

to the negro cow-sissies
who did tchaikovsky &
the beatles & live in

[*338*]

split-level homes & had
split-level minds & babies.
who committed the act of
love with their clothes on.

> (who hid in the bathroom to read
> jet mag., who didn't read the chicago
> defender because of the misspelled
> words & had shelves of books by
> europeans on display. untoched. who
> hid their little richard & lightnin'
> slim records & asked: "John who?"

> instant hate.)

they didn't know any better,
brother, they were too busy getting
into debt, expressing humanity &
taking off color.

> SCREAMMMM/we-eeeee/screech/teee   improvise
> aheeeeeeeee/screeeeeee/theeee/ee   with
> ahHHHHHHHHH/WEEEEEEEE/scrEEE feeling
>   EEEE
> we-eeeeeeWE-EEEEEEEEWE-EE-EEEE

the ofays heard you &
were wiped out. spaced.
one clown asked me during
my favorite things if
you were practicing.
i fired on the muthafucka & said,
"i'm practicing."

naw brother,
i didn't cry.
i got high off my thoughts—
they kept coming back,
back to destroy me.

& that BLIND man
i don't envy him anymore
i can see his hear
& hear his heard through my pores.
i can see my me. it was truth you gave,
like a daily shit
it had to come.

        can you scream—brother?   very
        can you scream—brother?   soft

i hear you.
i hear you.

and the Gods will too.

Move Un-Noticed to Be Noticed:
A Nationhood Poem

move, into our own, not theirs
into our.
they own it (for the moment): the unclean world, the
                         polluted space, the un-censor-
                         ed air, yr/foot steps as they
                         run wildly in the wrong
                         direction.
move, into our own, not theirs
into our.
move, you can't buy own.
own is like yr/hair (if u let it live); a natural extension of
        ownself.
own is yr/reflection, yr/total-being; the way u walk, talk,
             dress and relate to each other is *own*.
own is you,
cannot be bought or sold

                              can u buy yr/writing hand
                              yr/dancing feet, yr/speech,
                              yr/woman (if she's real),
                              yr/manhood?

own is ours.
all we have to do is   take it
take it the way u take from one another.
          the way u take artur rubinstein over thelonious
              monk
          the way u take eugene genovese over lerone bennett,
          the way u take robert bly over imamu baraka,
          the way u take picasso over charles white,
          the way u take marianne moore over gwendolyn
              brooks,
          the way u take *inaction* over *action*.
move. move to act   act.
act into thinking and think into action.
try to think. think.   try to think think think.
try to think. think (like i said, into yr/own) think.
try to think. don't hurt yourself, i know it's new.
try to act,
act into thinking and think into action.
can u do it, hunh? i say hunh, can u stop moving like a drunk
          gorilla?
                              ha ha   che che
                              ha ha   che che
                              ha ha   che che
                              ha ha   che che
move
what is u anyhow: a professional car watcher, a billboard for
          nothingness, a sane madman, a reincarnated clark gable?
either you is or you ain't!

the deadliving
are the worldmakers,
the image breakers,
the rule takers: blackman can you stop a hurricane?

                                                        [*341*]

"I remember back in 1954 or '55, in Chicago, when we had
13 days without a murder, that was before them colored
people started calling themselves *black*."
move.
move,
move to be moved,
move into yr/ownself, Clean.
Clean, u is the first black hippy i've ever met.
why u bes dressen so funny, anyhow, hunh?
i mean, is that u, Clean?
why u bes dressen like an airplane, can u fly,
i mean,
will yr/blue jim-shoes fly u,
& what about yr/tailor made bell bottoms, Clean?
can they lift u above madness,
turn u into the right direction.
& that red & pink scarf around yr/neck what's that for, Clean,
hunh?   will it help u fly, yeah, swing, swing   ing swing
swinging high above telephone wires with dreams
of this & that and illusions of trying to take bar-b-q
ice cream away from hon minded niggers who
didn't event know that *polish* is more than a
sausage.
"clean as a tack,
rusty as a nail,
haven't had a bath
sence columbus sail."

when u going be something real, Clean?
like yr/own, yeah, when u going be yr/ownself?

the deadliving
are the worldmakers,
the image breakers,
the rule takers: blackman can u stop a hurricane, mississippi
couldn't.

blackman if u can't stop what mississippi couldn't, *be it, be it.*
blackman be the wind, be the win, the win, the win, win win:

      wooooooooooowe boom boom   wooooooooooowe bah
      wooooooooooowe boom boom   wooooooooooowe bah
if u can't stop a hurricane, be one.
      wooooooooooowe boom boom   wooooooooooowe bah
      wooooooooooowe boom boom   wooooooooooowe bah
be the baddddest hurricane that ever came. a black hurricane.
      wooooooooooowe boom boom   wooooooooooowe bah
      wooooooooooowe boom boom   wooooooooooowe bah
the badddest black hurricane that ever came, a black
          hurricane named Beulah,
go head Beulah, do the hurricane.
      wooooooooooowe boom boom   wooooooooooowe bah
      wooooooooooowe boom boom   wooooooooooowe bah
move
move to be moved from the un-moveable,
into our own, yr/self is own, yrself is own, own yourself.
go where you/we go, hear the unheard and do,
do the undone, do it, do it, do it *now,* Clean
and tomorrow your sons will
be alive to praise
you.

CAROLYN RODGERS

5 Winos

sitting on the stone gray church steps
cupped in expensive shrubbery and lilac
looking from my third floor window
into a forest scene it is 1 A.M.
blue monday and the wolves are howling . . .

but they are singing.
crooning, straining & cursing
to harmonize, hit the perfect
sound, what is in their heads
that hovers around the hours &
years, spaced out-along side their dreams.
     and for some reason
     which is not the hour
     or the night
i too am straining, crooning, hoping—
let them hit 7-11 tonight, yeah.
let them hit, top the perfect note Babeeee its uuuuu
let 'em be the Temptin T's or the Fab-u-lous Im-
pressions, tonight . . .
let them nap up the air with their sound and ice
the other night noises into their places
     if they could just hit . . . for . . . one . . .
       mo-ment . . .

but the howling goes on,
and the straining & then cursing
and soon,
a bottle screams on the concrete,
scattering their mouths and juggling
their music into the most carefully
constructed a-melodic coltrane psalm . . .

Me, In Kulu Se & Karma

it's me,
bathed and ashy
smelling down with
                    (revlons aquamarine)
me, with my hair black
and nappy good and rough
as the ground
me sitting in my panties
no bra sitting on my am-vets
sofa with the pillows i stuffed
the red orange gold material i bought
from the little old jew i got lost and found
in new york looking
for the garment district i never found but
found skullcaps lining up the both sides
of the street with stores that make you sneeze it's
me i bought the yellow gold and got the wrong foam
and stuffed it and sewed it but the little pieces
keep coming out but u can sit on it anyway and listen
to pharoah ring into ur room like now, it's me sitting
on the thin thin wrong pillows hearing the trills and
the honey rolling through the air and the gravel roll-
ing and fluting and sweeet sweeet sweeeeeet and it's
me in the sky moving that way going freee where pha-
roah and trane playing in my guts and it's me and my
ears forgetting how to listen and just feeling oh
yeah me i am screammmmming into the box and the box
is screammmmmming back, is slow motion moving sound
through the spaces in the air and oh yeah it's me feel-
ing feeling rise, its rise feeling rise feeling feel-
ings rise rise rise in my throat and feeling throats
my head back and feeling laughs alloverme and feeling

[345]

screams mejoy and me flies feelings wild and laugh and
it's me oh yeah it's me rise feeling it's me being music
in kulu se & karma land

The Last M. F.

they say,
that i should not use the word
muthafucka anymo
in my poetry or in any speech i give.
they say,
that i must and can only say it to myself
as the new Black Womanhood suggests
a more reserved speaking self. they say,
that respect is hard won by a woman
who throws a word like muthafucka around
and so they say because we love you
throw that word away, Black Woman . . .
i say,
        that i only call muthafuckas, muthafuckas
so no one should be insulted. only
pigs and hunks and negroes who try to divide and
destroy our moves toward liberation.
i say,
that i am soft, and you can subpoena my man, put him
on trial, and he will testify that i am
soft in the right places at the right times
and often we are so reserved, i have nothing to say
but they say that this new day
creates a new dawn woman,
one who will listen to Black Men
and so i say
this is the last poem i will write calling

all manner of wites, card-carrying muthafuckas
and all manner of Blacks (negroes too) sweet
muthafuckas, crazy muthafuckas, lowdown muthafuckas
cool muthafuckas, mad and revolutionary muthafuckas.
But anyhow you all know just like i do (whether i say
it or not), there's plenty of MEAN muthafuckas out
here trying to do the struggle in and we all know
that none of us can relax until the last m. f.'s
been done in.

Poems for Malcolm

Poems for Malcolm
poems for Malcolm
No words, no lines, no poetic phrases,
I'm asking for Real poems for Malcolm
Black poems for Malcolm
Poems for the pimp who sold us ourselves
Poems for the hustler, who whipped the games on
the nigger psychoses in our minds, yeah,
I want a poem for that dope-pusher who
turned us on to the heaviest tuffest high, high truth
got us hooked on revolution, can't git enough
fixes till Liberation, yeah
I want a poem for the convict who did time,
so we could have time, this our time
Revolutionary times, Black Nationalist times
I want a poem for a Muslim brother who made me a sister
and you a brother, I want a poem for the Mightiest
        cleanser
who taught us pigology (human & otherunhumanwise)
I want a poem for the eternal Red, Big Red, dead Red,

a-live Red in our hearts, his ending,
our beginning, yeah
                    I want a poem that don't be cryin
                    or scream/preachin/rappin
                    for the end of scream/preachin/
                    rappin or protestin for the cause
                    of protestin or lyin for the
                                white pigs,
                                        I want a mean poem.
un cool muthafucka poem
uh we all black & love each otha poem
uh beatiful Luqman poem
uh seer Andy Thompson poem
uh gang banger's poem
uh stupid negro's poem
uh leave whitey in his own shithouse poem
uh black university poem
uh get your guns poem
uh Karenga poem, a LeRoi poem
uh Panther poem, uh NAACP poem, uh
where is Rap Brown poem
                    I want uh love poem
                    I want uh trust poem
                    I want uh unity poem
                    I want uh Liberation poem
uh blackhood poem
uh selfhood poem, uh building poem
uh let's fuck more babies poem
for a black strong Nation poem
I want a Nationhood poem
no lines, no cute words, no tired rappin fuh days will do,
        I want Black bodies poems
        I want Black hands poems
        I want Black minds poems
        I want Black actions poems
I want us to be a Black Nationhood Poem
                    for
El Hajj Malik El Shabazz

EBON (THOMAS DOOLEY)

The Prophet's Warning or Shoot to Kill

it is not enough
that we sing
and dance
and smile.
it is not enough
that we proclaim our beauty . . .

for I have seen
the faces of the enemy.
and they are red,
and white,
and blue.
patriotically evil faces,
bilious
and palely foul!
I have walked the streets
at noon
in the bright glare
of their sun
and watched the dumb,
the lame,
the rich . . .
prospect for hate
in the deep black soil
of america.

and we must Be that hate,
coiled about their hearts
like a striking cobra!
black poisons to fill their veins,
bringing bullet holes
and death
and apple pie!

Wednesday Night Prayer Meeting or Rappin' to My Boy

Charcoal stumps in the drifting snow!
death quick motion in the drizzling night!
great Anthracite!
black ancestral spirit
weaving through the weeping trees
and startled night!
Grant us your ear, O god!

let ebony blades of anger
encircle Our brow,
and drip death drops of darkness
upon the enemy!
grant us revenge, O god!

help us create
bronze astroids of destruction,
horizontally spiraling
from black infinities!
guide us to victory, O god!

black suns
and ebony evenings
encircle our heart, O god!
give us back our element,
those moonless nights and muddy days,
where peace and death
can stalk the path'.
let THEM die my god!

let US
see the dead
and the dying dead,

interwoven
in a tapestry of evil, O god!
let them suffer, my god!

in thy name,
we ask these
and other blessings,
amen.

Presidential Press Parley

greased turds
slid from his ear lobes
like little white lies,
blood-dripped and deathly.
screamed
insane inanities
while
tree-tops blow-jobbed
hand grenades
in vietnam

"we shall overcome"

and black Truth bombs
explode
in the back,
           alleys,
       of Newark's Asshole
to burn in Detroit
that
     pale
        cold
          white
unfeeling
       pus
of america's cancer.

JOHARI AMINI (JEWEL LATTIMORE)

Identity
(For Don L. Lee)

I saw a man   once
tall
  —wearing a crown
   of natural
a prophet
    creator of change
showing identity
      to negroes (the
  whiteminded ones)
a Black Gospel he had
to give
the message to save
them
his name was   Poet

he said   —what are you—
I felt fear for
what could I say
to him   or
  how should I
answer what he asked
(how about "a negro"
  no   something is
  wrong with that one)

I gathered nerve
  and ventured   —I am a people—
hoping he would
  ask no further
as birth

```
    is a
      painful
    process

he said                    —are you B l a c k—
sharp pain cut like
  ground glass
(should I lie and say
    yes    or . . .
no I must stall for
time)                      —what do you mean—
(but I didn't want
  to hear)                 —do you THINK BLACK—


I knew      I
knew      what he meant
I knew but I
could not say yes
in my   imitationwhite
      hair
I knew      but my
  curl free      bouffant
    flip      said
    no
without my answering       —why Poet
                              must you cause
                                such pain—


(I used to be
    comfortable)


he said

                           —Malcolm DuBois
                              African-American
                              Baldwin LeRoi Third
                              World Patrice Stokely
                              Black El-Hajj Malik
                              El-Shabazz—
```

the pain
      stopped
I took a breath of
   life
birth was   completed
  growth was   begun
I was   sister
    I had   Black
       Proud   IDENTITY

Upon Being Black One Friday Night in July

Bus stop waits are
not for
obviouslyBlacks

negro tomcops wearing
anybody's car
accost obviouslyBlacks
        what can you do? (when
        carrying literature saying
        be very black . . . live love
        disseminate black
        ? be courteous answering
                questions)

DO YOU HAVE IDEN TI FI CA TION !!!!
        what did you have
        in
        mind . . . votersregistration
           responsibilemember of body politic
             . . . churchmembership
          it ranout when i ranout
            . . . socialsecurity

to aid and abet The Plan for aged starvation
. . . bluecrossblueshield
insured myself against hsptls & m.ds
but no tomcops)

IS THIS YOUR PRES ENT AD DRESS !!!!!!
(crap)

WHERE DO YOU WORK !!!!!!!!
(they are 3 be cool this
summer and come
from out no bags)

WHAT IS YOUR HEIGHT !!!!!!!!!!
(all black ft. and damn proud ins!)

WHAT IS YOUR WEIGHT !!!!!!!!!!!!
(a   third   world)

note: tomcops
looking like are-black
= taking shorthand =

observe pattern: faux skin-hair-Afrodress
deceive
infiltrate
watch   (obviouslyBlack's
militant i's stamp
nationalism)
listen   (good friends
have bugged pads)

ATTENTION !!!!
ATTENTION !!!!
ALL KNOWN OBVIOUSLYBLACKS MUST BE KEPT
UNDER STRICT SURVEILLANCE !!!!

LADELE X (LESLIE POWELL)

O-o-oo-ld Miss Liza

> O-o-oo-ld Miss Liza
> Miss Liza Jane
> Old Miss Liza ain't got no Hair
> Miss Liza Jane

We grooved in the sun
watching Old Josh go about his business going straightway
across the summer day with no one to guide him and no cops
to stop him and we knew he must be a Bad Nigger cause God
the Om-ni-po-tent won't even fucking with him.

Then some flirting skirt
whispering by in Hollywood strides testing our manhood and
her readiness and off to play hide and go seek with a nigger
bend and doctor and the lady behind the woodshed and
feeling sure that bitch won't fuck with you again.

> O-o-oo-ld Miss Liza
> Miss Liza Jane
> Old Miss Liza ain't got no Hair
> Miss Liza Jane

Using the Evil Eye
that bad-ass right eye hitting everythang we threw at
in the mid-summer moonlight and off into the bushes to
discuss our victory when the statetrooper got too scared to
follow us to our Bad Nigger backwoods night retreat.

And we never knew
until that sweet young lady with the promising future got a
temporary migraine headache from a .22 automatic from a

Bad Nigger missing another Bad Nigger that the .38's the men-in-blue and gray wore was a motha-fucka.

And the dead don't groove
they just grow longer hair and fingernails and anythang green you plant above them until they rot and you only die once regardless of what james bond does and Bad Niggers don't always have the right eye and bullets don't play and death ain't got no mercy and the sun gonna die too and you can't be pussy-footing around and no hair ain't so bad after-all.

GERALD W. BARRAX

For a Black Poet

BLAM! BLAM! BLAM! POW! BLAM! POW!
RATTTTTTTAT! BLACK IS BEAUTIFUL, WHI
TY! RAATTTTTTTAT! POW! THERE GO A HON
KIE! GIT'M, POEM! POW! BLAM! BANG!
BANG! RATATAT! BLAM! COME ON, POEM! GET
THAT WHI-TE BEAST! BLAM! BLAM! POW!
ZAP! BANG! RAAATTTTTTTATAT! BLAM! BLAM!

How many fell for you, Brother?
How many did you leave
in the alley ballsmashed
headkicked in by your heavy feet?

The things we make as men
are guns triggered more efficiently than poems
and knives / and targets for the fires.

Men make revolutions
Poems will brings us to resurrection

There is prophecy in fire
and a beauty you can not see
  a sound you cannot hear
  below the exploding level of your poems
                    dress to kill
                    shoot to kill
                    love to kill
                    if you will
                    but write to bring back
                      the dead

And you are beautiful, Brother
not because you say so but because

black is the beauty of night a Black woman
the way a woman knows her beauty
    whose blackness falls
    softly from the spaces between stars
    who confirms our terror at her beauty in silence
and whose deepest blackness is the matrix
for the pendant worlds that hang
                                spinning from her ears.

And Black, like the swan
the shadow of itself who knows the secret
in the middle of its beauty is doubled silence
rarer than the white rush of lust
that led Leda's swan children
slouching thru their cycles of destruction.

The black panther.
His soft walk of lithe strong paces
a way of knowing   the hunter
                             the hunted

the beautiful) (silent (terrible beauty)quiet(terror
from   fear) the
panicked   (fear
beast / 's   (fear
crash / ing   (fear
bel / low   (fear and
ug / ly   fear

Beautiful as
a Black poempoetperson should be who
    knows what beauty lurks in the lives of men who
    know what Shadow falls between promise and praise.

The things that make us men.
Your child's questioning black fingers
touching you
is the poem

and more terror and beauty
because of the Shadow between you
than all your words.

   The way blackness absorbs   swallows everything
   and you Brother bring back up only upper cases
undigested at that
                              while beaten far below
                              the level of your voice
                              your life's deepest mean-
                              ings lie fallow.

What I mean is the way some things scream
at you   when synesthesia destroys   sometimes the be-
                                        holder   and   the
                                        beauty
and the sense of beauty is not truth
and no longer hurts
and frightens instead of making us
feel its terror.

The Dozens
A Small Drama in One Act, One Scene

Big Boy   Sophisticated, worldly-wise with the knowledge
          learned from listening to the hip talk of other
          big boys):
          Yo momma yo momma yo momma
          yo mom ahhh yo maaa yo mommmmmmmmmm
             UHma
          momma yo yo mommamommamomm
          ahhhhhh yo momma yoooOOOOOHHHHH
             MAN
          yo MOMMA!

Little Boy   (The Innocent who hasn't heard the hip talk of the Big Boys. He doesn't understand why there are tears in his eyes, but he knows, vaguely, that he must reply):

An' . . . an' . . . and you is ANOTHER one!

LEO J. MASON

It Was a Hot Day

It was a hot day
And I lay in the shade of my dreams.
"What you know, little pimp?"
"Nothing to it E.R."
"Say, I want you to meet
2 ladies, little pimp."
"You know Carol, this is
Conrad's ole lady, right?"
"And may I add she adds
A smile to my face."
This is Ann, she's from New York.
How yo doin', Ann?
"Much better now."
"And I'm not doin too bad myself.
Never been to New York
Here it's pretty fast down there."
And then I begin to play the game.
Ann had one thing going for her;
She was with one of the baddest boosters in Michigan.
Carol was one of those high-classed whores
One of those Cadillac buyer' bitches.
Yea, she was sweeter than the sound of music
'Cause her very presence was money.
It has even been said that the bitch would do anything
For Conrad, her man.
Yea, she ain't the kind of woman to be with nobody,
She's always with somebody.
So then I had to be about something myself.
So then I looked at my watch which had enough diamonds
To blind you.
I began to look really serious

As if I had someplace to go
Knowing all the time I had
No place to go.
So I kissed the day
And began to play
Popped my finger
Had someplace to go
Going to step into Ann's life.
Four days later I had the whore.
Found out she was fifty years old
If not older.
Told her a quick lie,
Gave her a short story,
Wounded her with charm,
Amazed her with ignorance
Got a lot of money in a short time
Lost it in two months time
Hot summer day
Can't find no shade in my dreams.

JUDY SIMMONS

Poem for Larry Ridley

awriiiight
mm   yeah
caught the black boys talkin
hands stroke the air/the word is
made, not spoken
quick heads duck, the
shoulders Frazier-feint

you missed the beat? message gone
wiped out with a wave   a
magic hand

awriiiight
mm   yeah
you slipped it to her
up to the neck, pluck the string
like
a nipple
a slick secret nib in that old
mystery, have
mercy! don't touch a
woman like you play

bass

The Answer

I don't want to touch your little sentiments:
Tiny Tims of feeling limping through your Sunday heart
Crutched by appropriate pity and popular joy
Dosed with acceptable passion

Let that proper pity be your justice
When *sane* men bomb your daughters, add their blood
To consecrated wine for your Communion,
Transubstantiation guaranteed

Indeed

Announce with modest anger, dignity, that
You "deplore" these senseless acts beyond your ken
Walk your private Via Dolorosa
To strains of "I'll Be Seeing You Again"

Amen

Then
Ask me why I don't write joyous verses
On childhood rambles; odes to tenderness
Politely touched with bearable nostalgia
For little loves and little pains and freight trains

All of which are proper in their place

As guns and deadly poems are
For my race

HENRY DUMAS

Genesis on an Endless Mosaic

I
starting on Kilimanjaro seven seasons hence
I chew our songs and blow you out in green
the wild oryx holds up the sky with two horns
Ngai has skinned the day sweating his clouds
the night is his blanket, he spreads a fence
you have traveled far from that star
starting at Kilimanjaro seven seasons hence

II
I am your paint upon the zebra and the firebird
the wild you in the seas climbing up the sun
we beat bone and bush til earth swell mountain
you are my river raining towards the seas
the eye and the mouth together must be heard
you have traveled far from that star
starting at Kilimanjaro seven seasons hence

III
dip with my dipper on the plain of lost reasons
eons ribbed in pearls, our diamond teeth
for my blood the wild beast lets fall the sky
in the beginning I danced these red bodies
O! Ngai, Lord of my skin temple
you have traveled far from that far
if love is endless all reasons run wild hence!

IV
starting at Timbuktu seven seasons hence
i dreamed of three kings wearing crowns of ice
my tongue is talking outside of my face

yet i taste my blood and still see the knife
these devils are devils and sons of devils
now i must make tongues with my eyes
starting at Timbuktu seven seasons hence

V

starting down the Congo with tri-god sails
i dream of three kings wearing crowns of ice
they are eating my baby from her belly
the sharks grow legs and bark upon this ship
the healing Mississippi has a new breed of shark
on my eyeball i can write with my lashes
starting down the Congo seven seasons hence

VI

starting on this journey long and long-short
i spit out three chewed devils laughing at me
i dream them back when the sea turns red
starting up the Caribbean they're still ahead
i remember the wild oryx holding up the sky
and i chant to Ngai it is better that i die
starting on this journey long and long-short

VII

the elephant is wild where the sidewalk ends
riding and riding my back is the laughing crow
"a bible for you and you and you" says he
under the tent of the tusk and the totem
the cotton blows, bowing, jerking,
the elephant is wild, eating bricks and sand
riding and riding my back is a phantom

VIII

starting in Gemini the sons of seasons
crazy horses with hoofs of steel
the scales of time shed and weigh
the earth tribes gather under lost reasons

a wild comet comes to break the seal
starting on this journey long and long-short
the child is watching the scales of time

IX
diction in gestures transposed to music
starting and ending in the black beyond
metamorphosis, said the preacher
is starting under the sign of the cross
wings, dreamed I are what we early lost
transition from waves long and long-short
starting in the galaxy moving toward the edge

X
geometry sounding, space between electrons
light makes
starting up the milky way on a cosmix eye
measured by the shadow of the earth
pin-pointed in the umbra
whispered in the penumbra
eclipsed by the sound of the universe on fire

XI
starting and starting and never ending
taking the light in the beginning of its bending
riding the firehorse to the garden of the stars
winking in the instant the transposed reflection
meta morphosis at the speed of light
starting and starting seven seasons hence

XII
I am the trans molecular on the long and long-short
eons and distances I have swallowed with my light
the spectrum of color and sound energized
teaching the drunken earth the music of the stars
I have traveled far from that far

[*368*]

I am coming I am coming, cosmic sperm
I am coming laced in the energy of the sun

the whole was once mine
(eons passing with dragon eyes)

now i count the blinks of your eyes
a bat waiting for the darkness to fall

I Laugh Talk Joke

i laugh talk joke
smoke dope skip rope, may take a coke
jump up and down, walk around
drink mash and talk trash
beat a blind baby over the head
with a brick
knock a no-legged man to his
bended knees
cause i'm a movin fool
never been to school
god raised me and the devil
praised me
catch a preacher in a boat
and slit his throat
pass a church,
I might pray
but don't fuck with me
cause i don't play

Keep the Faith Blues

They say if you ain't got no faith
                    you keep the blues most all the time
If you ain't got no faith, you keep the blues most all the time
Must be the reason I'm almost bout to lose my mind

I'm trying to hold on, people, tryin to keep what I got
Yeah, tryin to hold on, tryin hard to keep what I got
But you know the man is steadyin pressin me
                    bout to bust my natural back

Heard a man say once, you better hold on and keep the faith
He said hold on baby, and keep the faith
People, I swear I'm hold on and all I got *left* is faith

Yes the world gone crazy, they even talk about God is dead
Yes the world is gone crazy, some say worship the Devil
    instead

Well, I'm keepin my own faith, people
Can't let religion
                    bust open my head.

EUGENE REDMOND

Parapoetics
(For my former students and writing friends
in East St. Louis, Illinois)

Poetry is an *applied science:*
  Re-wrapped corner rap;
  Rootly-eloquented cellular, soulular sermons.

  Grit reincarnation of
  Lady Day
  Bird
  & Otis;
  Silk songs pitched on 'round and rhythmic rumps;
  Carved halos (for heroes) and asserted maleness:
  Sounds and sights of fire-tongues
  Leaping from lips of flame-stricken buildings in the night.

  Directions: apply poetry as needed.
  Envision.
  Visualize.
  Violate!
  Wring minds.
  Shout!
  Right words.
  Rite!!
  Cohabitate.
  Gestate.
  Pregnate your vocabulary.
  Dig, a parapoet!

Parenthesis: Replace winter with spring, move Mississippi
  to New York, Oberlin (Ohio) to East St. Louis, Harlem to

the summer whitehouse. Carve candles and flintstones for
flashlights.

Carry your poems.
Grit teeth.   Bear labor-love pains.
Have twins and triplets.
Fertilize poem-farms with after-birth,
Before birth and dung (rearrange old words);
Study/strike tradition.

Caution to parapoets:
Carry the weight of your own poem.
. . . it's a *heavy lode.*

Wind Goddess: Sound of Sculpture
(For Doris Mayes [Mezzo-Soprano], after March 17 [1970]
recital, Conservatory, Oberlin College)

In *Beulahland!*
You highlystand.

Raped wind-hordes
Walled & wailing against *unforgotten* gates
At your back.

Meticulously led,
These rough airs
Come sculpted,
Amplified,
Like African arrows,
From the silkly camouflaged turbulence
& beauty of your middlecountry.

Here is no sun-forsaken soul,
As that ancient light leaps

& smiles its rainbow of sounds
From your—
Now choiric/ancestral
Then epic/soulo—
Voice,
Vexing cured chant, and . . .
"*Everytime* I feel the spirit. . . ."

Definition of Nature

In this stoned and
Steely park,
Love is an asphalt
Fact:
      flowers
      birds
      trees
      rushing or creeping brooks
are framed on walls and tv tubes.

But each night when the city shrinks,
      the stars roof us,
And any bush becomes
      our Bantu wonderland.

SHARON BOURKE

I Remember That Day

Abbie,
Jerry.
When Ossie spoke a man began to cry,
As if the words, because they were so brave,
Made his face crumble.

Our measure of reality,
The mud wasn't so bad.

Folks went around hawking papers, chanting power,
And a woman
(Agent)
Went whispering through the crowd,
Between threads of rain.

People of Gleaming Cities, and of the Lion's and the Leopard's Brood

We have never stopped being Africans;
Speaking, minus our tongues,
With the drums of mental telepathy;
Planting, minus our whole seed,
The flowering cuttings of tribalness;
Wanting, minus hills and rivers that know us,
A land once more
Of leopard's boldness and lion's pride.
We have never stopped wearing the life masks of ancestors
Who, through us, gaze out over all human time.

For a long while we have brewed in our heart memory's
    herbs,
Prepared the drink of peoplehood.
We have never stopped being what we have preserved.
And now we flourish.

I Know She Will Pray for Me

Sometimes, when I become others of my people,
I become fervent in a different way,
Believing that if only we believe enough,
We can never be hurt,
That if only we are clean enough,
We can never be sullied,
That if only we love enough,
We shall be loved.

When I become these others of my people,
The bright, metallic discs of understanding, Yes, Lord,
Somehow shake and tremble on the tambourine,
And the rhythm, older than hymnals,
Is of a different Good.
Then the discs flash in the sun,
And my fervor becomes once more my fervor,
And I want to hurt and to sully,
Hating that vision of infinitely patient love.

Sopranosound, Memory of John

Soft
The stars are melting,
Smooth becomes the night
Around his shoulders.

Like two coins resting on his eyelids
Is the light,
And sound now, utterly,
He stays.

Listen to the reed,

To his mind
As it opens and closes the valves of the universe,

To his breath
Softly, smoothly spiraling,

To his song
From the throat of future time,

Listen
To John.

Biographical Notes

MARGARET WALKER ALEXANDER is a dynamo of energy. She has published two books of poetry, *For My People*, which won the Yale University Prize for Younger Poets in 1949; and *Prophets of a New Day*, Broadside Press, 1970. In addition, she has published a novel, *Jubilee*, which is the result of years of research in Southern, and her own family, history. In both her poetry and her fiction Miss Walker displays a profound knowledge of Black folk life and an unusually sensitive identification with it. Her handling of the ballad, like her handling of the novel, is masterful. Despite intimate knowledge of racism in the South, she nevertheless loves the region, especially her city of Jackson. Miss Walker was born in Birmingham, Alabama, the daughter of a Methodist minister. Her poetry, especially in the latter volume, and in the rhythms of "For My People," the title poem of the first, reveals a saturation in the King James Version of the Bible. At present, she lives in Jackson, Mississippi, with her husband and four children. She is chairman of the Division of Humanities of Jackson State College and Director of The Institute for the Study of History, Life, and Culture of Black People.

SAMUEL ALLEN (PAUL VESEY) (1917–   ) has had a distinguished career as poet, lawyer, teacher, and literary scholar. As a student at Fisk University, he studied literature under James Weldon Johnson. As a young poet, his work was first published by Richard Wright in *Presence Africaine*. Years later (1958) a collection of his poems, with German translations, was published under the title *Elfenbein Zahne (Ivory Tusks)*, in Heidelberg. In addition to law and poetry, Allen has served as Avalon Professor of the Humanities at Tuskegee Institute, and as professor of literature at Wesleyan University and at Boston University.

RICH AMERSON was recorded in Livingston, Alabama, in 1950, when he was well over sixty years old, by Harold Courlander. Courlander's purpose was to study Black folk music in a limited area so as to document its range and nature, and especially to investigate how the songs were "really sung in their natural setting." Amerson's songs can be heard on *Negro Folk*

Music of Alabama: Secular, Ethnic Folkways Library FE 4417. Courlander's sympathetic commentary can be found in his *Negro Songs from Alabama,* Oak, 1963, and *Negro Folk Music U.S.A.,* Columbia, 1970.

JOHARI AMINI (JEWEL LATTIMORE) has published three collections, *Images in Black,* 1967; *Black Essence,* 1968; and *Let's Go Somewhere,* 1970. In addition, she has published a broadside *For My People, A Fable.* She is presently living in Chicago, where she helps to manage Third World Press. Her poems have appeared in *Journal of Black Poetry* and *Negro Digest/ Black World.*

IMAMU AMIRI BARAKA (LE ROI JONES) (1934–   ) is the central figure of the new Black literary awakening. He is a prolific writer and speaker, and an effective political organizer. Under the name LeRoi Jones he became famous as an avant-garde poet of the post-Beat school. Later, he declared his independence from white cultural influences and deliberately set out to explore the revolutionary potential of Black Consciousness. His first success came with the Black Arts Movement, in the theater, but later he emerged as a music critic, a cultural historian, and essayist. Baraka's work is marked by a restless linguistic inventiveness, a tough and subtle mind, and a deep spirituality. This spirituality is especially evident single influence on the young artists who emerged in the 1960's. His major collections of poems include *Preface to a Twenty Volume Suicide Note,* 1961; *The Dead Lecturer and Other Poems,* 1964, and *Black Magic Poetry,* 1969.

GERALD W. BARRAX has written some tough and lyrical poems which have appeared in *Poetry,* the *Journal of Black Poetry,* and in various anthologies, including *Kaleidoscope.* He has published an important collection of poems under the title *Another Kind of Rain,* University of Pittsburgh Press, 1970.

LILLIE KATE WALKER BENITEZ attended Spelman College, where she majored in Fine Arts. She is an accomplished dancer and painter and has exhibited her work in the Atlanta area, where she has won several prizes during the Atlanta University annual competitions. She has reecntly married and makes her home in the Virgin Islands.

LEBERT BETHUNE (1937–   ) was born in Kingston, Jamaica, but has spent a good deal of his adult life in New York. He received an undergraduate degree from New York University, studied at the Sorbonne, and has traveled widely throughout Europe and the Middle East. He has made films for the government of Tanzania, produced a documentary on Malcolm X, and has published a collection of lyrical black poetry entitled *Juju of My Own,* which synthesizes his experiences in the United States and Europe with those in Africa and his memories of Jamaica.

LEWIS BLACK is hardly more than an entry in a discography and a handful of songs. Unfortunately, this is all too true of many talented performers.

[*380*]

The Goodrich and Dixon entry is stark: "Vcl acc by own gtr. Memphis, Saturday 10 December 1927." Along with the "matrix" numbers and the "issue" numbers, four songs are listed: "Rock Island Line Blues," "Gravel Camp Blues," "Corn Liquor Blues," and "Spanish Blues."

SHARON BOURKE is a native of New York City, where she attended Hunter College. She has published poetry in *Black Dialogue, Negro Digest/Black World,* and *Soulbook.* A professional editor during the past two years, she has been in charge of publications at The Institute of the Black World, Atlanta, Georgia.

GWENDOLYN BROOKS is a poet of immense influence, not only because of the national acclaim which attended her upon receipt of the Pulitzer Prize in 1949 but chiefly for her identification with and effect upon a new generation of poets and artists. Those most immediately influenced by her are the OBAC group, some of whom—Carolyn Rodgers, Johari Amini, Ebon, and Don L. Lee—are included in this collection. Miss Brooks's major publications include *A Street in Bronzeville,* 1945; *Annie Allen,* 1949; *Maud Martha,* 1953; *The Bean Eaters,* 1960; *In the Mecca,* 1968; *Riot,* 1969; *Family Portraits,* 1971, and *The World of Gwendolyn Brooks,* 1972. Miss Brooks has been Poet Laureate of the state of Illinois, but the more significant honor perhaps is that voiced by Don L. Lee and by Etheridge Knight in his *Poems from Prison.*

H. RAP BROWN (1943–   ) was born in Baton Rouge, Louisiana, where he received his early education. Later, he attended Southern University and became one of the most important voices in the Black Power Movement. He joined SNCC in 1963 and in 1966 served as State Project Director in Alabama for that organization. He succeeded Stokely Carmichael as chairman of SNCC, serving 1967–1968. He is presently awaiting trial in Maryland on charges of arson and inciting to riot. In 1968 Brown was convicted on a gun-carrying charge and sentenced to five years in jail and fined $2,000. His case is being appealed. Whatever the establishment's view of Brown may be, he remains for the present generation of Blacks an example of manhood and revolutionary zeal.

STERLING A. BROWN (1901–   ) has distinguished himself as a poet, scholar, critic, and teacher. The names of his students read like a roster of Who's Who in Black America. Brown is the author of an important book of poems, *Southern Road,* 1932, as well as two scholarly book-length studies, *The Negro in American Fiction* and *American Negro Poetry and Drama.* With A. P. Davis and the late Ulysses Y. Lee, he edited the classic collection of Black literature, *The Negro Caravan,* 1949, which perhaps more than any single text defined the range and content of Black literature. In addition, Brown has served in many editorial and consultative capacities. He was consultant on Black culture to Gunnar Myrdal during the preparation of *An American Dilemma.* A powerful and expressive reader of his own poetry, as well as that of others, he has been a significant influence upon at least three generations of writers, including the Negritude poets, the *Dasein* poets, and the present generation. This influence has been moral as well as technical, and he has been honored by them for it. Brown's poetry has been very widely anthologized, and appears not only in books, but also on record liner notes and on revolutionary posters. His deep knowledge of Black folk life—both rural and urban—is apparent in his virtuoso explorations in *Southern Road.* His poetry is characterized by a robust, infectious sense of humor and sharp craftsmanship. His character portraits—suggested from "the life"—are unforgettable, and include Ma Rainey, Sportin' Beasley, and fabulous Slim Greer. Brown was born in Washington, D.C., where he still resides and where he taught for over forty years at Howard University.

REGINALD BUTLER. I have little biographical material on Butler. He was born in Richmond, Virginia, about thirty years ago, is self-educated for the most part, and is a jazz buff and amateur musician. Presently he is living in California.

KARL CARTER is a young graduate of Howard University Law School. He is presently studying for his bar examination. His poetry has appeared in *Presence Africaine.*

"BIG BILL" BROONZY (WILLIAM LEE CONLEY) (1893–1958) was born in Scott, Mississippi, and grew up on a farm in Arkansas. As a child he learned songs from older relatives, which he played on a cigar-box fiddle. As a young man in Chicago, he learned to play blues on the guitar and established himself as a highly skillful entertainer before he made his recording debut in 1930. His music is characterized by good-timey electric excitement, though many of his blues and protest songs have all of the poignant depth of feeling associated with the Delta singers. His concert tour of Europe in 1951, according to Paul Oliver, marks the beginning of the blues revival which was to bring back before the public long-forgotten, legendary figures like John Hurt, Skip James, and "Son" House. Broonzy's autobiography, *Big Bill's Blues* (Oak, 1964), is important not only as a personal and social document, but also as a clue to the process of composition. A representative sample of his performances can be found on Yazoo, Mercury, Folkways, and Verve recordings.

COUNTEE CULLEN (1903–1946) was born in New York City, where he was reared by foster parents in a Methodist parsonage. A precocious student and brilliant poet, he early distinguished himself. Before his graduation from New York University, in 1925, he had already been published in national magazines and had published his first book, *Color.* He took an M.A. at Harvard, where he studied versification under Robert Hillyer, who later praised his virtuosity with traditional verse forms. *Copper Sun* and *The Ballad of the Brown Girl,* two books of poems, were published in 1927, the same year that he edited the important anthology, *Caroling Dusk.* Other publications include *The Black Christ,* 1929, written on a Guggenheim Fellowship; a novel, *One Way to Heaven*, 1932; *The Medea and Some Poems*, 1935; *The Lost Zoo*, 1940, children's verse; *My Nine Lives and How I Lost Them*, 1942, children's stories. He also collaborated with Arna Bontemps on *St. Louis Woman*, a dramatization of Bontemps' novel, *God Sends Sunday*. A collection of his poetry, *On These I Stand*, was published in 1947.

WALTER DANCY was born in Tuskegee, Alabama, and grew up in Akron, Ohio. He attended Morehouse College until he was forced to leave because of ill health. A brilliant, original student with a wide range of interests, including mathematics, science, philosophy, and literature, his poems in this volume have not previously been published.

MARGARET DANNER was born in Pryorsburg, Kentucky, although she has spent much of her life in Chicago and Detroit. In Chicago she was associated with *Poetry: The Magazine of Verse*, which also published a series of her poems, entitled "Far from Africa." Her other published work includes *To Flower and Other Poems, Poem Counter Poem* (with Dudley Randall), *Impression of African Art Forms*, and *Iron Lace*. Mrs. Danner is a highly effective reader of her poetry and has appeared before numerous audiences. Recently she has served as poet-in-residence at Virginia Union University, Richmond, Virginia.

FRANK MARSHALL DAVIS (1905–   ) is a much neglected poet, probably because his books have been out of print for so long, but perhaps also because his work is inadequately represented in existing anthologies. This is unfortunate because he has a great deal in common with the present generation, especially the OBAC poets. The Chicago toughness is there although its relationship to Sandburg and the Imagists is apparent too. His poetry has a certain unevenness which has kept some anthologists and critics at bay; but there is much to be gained from a reading of his work, which includes *Black Man's Verse*, 1935; *I Am the American Negro*, 1937; and *47th Street*, 1948. Davis has been a professional journalist and was one of the founders of *The Atlanta Daily World*, one of the few Black dailies in the country. At present, he lives in Hawaii, where he is preparing an autobiography and a collection of his poems.

WALTER DE LEGALL (1936–   ) was born in Philadelphia, Pennsylvania. He is a mathematician and a data processing specialist. At Howard University, he edited the quarterly *Dasein*, where his early work was published. He has also been published in *Beyond the Blues* and *Black Fire*.

OWEN DODSON (1914–   ) has distinguished himself as a playwright, a teacher, a novelist, and a poet. Until failing health recently forced him to relinquish his post, Dodson was for years head of the department of drama at Howard University, Washington, D.C., where the Ira Aldridge Theatre, under his direction, played a major role in the cultural life of the city. Dodson's work displays dazzling gifts of language and invention, and a nearly impeccable ear for the poetry of Black speech. His chief writings are *Divine Comedy, Garden of Time, Loup Garoo, Antigone,* all plays; *Powerful Long Ladder,* 1946, a collection of poems; and *Boy at the Window,* 1949, a novel.

HENRY DUMAS (1934–1968) was born in Sweet Home, Arkansas, and was killed by New York policemen on a subway. He was one of the most promising writers of his generation as his two posthumously published volumes show. They are *Poetry for My People,* a book of poems, and *Ark of Bones and Other Stories,* Southern Illinois University Press, 1970. Dumas was a free-lance writer and a teacher at Southern Illinois University and had published in various little magazines. He was also a member of the editorial staff of the *Hiram Poetry Review.* His work has to be read in its entirety for a sense of his range and potential growth. Jay Wright and Amiri Baraka write eloquent testaments of appreciation and elegaic loss in the introduction and the preface to the poetry.

PAUL LAURENCE DUNBAR (1872–1906) was born in Dayton, Ohio, and is best known for his dialect poems. Although he had some reservation about their popularity, Dunbar achieved a national reputation because of them among whites and Blacks alike. Only a few years ago the generation of World War II maturity knew his poems by heart and recited them on school and church programs. A serious attempt to assess the quality of consciousness of the total Black Community must honestly consider this audience. Included in this book are some of his most popular pieces as well as others chosen to illustrate a specific critical point. It is interesting to speculate how Dunbar might have developed as a poet had he lived longer, whether he would have given up dialect altogether or would have moved in the direction of writers like Hughes, Brown, Horne, Davis, and Fenton Johnson. Dunbar's chief poetry publications include *Oak and Ivy,* 1893; *Majors and Minors,* 1895; *Lyrics of a Lowly Life,* 1896. His *Complete Poems* appeared in 1913. In addition, his prose works like *The Strength of Gideon and Other Stories,* 1900, show his skill in that medium too.

EBON (THOMAS DOOLEY) gave up a career in law to become a "poet/mover." He was a member of OBAC and published a volume of poems, *Revolution,* at Third World Press. For the past two years he has been living and working both at the Atlanta Center for Black Art and at his bookstore, Timbuktu, which is the best of its kind in the area.

JAMES A. EMANUEL (1921–   ) has distinguished himself as a professor of American literature, a critic, a scholar, and a poet. His doctoral dissertation on the short stories of Langston Hughes has been expanded into a sensitive full-length treatment of that poet *Langston Hughes,* Twayne Publishers, 1967. With Theodore L. Gross, his colleague at the City University of New York, he edited *Dark Symphony,* one of the best anthologies of Afro-American literature to appear since Brown, Davis and Lee's *The Negro Caravan.* He has published two volumes of poems, *The Treehouse and Other Poems,* 1968, and *Panther Man,* 1970. Presently he is writing and studying in France and upon his return will serve as general editor of Broadside Press's critical series.

MARI EVANS is one of the most widely anthologized poets in the country. A frequent contributor to *Negro Digest/Black World,* she has published a volume of poetry, *I Am A Black Woman,* William Morrow & Co., 1970. This volume has been highly praised and given the 1970 award in poetry by the Black Academy of Arts and Letters. Mari Evans is a native of Toledo, Ohio, but makes her home in Indianapolis, Indiana, where she is producer/director for "The Black Experience," a weekly presentation of WTTV, and is writer-in-residence and assistant professor at Indiana University.

SARAH WEBSTER FABIO is well known as a gifted teacher as well as a poet. She is a native of Tennessee and graduated from Spelman College, in Atlanta, and the Iowa Writers Workshop. She brings to her readings a sensitive knowledge of music, and has read her poems with rock and jazz bands. *Black Wild* employs a multimedia approach in the teaching of Black history. Her work has appeared in *Negro Digest, College Composition and Communication, The Black Aesthetic,* ed. Addison Gayle, and *Dices or Black Bones,* ed. Adam David Miller. A collection of her poetry, entitled, *A Mirror: A Soul,* was published in 1969.

BETTY GATES is a member of the humanities and English faculty at Miles College in Birmingham, Alabama. She is a dynamic teacher and has helped to raise the level of consciousness in the Birmingham area.

NIKKI GIOVANNI was born in Knoxville, Tennessee, but grew up in Cincinnati, Ohio. Her formal education includes undergraduate work at Fisk University, where she studied creative writing under John O. Killens, and graduate study at the University of Pennsylvania. She has taught English in the SEEK program at Queens College in New York and at Livingston College, in New Jersey. Her writings—essays and poems—have appeared in *Essence, Negro Digest/Black World, Black Review No. 1, The Journal of Black Poetry,* and *Encore.* She has also published the following collections of poetry: *Black Feeling, Black Talk; Black Judgement,* Broadside Press, 1968 (published by William Morrow in 1970, in an edition which combined the two); *Re:Creation, Broadside,* 1971, and *My House,* William Morrow, 1972. *Truth Is on Its Way,* Right-On Records, RR 05001, is an important experiment with poetry and gospel music which suggests by its popularity the further expansion of Black poetry as a communal art form.

OSWALD GOVAN was also one of the Howard Poets. Born in New York, he presently makes his home in suburban Washington, D.C. A philosopher-mathematician, he still writes poetry but he hasn't been represented in any other publication since early appearances in *Dasein* and *Burning Spear.*

DONALD L. GRAHAM (DANTE) (1944–1971) was born in Gary, Indiana, and attended Fisk University, where he distinguished himself as a writer, artist, and musician. A protégé of John O. Killens, he succeeded Killens as director of Fisk Writers Workshop when Killens returned to New York. Graham, a highly imaginative theorist as well as a poet, was killed in an automobile accident while returning to Fisk from a reading engagement. At the time of his death, he was working on a novel and an oral history project that involved Black painters and musicians. He published three volumes of poetry, *Black Song*, 1966, *Soul Motion I*, and *Soul Motion II*. His poems have appeared in *Journal of Black Poetry, Black Fire*, and *Kaleidoscope*, R. Hayden, ed., 1967.

GREGOR HANNIBAL is a member of the *Ex Umbra* staff at North Carolina Central University, and has appeared in its more recent issues.

MICHAEL HARPER (1938–   ) was born in Brooklyn, New York, and moved to Los Angeles, California, in 1951. He has taught at several California colleges, has been poet-in-residence at Lewis and Clark, and is presently teaching at Brown University. His poems have appeared in *Burning Deck, Carolina Quarterly, Negro Digest/Black World,* and *Poetry*. His first volume, *Dear John, Dear Coltrane,* was published in 1970. His second volume, *History Is Your Own Heartbeat,* appeared in 1971. In 1972 he received a grant from the National Academy of Arts and Letters.

ROBERT HAYDEN (1913–   ) has consistently written and published poetry of a very high order. For this he has received important fellowships and awards as well as the respect of fellow craftsmen. For over twenty years he taught literature and creative writing at Fisk University, where his impact on his students has been great. His poetry has appeared in national periodicals and has been widely anthologized, especially his "Middle Passage." His major publications include *Heartshape in the Dust,* 1940; *The Lion and the Archer,* 1948; *A Ballad of Remembrance,* 1962; *Collected Poems,* 1966; *Words In the Mourning Time,* 1971, and an anthology of black poetry, *Kaleidoscope,* 1968. Hayden is only just now beginning to receive the general acclaim which is his due as a major voice. Although he has no special desire to be singled out as a Black poet, it is obvious that his inspiration is drawn largely from the Black Experience, personal, historical, and mythic. Hayden was born in Detroit, Michigan, where he attended Wayne State University and the University of Michigan. At present he is living in Ann Arbor, Michigan.

DAVID HENDERSON (1942–   ) was born in Harlem and attended Hunter College and the New School for Social Research. His poetry has been highly praised for its power and virtuosity. He has two collections, *Felix of the Silent Forest,* Poets Press, 1967, and *De Mayor of Harlem,* E. P. Dutton, 1970. He has been both lecturer and poet-in-residence at the College of the City of New York, and has worked with the Teachers and Writers Collaborative at I.S. 55 in Ocean Hill and with the Free Southern Theatre. He is editor and founder of the important poetry journal *Umbra*.

[*386*]

PAMELA WOODRUFF HILL was a student at North Carolina Central University when the poems in this volume were written. Her work appeared regularly in the pages of *Ex Umbra*, a literary magazine.

EDDIE "SON" HOUSE (1902–   ) was born in Lyon, Mississippi, and raised in the New Orleans area. As a youth, he worked as a field hand until moving in 1922 to East St. Louis. When he returned to Mississippi five years later, he learned to play the guitar. In 1930, he recorded some of the most powerful and moving blues of the time, "My Black Mama," "Preachin' the Blues," and "Dry Spell Blues." The latter records an actual drought following a season of flooding and one of devastation by the boll weevil. He was recorded again in 1941 and 1942 by Alan Lomax for the Library of Congress, but twenty years passed before he was recorded again. He was "rediscovered" in the sixties and recorded for Columbia and for Roots Records. Important streams of the Black Experience converge in this man: the preacher, the poet, the peasant; the saint, the sinner, the teacher. He forms a link between the ancestral Charlie Patton and the haunted Robert Johnson, whom he influenced. "Son" House made his final public appearance in 1970 at the Ann Arbor Blues Festival.

LANGSTON HUGHES (1902–1967) is probably the best known of all Black American poets and, certainly, the most prolific. His major works include *The Weary Blues*, 1926; *Fine Clothes to the Jew*, 1927; *The Dream Keeper*, 1932; *Shakespeare in Harlem*, 1942; *Fields of Wonder*, 1947; *One-Way Ticket*, 1949; *Montage of a Dream Deferred*, 1951; *Ask Your Mama: Twelve Moods for Jazz*, 1961; *The Panther and the Lash*, 1967. In addition, Hughes endeared himself to the Black public with his character Jesse B. Semple. These sketches of a simple, kind of Black Everyman provided the author with a sensitive and flexible instrument for a perceptive commentary on American life. Hughes's passionate involvement with the lives of his people is further reflected in volumes like *The Book of Negro Folklore*, edited with his longtime friend, Arna Bontemps; *The Sweet Flypaper of Life*, a picture poem book, done with Roy De Caravara, *The Book of Negro Humor*, as well as various anthologies, including his famous *An African Treasury*. Hughes's influence has been enormous, both on poets in this country and abroad. His effect on the *Negritude* poets, for example, has been openly acknowledged by the three major founders of the movement, Senghor, Damas, and Cesaire. One can only speculate about the extent of his influence on modern American poetry in general, since it is not likely to be admitted. Notwithstanding, Hughes called attention to the fact that he was reading poetry with a jazz orchestra long before the Beat poets got around to it. In fact, even the early poems, like those in this volume, repay serious study, not only for what they accomplish by way of wedding musical and poetic form, but also for what they attempt, and what they suggest. Three indispensable works for the study of Langston Hughes are Dickinson's *Bio-bibliography of Langston Hughes* (though his conclusion is highly questionable); James Emanuel's thoughtful and articulate study, *Langston Hughes*, and

Langston Hughes: Black Genius, A Critical Evaluation, edited by Therman B. O'Daniel.

TED HUNT, a student at North Carolina Central University when the poems in this volume were written, was an editor for the college literary magazine, *Ex Umbra.*

MISSISSIPPI JOHN HURT (1894–1966) has been called "the most impressive representative of the 'songster' generation on record," and his recordings provided a transition between the "old-time songs" and the blues. His repertoire consists of ballads, religious songs, blues, and original lyrics. First recorded in 1928, he dropped out of sight until rediscovery by blues enthusiasts in 1963. In that year, he began a new career at the Newport Folk Festival, where he captured the audience with his gentle, unassuming manner, his sly humor, and his faultless virtuosity. Before his death, he reworked old songs and re-recorded others, in addition to recording several new dances and songs. His work is represented on Folkways, Piedmont, and Vanguard.

LANCE JEFFERS (1919–   ) was born in Fremont, Nebraska, and reared there and in San Francisco. He was educated at Columbia University. Although older than most of that group, he was one of the Howard Poets, when as an instructor in the English Department, he both influenced and was influenced by them. His most famous poem, "My Blackness Is the Beauty of This Land," appeared in the initial issue of *Dasein.* A volume of the same name was published by Broadside Press in 1970. A second volume is ready for publication. Other works, short stories, novel excerpts, criticism, as well as poems, have appeared in *The Best American Short Stories of 1948, The New Black Poetry, Nine Black Poets, Black Voices, a Galaxy of Black Writing, New Black Voices,* and *Confrontation.* He lives with his family in suburban Maryland and teaches at Bowie State College. Jeffers is a jazz pianist.

TED JOANS (1928–   ) was born on the Fourth of July on a riverboat in Cairo, Illinois (his father was a riverboat entertainer). Jazz, he says, is his religion, and his poetry reflects this dedication. He has traveled around the world, most recently in Africa, and is an accomplished painter, poet, and musician. Joans is one of the most inventive of contemporary poets, and his work is on the growing edge of the poetry/jazz synthesis. His volumes of poetry are *The Hipsters, Black Pow-Wow,* 1969, and *Afrodisia: New Poems by Ted Joans,* 1971.

JAMES WELDON JOHNSON (1871–1938) was born in Jacksonville, Florida, and led a varied and significant life. He was a high school teacher and administrator, a songwriter with his brother Rosamond Kay, American consul in Venezuela and Nicaragua, an Executive Secretary of the NAACP, and a professor of creative writing at Fisk University. His critical awareness of the possibilities of Black speech and music are incisive and extremely valuable to the present day. His major publications include *Black Manhat-*

[*388*]

tan (1930), *Autobiography of an Ex-Coloured Man* (1912, 1927); *Fifty Years and Other Poems* (1917); *Book of the American Negro Poetry* (1922); *Books of Negro Spirituals* (1925, 1926); and *Along This Way*, an autobiography (1933).

PERCY E. JOHNSTON (1930–) was born in New York City into a musical family, the son of a jazz drummer and a concert harpist. He was educated in New York, Jersey City, New Jersey, Richmond, Virginia, and Washington, D.C. He studied history, philosophy, and literature at Howard University and was a key figure in the group known as the Howard Poets, publishing their work in *Dasein*, a quarterly of the arts, and later in *Burning Spear*, an anthology, published by his Jupiter Hammon Press. A section of his impressive poem "Concerto for Girl and Convertible," 1960, appeared in Rosey E. Pool's *Beyond the Blues*, 1962. The work of Johnston and the Howard Poets is artistically and historically very significant, but unfortunately too little known.

BOB KAUFMAN is a poet's poet. He has been closely identified with the Beat Movement and, in fact, has been called one of the chief architects of the movement as well as its best poet. Notwithstanding, there is no attempt on Kaufman's part to disassociate himself from his Blackness. On the contrary, numerous poems and statements call specific attention to it. It is strange, then, that his work appears so seldom in Black anthologies, and many Black readers do not know him at all. His major publications are *Solitudes Crowded Loneliness* and *The Golden Sardine*.

W. KEORAPETSE KGOSITSILE (1938–) was born in Johannesburg, South Africa, and has lived in exile since 1961. He has studied at various universities in the United States and has come to understand the American scene with considerable clarity. A powerful, sensitive, and moral writer, his poems and essays have appeared in *Journal of Black Poetry, Negro Digest/ Black World, Soulbook, For Malcolm*. He has read and lectured all over the country and is presently writer-in-residence at North Carolina A. & T. University, in Greensboro, North Carolina.

ETHERIDGE KNIGHT (1933–) was born in Corinth, Mississippi, and is well known for his *Poems from Prison*, written while serving time in Indiana State Prison. His work has appeared in *Negro Digest/Black World, Journal of Black Poetry, The Lakeshore Outlook, Prison Magazine, For Malcolm X, Potere Negro, The New Black Poetry*. Since his release from prison Knight has taught at Rutgers and at Lincoln University, Jefferson City, Mo. He is a sensitive, powerful poet, who is still growing.

LADELE X (LESLIE POWELL) is a native of Staunton, Virginia and a graduate of Wesleyan College, where he majored in history. He spent a year at The Institute of the Black World, Atlanta, Georgia, in 1970–71 as an intern. His poem in this collection has not been previously published.

[*389*]

HUDDIE LEDBETTER ("LEADBELLY") (1885–1949) is one of the greatest figures in Black folk song. Born near Mooringsport, Louisiana, he was a giant of a man, with prodigious energy and is reported to have regularly picked a thousand pounds of cotton a day. His pride, his way with the women, and his rambling mind kept him in trouble. Sentenced to Shaw State Farm on a murder conviction, he sang his way to a pardon. Sentenced again in 1930 for attempted murder, he was serving time at Angola State Prison Farm, when he was discovered by John Lomax, who was instrumental in his securing a reprieve. With Lomax and his son Alan, Leadbelly traveled and recorded through the South and in Washington, D.C. These works, extensive in their variety and execution, form one of the cornerstones of American folklore. Leadbelly's instrument was the twelve-string guitar, of which he was undisputed master. His songs include hollers, barrelhouse, square dances and reels, prison songs, blues, spirituals, popular numbers, and songs of protest. He recorded chiefly for Folkways and the Library of Congress.

DON L. LEE (1942–) was born in Arkansas and grew up in Detroit and Chicago. Lee is probably the best known of the poets who emerged during the 1960's and has traveled widely, here and abroad, reading his work in a powerful, staccato style. He has published six books, four of them poetry: *Think Black*, 1967; *Black Pride*, 1968; *Don't Cry, Scream*, 1969; *We Walk the Way of the New World; Direction Score*, 1971; and a book of criticism, *Dynamite Voice #1*, which is indispensable reading for anyone who is seriously interested in the new Black poetry. All were published by Broadside Press. His books have sold phenomenally well. Lee has been writer-in-residence at Cornell, Northeastern Illinois State University, and the University of Illinois, and is currently writer-in-residence at Howard University. Lee has made important and seminal statements on the role of the Black writer in numerous Black publications. Recently, he has expanded his theory to more direct action and has founded a publishing firm, Third World Press, which provides another forum for Black writers.

AUDRE LORDE was born in Manhattan and received her undergraduate degree from Hunter College and a master's degree from Columbia. She has also studied at the University of Mexico. A meticulous, skillful poet, her work should be better known. She has published two books, *The First Cities*, Poets Press, 1968, and *Cables to Rage*, Paul Bremen, 1970. In 1968, she was poet-in-residence at Tougaloo College in Mississippi. Presently she works as a librarian and teaches at the City University of New York.

LEO J. MASON (1947–) was born and raised in Detroit. Presently living and writing in Atlanta, he has written plays as well as poems. This is his first publication.

CLAUDE MC KAY (1891–1948) was born in Clarendon, Jamaica, the youngest of eleven children. His first book of poetry, *Songs of Jamaica* (1912) was written in Jamaican dialect. They were popular and won him an award from the Institute of Arts and Sciences. He came to Tuskegee Institute the following year, but spent only a few months before moving on to Kansas State University, where he remained for two years. Afterwards he came to New York, and finally traveled to Europe, spending a year in London, where he published *Spring in New Hampshire*, 1920. After his return to the United States in 1921, he worked with Max Eastman as associate editor of the *Liberator* and in 1922 wrote *Harlem Shadows*, his first book of poems published in the United States. He returned to Europe shortly thereafter and remained there for about ten years. His output during that time was chiefly in prose and included *Home to Harlem* (1928), *Banjo* (1929), *Gingertown* (1932), *Banana Bottom* (1933), *A Long Way from Home* (1937), and *Harlem: Negro Metropolis* (1940). A posthumous volume of his poetry, *Selected Poems of Claude McKay*, was published in 1953.

LARRY NEAL (1937–   ) was born in Atlanta, Georgia, and grew up in Philadelphia, Pennsylvania. A graduate of Lincoln University, he has done graduate work in folklore at the University of Pennsylvania. Neal is one of the most important theoreticians of the present movement in Black art. He is one of the few to bring a comprehensive analysis and knowledge of folk-life into present aesthetic and ideological considerations. Neal has published widely both as a poet and an essayist. His works have appeared in *Freedomways*, *Negro Digest/Black World*, the *Tulane Drama Review*, *Soulbook*, the *Journal of Black Poetry*, and *The Cricket*, of which he is an editor, along with Amiri Baraka (LeRoi Jones) and A. B. Spellman. With Baraka he edited the powerful anthology *Black Fire*, for William Morrow & Co., 1968. He has also served as arts director of *Liberator* magazine. In 1968 the *Journal of Black Poetry* published his *Black Boogaloo*, a major poetic statement.

DAPHNE DIANE PAGE is a graduate of North Carolina Central University, where she was one of the chief writers for the impressive student publication, *Ex Umbra*.

GERTRUDE "MA" RAINEY (1886–1939) was born in Columbus, Georgia, and began singing in a local talent show at the age of fourteen. Four years later, she married Will Rainey, whom she joined in a traveling show. This set the pattern of her performances, and she worked with the Rabbit Foot, C. W. Parks, and Al Gaines' Minstrels. Later she formed her own troupe and traveled throughout the South. She taught Bessie Smith and her influence is immediately apparent to anyone who listens to the two singers. While Bessie Smith played the theaters in the North as well as the large cities of the South, "Ma" Rainey remained close to the country roots of the blues, both the land and the people. Her essential majesty is caught by Sterling Brown's moving poem.

DUDLEY RANDALL (1914–   ) is the publisher of the important Broadside Press, where many of the poets of the present generation first broke into print. Among these are Don L. Lee, Sonia Sanchez, Nikki Giovanni, and

Etheridge Knight. The importance of this venture is easily grasped when one tries to imagine what the state of Black publication would be without the Broadside poets, and without works like the collection, *For Malcolm: Poems on the Life and Death of Malcolm X*, which he edited with Margaret Burroughs. Randall was born in Washington, D.C., but has spent most of his life in Detroit, where he is a librarian with the Wayne County Public Library. His publications include translations of the Russian poet Pushkin as well as *Poem Counter Poem* (with Margaret Danner), *Cities Burning*, and *Love You*.

EUGENE REDMOND is a native of East St. Louis, Illinois, where he has been involved in numerous community activities. He was Senior Consultant to Katherine Dunham at the Performing Arts Training Center in East St. Louis and is contributing editor to the *East St. Louis Monitor*. Redmond has been writer-in-residence at Oberlin College and Southern University and presently is Professor of English and Poet-in-Residence in Ethnic Studies at Sacramento State College, California. He is a journalist, a playwright, and an editor. His first book of poetry is *Sentry of the Four Golden Pillars*, 1970, and his latest is *River of Bones and Flesh and Blood*, 1971. With Hale Chatfield he co-edited *Poetry for My People* and *"Ark of Bones" and Other Stories*, both by the late Henry Dumas.

NATHAN A. RICHARDS was born in Kingston, Jamaica. He matriculated at Howard University where he studied economics, and was managing editor of *Dasein*, a literary magazine. His work has appeared there and in *Burning Spear*, as well as in the West Indian publication *New World*. He is presently living in New York City.

CONRAD KENT RIVERS (1933–1968) was born in Atlantic City, New Jersey, and attended schools in Pennsylvania, Georgia, Ohio, and Indiana. As a high school student he won the Savannah, Georgia, State Poetry Prize in 1951. His work subsequently has appeared in *Antioch Review, Kenyon Review, Ohio Poetry Review, Negro Digest*, and several well-known anthologies. His collections include *Perchance to Dream, Othello*, 1959; *These Black Bodies* and *This Sunburnt Face*, 1962; *Dusk at Selma*, 1965; and posthumously, *The Still Voice of Harlem*, 1968.

CAROLYN M. ROGERS was born and raised in Chicago, where she was a founding member of OBAC (Organization of Black American Culture). She has a wide range of talent and has written memorable short stories and important criticism. Her intense love for music and for her people is everywhere evident in her work. In 1968 she won the Conrad Kent Rivers Writing Award. Her work has appeared in *Negro Digest/Black World, Journal of Black Poetry*, as well as in anthologies like *Natural Process* and *For Malcolm X*. In addition, she has published two collections, *Paper Soul*, 1968; *Songs of a Blackbird*, 1969, by Third World, and a broadside, *2 Love Raps*.

SONIA SANCHEZ was born in Birmingham, Alabama, and is one of the strongest voices of the New Black Poetry. She lectures and reads her poetry to audiences all over the country and spends a great deal of time talking with young people. She is a graduate of Hunter College and has taught at San Francisco State College and Rutgers. Her collections of poetry include *Homecoming* and *We a BaddDDD People*. In addition to poetry, she has written and published plays and short stories.

JUDY DOTHARD SIMMONS was born in Westerly, Rhode Island, grew up in Alabama and received a bachelor of arts degree in psychology at California State University at Sacramento. *Judith's Blues*, her first volume of poetry, was published by Broadside Press.

A. B. SPELLMAN (1935–   ) was born in Nixonton, North Carolina, but grew up in Elizabeth City, North Carolina. He spent six years at Howard University, and earned a B.A. in political science and history. He also attended Howard's school of law and worked on a master's degree. Poetry and jazz criticism are Spellman's chief publications. He wrote the liner notes for Coltrane's *Ascension* and some eighty-odd other albums. His searching study *Four Lives in the Bebop Business* is his major work of criticism/history. Spellman's poetry has been translated in several languages and published in *Black Dialogue, Umbra, The Journal of Black Poetry*, as well as in several major anthologies. He is an editor of *The Cricket*, a journal of Black music, along with Amiri Baraka and Larry Neal. In 1969, he organized the Atlanta Center for Black Art, which publishes *Rhythm*.

LE ROY STONE (1936–   ) was born in Montego Bay, Jamaica, and is keenly interested in music, as the title of his famous poem "Calypso" indicates. His jazz criticism has appeared in *Down Beat* and *Metronome*. He studied sociology at Howard University, where he was one of the Howard Poets.

MELVIN B. TOLSON (1900–1966) was born in Moberly, Missouri, and was educated at Fisk, Lincoln, and Columbia universities. Early in his career he distinguished himself in speech, debate, dramatics, and the study of classical literature. His poetry is informed by this study and by his general erudition. *Dark Symphony*, a long poem, won a national contest sponsored by the American Negro Exposition in Chicago. Other works of his include *Rendezvous with America* (1944); *Libretto for the Republic of Liberia* (1953); *Harlem Gallery* (1965); and dramatizations of novels by George Schuyler and Walter White. Tolson is a complex, almost anomalous poet and his work remains to be properly evaluated. When that is done, it should not only reveal a great deal about the man, but about a whole tendency in Afro-American life and thought. Langston Hughes once said of him: ". . . Tolson is no highbrow. Students revere him and love him. Kid. from the cottonfields like him. Cowpunchers understand him. . . . He's a great talker. There is only one Tolson" (from the jacket of *Harlem Gallery*).

JEAN TOOMER (1894–1967) was born in Washington, D.C. One of the most enigmatic personalities associated with the Harlem Renaissance, his reputation rests upon a single book, *Cane,* a collection of stories, poems, sketches, and a play, dealing with Afro-American life. About ten years after the enthusiastic reception of his book, Toomer dropped from public sight, and reappeared, so to speak, just a short while before his death. He died in Bucks County, Pennsylvania. Interest in him has grown considerably since the reissue of *Cane* in paperback and the "discovery" of his unpublished manuscripts.

ASKIA MUHAMMAD TOURÉ (ROLAND SNELLINGS) is one of the cosmic-minded poets of the new Black movement. He is a Sunni Muslim and his religious thought suffuses his poetry. His works have appeared in the *Journal of Black Poetry, Black Theater* magazine, *Liberator, Freedomways, Soulbook, Negro Digest/Black World.*

JAY WRIGHT (1935–   ) was born in Albuquerque, New Mexico, and has led a varied and productive life. He has played minor league baseball, served in the army medical corps, studied theology and comparative literature, acted as an educational consultant, and has been poet-in-residence at Tougaloo College and Talladega College. He read his poetry on a tour of Black Southern colleges sponsored by the Woodrow Wilson Foundation and the National Endowment for the Arts in 1967 and has received various grants to sustain his writing, which includes poetry published in *New Negro Poets: USA, New American Poets, The Nation, Negro Digest/Black World, Union Seminary Quarterly, Black Fire, Umbra, National Process,* and *Journal of the New African Literature.* Aside from poetry, he has published several plays, two for radio. He has published two volumes of poems called *Death as History,* Poets Press, which is also the title of one of his unpublished plays, and *The Homecoming Singer* (Corinth Books). Wright has a passionate, disciplined, and far-ranging intelligence which may one day emerge as a major voice of this period. Further indication appears in his introduction to the posthumous book by Henry Dumas, *Poetry for My People.*

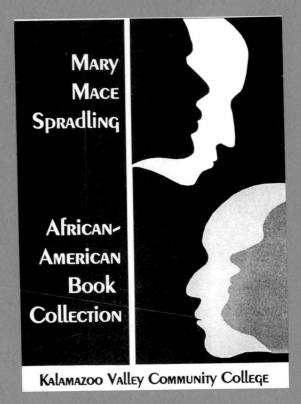

MARY
MACE
SPRADLING

AFRICAN-
AMERICAN
BOOK
COLLECTION

KALAMAZOO VALLEY COMMUNITY COLLEGE